Edward Money

The Cultivation and Manufacture of Tea

Edward Money

The Cultivation and Manufacture of Tea

ISBN/EAN: 9783743310490

Manufactured in Europe, USA, Canada, Australia, Japa

Cover: Foto ©ninafisch / pixelio.de

Manufactured and distributed by brebook publishing software (www.brebook.com)

Edward Money

The Cultivation and Manufacture of Tea

THE
CULTIVATION & MANUFACTURE
OF
TEA,

BY

LIEUT.-COL. EDWARD MONEY,

THE ORIGINAL MANUSCRIPT OF WHICH SECURED THE PRIZE OF THE
GRANT GOLD MEDAL AND Rs. 300, AWARDED BY THE AGRICULTURAL
AND HORTICULTURAL SOCIETY OF INDIA
IN THE YEAR 1871.

FOURTH EDITION,

REVISED AND SUPPLEMENTED BY ADDITIONAL CHAPTERS.

LONDON:
W. B. WHITTINGHAM & CO., 91, GRACECHURCH STREET.
CALCUTTA: THACKER & CO.
1883.

D. VAN NOSTRAND COMPANY,
NEW YORK.

PREFACE

TO

THE FOURTH EDITION.

SIX new Chapters are added. So much has been done in Tea since I last wrote, I found it impossible to embody all in the former book, and so preferred to give it separately. The new Chapters treat of—

- COUNTRIES OUTSIDE CHINA AND INDIA THAT PRODUCE TEA.
- TEA STATISTICS.
- MARKETS FOR TEA OUTSIDE GREAT BRITAIN.
- MAKING INDIAN TEA KNOWN IN THE UNITED KINGDOM.
- TEA MACHINERY.
- WEIGHING AND BULKING OF INDIAN TEAS AT CUSTOM HOUSE.

A separate and full Index of the subjects treated of in the additions to this Fourth Edition will be found at the end of the Book.

EDWARD MONEY.

EAST INDIA CLUB, ST. JAMES'S SQUARE,
July, 1883.

PREFACE

TO

THE THIRD EDITION.

The experience of four more years, which includes six months' residence in the Neilgherries, is embodied in the following, while the whole of the letter-press of the Second Edition has been corrected and revised.

EDWARD MONEY.

London,
April, 1878.

PREFACE

TO

THE SECOND EDITION.

THREE years' further experience, and visiting two Tea districts I had not seen before, have enabled me to amend whatever was faulty in the First Edition. The whole has been revised, and much new matter is added throughout. A new Chapter at the end on the Past, the Present, and the Future of Indian Tea will, it is hoped, be found interesting. An Index (a great want to the First Edition) is added, so that all information on any point can be at once found. The manufacture of Green Tea, of which I was ignorant when I last wrote, is given, and the advisability of that manufacture is discussed.

In its present form I hope and believe this little work will be found useful and interesting to all connected with Tea.

EDWARD MONEY.

DARJEELING,
May, 1874.

PREFACE

TO

THE FIRST EDITION.

THE following Essay was written with, *firstly*, the object of competing for the Gold Medal and the Money Prize offered by the Agricultural and Horticultural Society of India for the best treatise on the cultivation and manufacture of Tea; and, *secondly*, with the view of arranging the hundreds of notes on these subjects, which, in the course of eleven years, I had collected.

During all these years I have been a Tea planter, making first for myself and others a garden in the Himalayas, and for the last six years doing the same thing for myself in the Chittagong district.

Whenever I have visited other plantations (and I have seen a great number in many districts), I have brought away notes of all I saw. Up to the last, at every such visit, I have learnt *something*—if rarely nothing to follow, something at least to avoid. I have now tested all and everything connected with the cultivation and manufacture of Tea by my own experience, and I can only hope that what I have written will be found useful to an industry destined yet, I believe, in spite of the late panic—the natural result of wild speculation—to play an important part in India.

I have endeavoured to adapt this Essay to the wants of a beginner, as there are many of that class now, and may yet be more in days to come, who must feel, as I often have, the want of a really practical work on Tea.

To those who have Tea properties in unlikely climates and unlikely sites, I would say two words. No view I have taken of the advantages of different localities *can* in any way affect the results of enterprises already entered upon. But if the note of warning, sounded in the following pages, checks further losses in Tea, already so vast, while it fosters the cultivation on remunerative sites, I shall not have written in vain.

EDWARD MONEY.

Sungoo River Plantation,
 Chittagong,
  November, 1870.

CONTENTS.

CHAPTER		PAGE
I.	Past and Present Financial Prospect of Tea	1
II.	Labour, Local and Imported	10
III.	Tea Districts and their Comparative Advantages. Climate, Soil, &c., in each	13
IV.	Soil	31
V.	Nature of Jungle	34
VI.	Water and Sanitation	35
VII.	Lay of Land	37
VIII.	Laying out a Garden	42
IX.	Varieties of the Tea Plant	47
X.	Tea Seed	54
XI.	Comparison between Sowing in Nurseries and in Situ	57
XII.	Sowing Seed in Situ, id est, at Stake	59
XIII.	Nurseries	62
XIV.	Manure	67
XV.	Distances apart to Plant Tea-Bushes	71
XVI.	Making a Garden	73
XVII.	Transplanting	76
XVIII.	Cultivation of Made Gardens	81
XIX.	Pruning	86
XX.	White Ants, Crickets, and Blight	89
XXI.	Filling up Vacancies	92
XXII.	Flushing and Number of Flushes	97
XXIII.	Leaf-Picking	102
XXIV.	Manufacture. Mechanical Contrivances	109

CONTENTS.

CHAPTER		PAGE
XXV.	Sifting and Sorting	134
XXVI.	Boxes. Packing	147
XXVII.	Management, Accounts, Forms	152
XXVIII.	Cost of Manufacture, Packing, Transport, &c.	160
XXIX.	Cost of Making a 300-acre Tea Garden	163
XXX.	How much Profit Tea can give	168
XXXI.	The Past, Present, and Future of Indian Tea	174
XXXII.	Countries Outside China and India that Produce Tea	183
XXXIII.	Statistics regarding Indian Tea	194
XXXIV.	Markets Outside Great Britain	207
XXXV.	Making Indian Tea Known in the United Kingdom	218
XXXVI.	Tea Machinery	222
XXXVII.	Weighing and Bulking of Indian Teas at Custom House	272
	Addenda to Third Edition	293
	Index	299

PRIZE ESSAY
ON THE
CULTIVATION AND MANUFACTURE OF TEA IN INDIA.

PREMIUM, THREE HUNDRED RUPEES AND THE GRANT GOLD MEDAL.

CHAPTER I.

PAST AND PRESENT FINANCIAL PROSPECTS OF TEA.

Will Tea pay? Certainly, on a suitable site, and in a good Tea climate; equally certainly *not* in a bad locality with other drawbacks.

Why, then, has Tea only paid during the last few years (?) Simply because nothing will pay, which is embarked on without the requisite knowledge; and this was pre-eminently the case with Tea.

Nothing was known of Tea formerly, when everybody rushed into it; not much is known even now. Still, with those drawbacks and many others, the enterprise has survived, and it is very certain the day will never come that Tea cultivation will cease in India.

I believe there is nothing will pay better than Tea, if embarked on with the necessary knowledge in suitable places, but failing either of these success must not be hoped for.

It was madness to expect aught but ruin, under the conditions which the cultivation was entered on in the Tea-fever days. People who had failed in everything else were thought quite competent to make plantations. 'Tis true Tea was so entirely a new thing at that time, but few could be found who had any knowledge of it. Still, had managers with some practice in agriculture been chosen, the end would not have been so disastrous. But any one—literally any one—was taken, and tea planters in those days were a strange medley of retired or cashiered army and navy officers, medical men, engineers, veterinary surgeons, steamer captains, chemists, shop-keepers of all kinds, stable-keepers, used-up policemen, clerks, and goodness knows who besides!

Is it strange the enterprise failed in their hands? Would it not have been much stranger if it had not?

This was only one of the many necessities for failure. I call them "necessities" as they appear to have been so industriously sought after in some cases. I must detail them shortly, for to expatiate on them would fill a book.

No garden should exceed 500 acres under Tea. If highly cultivated one of even half that size will pay enormously, far better than a larger area with low cultivation. Add, say, 400 acres for charcoal, &c., making 900 or say 1,000 acres the outside area that can be required, and the outside that should ever have been purchased for any one estate. Instead of this, individuals and Companies rushing into Tea bought tracts of five, ten, fifteen, and twenty thousand acres. The idea was that, though it might not be all cultivated, by taking up so large an area all the local labour where there was any would be secured. Often, however, these large tracts were purchased where local labour there was none, and what the object there was is a mystery. I conceive, however, there was a hazy idea that *if* 500 acres paid well, 1,000 would pay double, and that eventually even two or three thousand acres would be put under Tea and make the fortunate possessor a *millionaire*. In short, there were no bounds, in fancy, to the size a garden might be made, and thus loss No. 2 took place when absurdly large areas were bought of the Government and large areas cultivated.

The only fair rules for the sale of waste lands were those of Lord Canning, which the Secretary of State at home, who could know nothing of the subject, chose to modify and upset. Instead of Rs. 2-8 per acre for all waste lands (by no means a low price, when the cost of land in the Colonies is considered) and that the applicant for the land (who had, perhaps, spent months seeking for it) should have it, the illiberal and unjust method of putting the land up to auction with an upset price of Rs. 2-8 was adopted, the unfortunate seeker, finder, and applicant, through whose labour the land had been found, having no advantage over any other bidder. The best, at least the most successful plan in those days, though as unfair and illiberal as the Government action, was to wait till some one, who was supposed to know what good Tea land was, applied for a piece, and then bid half an anna more than he did, and thus secure it. It *paid* much better than hunting about for oneself, and it was kind and considerate on the part of Government to devise such a plan!

In those fever days, with the auction system, lands almost always sold far above their value. The most absurd prices, Rs. 10 and upwards per acre, were sometimes paid for wild jungle lands. Tracts, which natives could have, and in some cases *did* lease from Government for inconceivably small sums, representing, say, at thirty years' purchase, 4 annas per acre, were put up for auction with a limit of Rs. 2-8, and sold perhaps at Rs. 8 or 10 per acre. Had the Government given land *gratis* to Tea cultivators the policy would have been a wise one. To do what they did was scarcely acting up to their professed wish " to develope the resources of the country."

Since the above was written, new rules have been published for the sale of waste lands. The objectionable auction system is continued, and the upset price is much enhanced, as follows :—

Schedule of Rates of Upset Prices.

	Upset price per acre.
Districts of the Assam Division	Rs. 8
Districts of Cachar and Sylhet	8
Districts of the Chittagong Division	6
Districts of the Chota Nagpore Division	5
The Soonderbuns	5
All other Districts	10

It is not likely that Government will sell much land at such exorbitant rates.*

Security of title, it is generally thought, is one of the advantages of buying land from the State; but I grieve to state my experience is that the reverse is the case, and will so remain until the following is done :—

First. The Government should learn *what is and what is not theirs to sell.* Such an absurdity, then, as Government ascertaining, years after the auction, that they had sold lands they had no right to sell, **could not be.**

Secondly. That before land is sold it be properly surveyed and demarcated; and what might so easily have been done, and which alone would have compensated for much of bad procedure in other respects, that the simple and obvious plan before the sale, of sending a European official to show

---

* Since the Second Edition went to press, further Rules for Waste Lands have been enacted. Generally speaking, they are only now leased to applicants

the neighbouring villagers and intending purchasers the boundaries of the land to be sold, be resorted to.

This last simple expedient would have saved some grantees years of litigation, and many a hard thought of the said grantees against the Government. It would naturally occur to any one at all conversant with the subject; but, *alas!* in India this is often not the condition under which laws are made.

But there is another difficulty at the back of all this.

Though the Waste Land Rules enact that the Government, and not the grantee, shall be the defendant in any claim for land within a lot sold, practically the said enactment in no way saves grantees from litigation. Claimants for land always plead that it is *not* within the boundaries of the land sold, and *ergo* the grantee is made the defendant to prove that it is. The villagers never having been shown the boundaries by any Government official (for it is not enacted in the Waste Land Rules), the question whether the land claimed is within or without the boundaries is an open one, not always easily decided, and the suit runs its course.

I even know of cases where, though survey has been charged for at the exorbitant rate of four annas an acre, the outer boundaries of the lot have never been surveyed at all, but merely copied from old Collectorate maps, which showed the boundaries between the zemindaree and waste lands.*
Is it strange, then, if buying lands from Government is often buying litigation, worry, loss of time and money.

In many countries, for example Prussia (there I know it is so, for I have tested it again and again), there are official records which can and do show to whom any land in question belongs. This may scarcely be practicable in India, but surely the question of title being, as it is, in a far worse

---

* I need scarcely observe it is impossible to define lands from maps alone without the field-book.

state in India than in most countries, any change would be for the better. Anyhow, the present mode the Government **adopts** in selling lands is a grievous wrong to the purchasers. Words cannot describe the worry and loss some have suffered thereby, and it might all be so easily avoided.

I have above detailed two of the drawbacks **Tea had to contend with** in its infancy; the absurdly high **price paid for land** was the third.

Again, companies and proprietors of gardens wishing to have large areas under cultivation gave their managers simple orders to extend, not judiciously, but in any case. What was the result? Gardens might be seen in those days with 200 acres of so-called cultivation, but with 60 or even 70 per cent. vacancies, in which the greater part of the labour available was employed in clearing jungle for 100 acres further extension in the following spring. **I have** seen no garden in Assam or Cachar with less than 20 per cent. vacancies, many with far more; and yet most of them were extending. I do not believe *now* any garden in all India exists with less than 12 per cent. vacancies, but a plantation as full as this did *not* exist formerly.

As **the** expenditure on a garden is in direct proportion to the **area** cultivated, and the yield of **Tea** likewise in direct **proportion to the** number of plants, it follows the course adopted was the one exactly calculated to entail the greatest expenditure for the smallest yield. This unnecessary, this wilful extension, was the fourth and a very serious drawback.

Under this head the fourth drawback may also be included—the fact that the weeds in all plantations were *ahead* of the labour; that is to say, that gardens were not kept **clean**. This is more or less even the case to-day; it was **the invariable rule then.** The consequence was twofold—*first*, a small yield of Tea; *secondly*, an increased expenditure; for it is a fact that the land fifty men can keep always clean, if the weeds are never allowed to grow to maturity and seed, will take nearer one hundred if the weeds once get ahead. The results, too, differ widely: in the first case the soil is always clear; in the second clear only at intervals. The first, as observed, can be accomplished with fifty, the latter will take nearly double the men.

The fifth drawback I shall advert to again later, *viz.*, the selection of sloping land, often the steepest that could be found, on which to plant Tea. The great mischief thus entailed will be fully described elsewhere. It was the fifth, and not the least, antagonistic point to success.

Number six was the difficulty in the transport of seed to any new locality, for nine times out of ten a large proportion failed; and again the enormous cost of Tea seed in those days, Rs. 200 a maund (Rs. 500 at least, deducting what failed, was its real price). This item of seed alone entailed an enormous outlay, and was the sixth difficulty Tea cultivation had to contend with. It was, however, a source of great profit to the old plantations, and principally accounts for the large dividends paid for years by the Assam Company.

Again, many managers at that time had no experience to guide them in the manufacture of Tea; each made it his own way, and often turned out most worthless stuff. There is great ignorance on the subject at the present time, but those who know *least* to-day, know *more* than the best informed in the Tea-fever period. Indian Tea was a new thing then; the supply was small, and it fetched comparatively much higher prices than it does now. Still much of it was so bad that the average price all round was low.

Tea manufacture, moreover, as generally practised then,

was a much more elaborate and expensive process than it is now.

This will be explained further on, under the head of "Tea Manufacture;" I merely now state the fact in support of the assertion that the bad Tea made in those days, and the expensive way it was done, was the seventh hindrance to successful Tea cultivation.

Often in those days was a small garden made of 30 or 40 acres, and sold to a Company as 150 or 200 acres! I am not joking. It was done over and over again. The price paid, moreover, was quite out of proportion to even the supposed area. Two or three lakhs of rupees (20,000*l*. or 30,000*l*.) have been often paid for such gardens, when not more than two years old, and 40 per cent. of the existing area, vacancies. The original cultivators "retired" and the Company carried on. With such drags upon them (apart from all the other drawbacks enumerated) could success be even hoped for? Certainly not.

I could tell of more difficulties the cultivation had to contend with at the outset, but I have said enough to show, as I remarked, "that it was not strange Tea enterprise failed, inasmuch as it would have been much stranger if it had not."

Do any of the difficulties enumerated exist now? And may a person embarking in Tea to-day hope, with reasonable hope, for success? Yes, certainly, I think as regard the latter—the former let us look into.*

People who understand more or less of Tea are plentiful, and a good manager, who knows Tea cultivation and Tea manufacture well, may be found. It will scarcely pay to

---

* Note to Third Edition.—Since the above was written, Teas, both Indian and Chinese, have had a heavy fall, due to the simple fact that the supplies have exceeded the demands. But with increased knowledge and experience, producers can afford to sell cheaper, and the present absurdly low prices ruling will, I think, work their own cure.

buy land of the Government at the present high rates, but many people hold large tracts in good Tea localities, and would readily sell.

There is plenty of flat land to be got, so no evil from slopes need be incurred.

Tea seed is plentiful and cheap.

The manufacture of Tea (though still progressing) is simple, economical, and more or less known. Anyhow a beginner now will commence where others have left off.

Of course to buy a made garden cheap is better than to make one; but the result in this case is of course no criterion of what profit may be expected from Tea cultivation.

As many of the items to be calculated under the heads of cultivation, manufacture, and receipts will be better understood after details on these subjects are gone into, I shall reserve the consideration of "how much profit Tea can give" to the end of this treatise.

CHAPTER II.

LABOUR, LOCAL AND IMPORTED.

WHEN the very large amount of labour required to carry on a plantation is considered, it is evident that facilities for it are a *sine quâ non* to success. Assam and Cachar, the two largest Tea districts, are very thinly populated, and almost entirely dependent on imported labour.* The expense of this is great, and it is the one, and consequently a great drawback to those provinces. The only district I know of with a good Tea climate and abundance of local labour is Chittagong.† Several other places have a good supply of local labour, but then their climates are not very suitable.

Each coolie imported costs Rs. 30 and upwards (it used to be much more) ere he arrives on the garden and does any work. After arrival he has to be housed; to be cared for and *physicked* when sick; to be paid when ill as when working; to have work found for him, or paid to sit idle when there is no work; and in addition to all this every death, every desertion, is a loss to the garden of the whole sum expended in bringing the man or woman. Contrast this with the advantages of local labour. In many cases no expense for buildings is necessary, as the labourers come daily to work from adjacent villages, and in such cases no expense is entailed by sick men, for these simply remain at home. There is no loss by death or desertions. When no

---

* Not so much so now as when this was first written.

† Note to Third Edition.—A portion of the Western Dooars may perhaps be added, but the labour, though adjacent, is not strictly local. Up to the present, however, I have had but little expense in importing coolies to the gardens there in which I am interested.

work is required on the garden, labour is simply not employed. All this makes local labour, even where the rate of wages is high, very much cheaper than imported.

The action of Government in the matter of imported labour has much increased the difficulties and expense necessarily attendant on it. It is a vexed and a very long question which I care not to enter into minutely, for it has been discussed already *ad nauseam;* still I must put on record my opinion, after looking very closely into it, that the Government has not acted wisely, inasmuch as any State interference in the relations of employer and employed (outside the protection which the existing laws give) is a radical mistake. As for the law passed on the subject to the effect that a coolie who has worked out his agreement and voluntarily enters into a new one shall be, as before, under Government protection, and his employer answerable as before to Government, for the way he is housed, treated when sick, &c., it is not easy to see why such enactments are more necessary in his case than in that of any other hired servant or labourer throughout all India.

All evidence collected, all enquiries made, tend to show that coolies are well treated on Tea estates. It is the interest of the proprietors and managers to do so, and self-interest is a far more powerful inducement than any the Government can devise. The meddling caused by the visits of the " Protector of Coolies " [*] to a garden conduces to destroy the kind feelings which should (and in spite of these hindrances often do) exist between the proprietor or manager and his men. I do not hesitate in my belief that imported coolies on Tea plantations would be better off in many ways were all Government interference abolished.

---

[*] What a designation! Who invented it, I wonder? A clever man, doubtless, for Government interference was probably his hobby, and he quickly perceived the very title would, more or less, render the office necessary.

I do not decry Government action to the extent of seeing the coolies understand their terms of engagements, and are cared for on their journey to the Tea districts; but once landed on the garden, all Government interference should cease.

The idea of the State laying down how many square yards of jungle each coolie shall clear in a day, how many square feet he shall dig, &c., &c.! Can *any* certain rates be laid down for such work? Is all jungle the same, all soil the same; and even if such rates *could* be laid down, how can the rules be followed? Bah! they are *not*, never will be, and the whole thing is too childish for serious discussion.

It is not difficult to sit at a desk and frame laws and rules that look feasible on paper. It is quite another thing to carry them out. Over-legislation is a crying evil in India, but there is still a worse, namely, legislation and official action on subjects of which the said officials are utterly ignorant.

I have said enough to show imported labour cannot vie with local, nor would it do so were all the evils of Government interference removed. I therefore believe Tea property in India will eventually pay best where local labour exists. This will naturally be the case when other conditions are equal, but so great are the advantages of local labour, I believe it will also be the case in spite of *moderate* drawbacks.

CHAPTER III.

TEA DISTRICTS AND THEIR COMPARATIVE ADVANTAGES, CLIMATE, SOIL, ETC., IN EACH.

The Tea districts in India, that is, where Tea is grown in India to-day, are—*

1. Assam.
2. The Dehra Dhoon.
3. Kumaon (Himalayas).
4. Darjeeling (Himalayas).
5. Cachar and Sylhet.†
6. Kangra (Himalayas).
7. Hazareebaugh.
8. Chittagong.
9. Terai below Darjeeling.
10. Neilgherries (Madras Hills).
11. Western Dooars.

In fixing on any district to plant Tea in, four things have to be considered—viz., soil, climate, labour, and means of transport. When—the district being selected—a site has to be chosen, all but the second of these have to be considered again, and the lay of land, nature of jungle, water, and sanitation are also of great importance in choosing a site.

I will first, then, discuss generally the Tea districts given

---

* Note to Third Edition.—I give them, as far as I know, in the order they became Tea districts. Though in the said order there is, I believe, no great error, I may be open to correction in one or two instances.

† These are virtually one, and I shall allude to both as Cachar.

above as regards the advantages of each for Tea cultivation. I have seen and studied Tea gardens in all the districts named, except No. 2. What I know of the Dehra Dhoon is from what I have read, and what is generally known of the climate.

Before, however, comparing each district, we should know what are the necessities of the Tea plant as regards climate and soil. Tea, especially the China variety, will grow in very varying climates and soils, but it will not flourish in all of them, and if it does not flourish, and flourish well, it well certainly not pay.

The climate required for Tea is a hot damp one. As a rule, a good Tea climate is not a healthy one. The rainfall should not be less than 80 to 100 inches per annum, and the more of this that falls in the early part of the year the better. Any climate which, though possessing an abundant rainfall, suffers from drought in the early part of the year is not, *cæteris paribus*, so good as one where the rain is more equally diffused. All the Tea districts would yield better with more rain in February, March, and April; and therefore some, where fogs prevail in the mornings at the early part of the year, are so far benefited.

As any drought is prejudicial to Tea, it stands to reason hot winds must be very bad. These winds argue great aridity, and the Tea plant luxuriates in continual moisture.

The less cold weather experienced where Tea is, the better for the plant. It can stand, and will grow in, great cold (freezing point, and lower in winter, is found in some places where Tea is), but I do not think it will ever be grown to a profit on such sites. That Tea requires a temperate climate was long believed and acted upon by many to their loss. The climate *cannot* be too hot for Tea if the heat is accompanied with moisture.

Tea grown in temperate climes, such as moderate elevations in the Himalayas, is quite different to the Tea of hot moist climates, such as Eastern Bengal. Some people like it better, and certainly the flavour is more delicate; but it is very much weaker, and the value of Indian Tea (in the present state of the home market, where it is principally used for giving "body" to the washy stuff from China) consists in its strength. Another all-important point in fixing on a climate for Tea is the fact, that apart from the strength the yield is double in hot, moist climes, what it is in comparatively dry and temperate ones. A really pleasant climate to live in *cannot* be a good one for Tea. I may now discuss the comparative merits of the different Tea districts.

Assam.

This is the principal home of the indigenous plant. The climate in the northern portions is perfect, superior to the southern, as more rain falls in the spring. The climate of the whole of Assam, however, is very good for Tea. The Tea plant yields most abundantly when hot sunshine and showers intervene. For climate, then, I accord the first place to Northern Assam. Southern Assam is, as observed, a little inferior.

The soil of this province is decidedly rich. In many places there is a considerable coating of decayed vegetation on the surface, and inasmuch as in all places where Tea has been or is likely to be planted it is strictly virgin soil, considerable nourishment exists. The prevailing soil also is light and friable, and thus, with the exception of the rich oak soil in parts of the Himalayas, Assam in this respect is second to none.

As regards labour we must certainly put it the last on the list. The Assamese, and they are scanty, won't work, so the planters, with few exceptions, are dependent on imported coolies; and inasmuch as the distance to bring them is enormous, the outlay on this head is large, and a sad drawback to successful Tea cultivation.

The Burhampootra—that vast river which runs from one end of Assam to the other—gives an easy mode of export for the Tea, but still, owing to the distance from the sea-board, it cannot rank in this respect as high as some others.

Cachar.

The indigenous Tea is also found in a part of this province. The climate differs but little from Assam. In one respect it is better; more rain falls in the spring.

The soil is not equal to Assamese soil; it is more sandy, and lacks the power. Again, there is much more flat land fit for Tea cultivation in Assam, and there can be no doubt as to the advantage of level surfaces.

As regards transport Cachar has the advantage, for it has equally a water-way, and is not so distant from Calcutta.

The labour aspect is much the same in the two provinces, both being almost entirely dependent on imported coolies; but Cachar is nearer the labour fields than Assam.

However, after discussing separately the advantages of each province, I propose to draw up a tabular statement, which will show at a glance the comparative merits of each on each point discussed.

Chittagong.

This is a comparatively new locality for Tea. The climate is better than Cachar in the one respect that there is less cold weather, but inferior in the more important fact that much less rain falls in the spring. In this latter respect it is also inferior to Assam, particularly to Northern Assam. There is one part of Chittagong, the Hill Tracts (Tea has scarcely been much tried there yet), which, in the fact of spring rains, is superior to other parts of the province, as also in soil, for it is much richer there. On the whole, however, Chittagong must yield the palm to both Assam and Cachar on the score of climate, and also, I think, of soil. For though good rich tracts are occasionally met with, they are not so plentiful as in the two last-named districts. Always, however, excepting the Hill Tracts of Chittagong; there the soil is, I think, quite equal to either Assam or Cachar.

As regards labour (a very essential point to successful Tea cultivation), Chittagong is most fortunate. With few exceptions (and those only partial) all the plantations are carried on with local labour, which—excepting for about two months, the rice-time—is abundant.

For transport (being on the coast with a convenient harbour, a continually increasing trade, ships also running direct to and from England), it is very advantageously situated.

Chittagong possesses another advantage over all other Tea districts in its large supply of manure. The country is thickly populated, and necessarily large herds of cattle exist. The natives do not use manure for rice (almost the sole cultivation), and, consequently, planters can have it almost for the asking. The enormous advantages of manure in Tea cultivation are not yet generally appreciated: it will certainly double the ordinary yield of a Tea garden. A chapter is devoted to this subject.

Terai below Darjeeling.

I have seen this, and the Tea in it, since I wrote the first edition of this Essay.

The soil is *very* good for Tea. The climate is also a good one, but there is not as much rain in the early part of the year as planters could wish. Much difficulty exists about labour, owing to the very unhealthy climate. As the jungle is cleared, however, this last objection will be in a measure got over. As it stands now, it is perhaps the most unhealthy Tea locality in India.

Communication will be very easy when the Northern Bengal Railway is finished, which it will be immediately.

Except in the point of salubrity (which is, however, an important one), I think this locality a favourable one for Tea.

The Dehra Dhoon.

I have heard the first Tea in India was planted here. The lucky men, two officers, who commenced the plantation, sold it, I believe, in its infancy, to a company for five lakhs of rupees. What visions did Tea hold forth in those days!

In climate the Dehra Dhoon is far from good. The hot dry weather of the North-west is not at all suited to the Tea plant. Hot winds shrivel it up, and though it recovers when the rains come down, it cannot thrive in such a climate. One fact will, I think, prove this. In favourable climates, with good soil and moderate cultivation, 18 flushes or crops may be taken from a plantation in a season. With like advantages, and *heavy* manuring, 22 or even more may be had. In the "Selections from the Records of the Government of India" on Tea, published in 1857 (a book to which many owe their ruin), the following appears, showing how small are the number of flushes in the North-west :—

Method of gathering Tea Leaves.—The season for gathering leaves generally commences about the beginning of April, and continues until **October**; the number of gatherings varies, depending on the moistness and dryness of the season. If the season be good, that is to say, if rain falls in the cold weather and spring, and the general rains be favourable, as many as five gatherings may be obtained. These, however, may be reduced to three general periods for gathering—viz., from April to June, from July to August 15, and from September to October 15. If the season be a dry one, no leaves ought to be taken off the bushes after October 1, as by doing so they are apt to be injured. If, however, there are good rains in September, leaves can be pulled until October 15, but no later, as by this time they have got hard and leathery and not fitted for making good Teas, and it is necessary to give the plants good rest in order to recruit. Some plants continue to throw out new leaves until the end of November; but those formed during this month are generally small and tough.

<small>Three general gatherings.</small>

When this was written, the experience detailed related to Dehra Dhoon, the Kumaon, and Kangra gardens, and we see that five flushes or gatherings are thought good. It however makes matters in this respect (far from a general fault in the said "Records") worse than they are. Ten and twelve flushes, with *high* cultivation, can be got in the North-west. But what is this as against twenty and twenty-five?

Labour is plentiful and cheap. The great distance from the coast makes transport very expensive.

KANGRA.

This is a charming valley, with a delightful climate

more favourable to **Tea** than the Dehra Dhoon, still it is not **a perfect** Tea climate. It is too dry and too cold. The **soil is good** for **Tea, better than that of the** Dhoon, **but** inferior to some rich soils in the Himalayan oak forests. Local labour is obtainable at cheap rates. Distance makes transport for export very difficult; but a good local market now exists in the Punjab, and a good deal **of Tea is bought at the fairs, and** taken away **by** the wild **tribes** over the **border.** With the limited cultivation there, I should hope planters will find a market for all their produce. Manure must be obtainable (manure had not been thought of **for** Tea when I visited Kangra), and if liberally applied, it will increase the yield greatly.

Kangra is strictly a Himalayan **district,** but the elevation is moderate, if I remember right, **about** 3,000 feet, and the land is so slightly sloping **it** may almost be called level. A great advantage this over the steep lands, on which most of the Himalayan gardens, many in Cachar, and some in Assam and Chittagong, are planted.

Kangra is *not* the best place for a man who wants to make money by Tea; but for one who would be content to settle there, and content to make a livelihood by it, a more desirable spot with a more charming climate could not be found. Land, however, is not easily procured.

The Teas produced in Kangra are of a peculiarly delicate flavour, and are consequently highly esteemed in the London market.

DARJEELING.

This, too, I have seen since I published the first edition of this Essay. The elevation of the station, 6,900 feet, is far too great; but plantations lower down do tolerably well (that is, well for hill gardens). The climate, like all hill climates, is too cold. As regards transport the Darjeeling plantations will be well situated when the railroad now constructing is finished. Like elevations in Darjeeling and Kumaon are in favour of the former, *first*, because the latitude is less; *secondly*, because Darjeeling has much more rain in the spring. I believe, therefore, that the hill plantations of Darjeeling have a better chance of paying than the gardens in Kumaon, but, as stated before, no elevated gardens, that is, none in the Himalayas, have any chance in the race against plantations in the plains, always providing the latter are in a good Tea climate.

In two respects, however, Darjeeling is behind Kumaon. The soil is not so good, and the land is much steeper. It is more than absurd, some of the steeps on which Tea is planted in the former; and such precipices can, I am sure, never pay. Gardens, barely removed above the Terai (and there are such in Darjeeling), can scarcely be called "elevated," and for them the remarks applied to the Terai are more fitting. As a broad rule it should be recognised that the lower Tea is planted in the Himalayas the better chance it has.

All the plants in the Darjeeling gardens, with but few exceptions, are China.

The China plant makes by far the best Green Tea, and I believe the Darjeeling gardens would pay much better than they do if they altered their manufacture from black to green. (See further on, under the head of Hazareebaugh, what has been done in this way.) All Himalayan gardens should, in my opinion, make Green Tea (Kumaon has awoke to the fact), for all have China plants, and can therefore make far better Green Tea than can be produced from the Hybrid which is so general in plain gardens.*

KUMAON.

It was in this district (a charming climate to live in, with magnificent scenery to gaze at) I first planted Tea in India, and I much wish for my own sake, and that of others, I had not done so. I knew nothing of Tea at the time, and I thought a district selected by Government for inaugurating the cultivation must necessarily be a good one. No hill climate *can* be a good one for Tea; but the inner part of Kumaon, very cold, owing to its elevation, high latitude, and distance from the plains, is a peculiarly **bad** one. Yet **there it** was Government made nurseries, distributed seed gratis, recommended the site for Tea (see the " Records " alluded to), and led **many on to** their ruin **by** doing so. The intention of the Government was good, but the officers in charge of the enterprise were much to blame, perhaps not for making the mistake at first (no one *at the first* knew what climate was suitable), but for perpetuating the mistake, when later very little enquiry would have revealed the truth. I believe it was guessed at by Government officials **long** ago, but it **was** easier to sing the old tune; and a very expensive song it has proved to many.†

I need scarcely, after this, add that I do not approve of Kumaon for Tea. An exhilarating and bracing climate for man is not suited to the Tea plant. The district has

* When this was written the demand for Green Teas in Europe was greater than it is now. Still Kumaon has found a local market for Green Tea over the border, that is, among the Asiatic tribes, and Darjeeling might do the same.

† Is it possible that the continued deception (it was nothing less) was owing to the fact that Government had gardens to sell there? They were advertised for sale a long time at absurd prices.

one solitary advantage—rich soil. I have never seen richer, more productive land than exists in some of the Kumaon oak forests, but even this cannot in the case of Tea counterbalance the climate. Any crop which does not require much heat and moisture will grow to perfection in that soil. Such potatoes as it produces! Were the difficulties of transport not so great, a small fortune might be made by growing them.

Could any part of Kumaon answer for Tea it would be the lower elevations in the outer ranges of the hills, but these are precisely the sites that have *not* been chosen. Led, as in my own case, partly by the Government example, partly by the wish to be *out* of sight of the " horrid plains," and *in* sight of that glorious panorama the snowy range, planters have chosen the interior of Kumaon. Some wisely (I was not one of them) selected low sites, valleys sheltered from the cold winds; but even their choice has not availed much. The frost in winter lingers longest in the valleys, and though doubtless the yield there is larger, owing to the increased heat in summer, the young plants suffer much in the winter. The outer ranges, owing to the heat radiating from the plains, are comparatively free from frost, but there again the soil is not so rich. Still they would unquestionably be preferable to the interior.

Labour is plentiful in Kumaon and very cheap—Rs. 4 per mensem. Transport is very expensive. It costs not a little to send Tea from the interior over divers ranges of hills to the plains. It has then some days' journey by cart ere it meets the rail, to which 1,000 miles of carriage on the railroad has to be added.

Since the above was written, Kumaon has secured a good local market, and I believe sells most of its Tea unpacked to merchants who come from over the border to buy it.

It has also improved its position greatly by making Green Teas, for which, as observed before, the China plant is so well fitted. With those two advantages, though the climate is inferior, I suspect that Tea there now pays better than in Darjeeling.

Gurhwall is next to Kumaon, and so similar that I have not thought it necessary to discuss it separately. The climate is the same, the soil as a rule not so good. There is one exception though, a plantation near " Lohba," the Teas of which (owing, I conceive, to its peculiar soil) command high prices in the London market. The gardens, both in Kumaon and Gurhwall, have been generally much better cared for than those in Eastern Bengal. As a rule they are private properties managed by the owners.

HAZAREEBAUGH.

This district I have resided in since I wrote the first edition of this Essay. The climate is too dry, and hot winds are felt there. A great compensation, though, is labour; it is more abundant and cheaper in this district than in any other The carriage is all by land, and it is some distance to the rail. But the Tea gardens at Hazareebaugh can never vie with those in Eastern Bengal, inasmuch as the climate is very inferior. The soil is very poor.

NEILGHERRIES.

The climate is superior to the Himalayan, for the frost is very slight. Were, however, more heat there in summer, it would be better.

Some of the Teas have sold very well in the London

market, for as regards delicacy of flavour they take a high place.

The soil is good, but the temperate climate which holds on these "blue mountains" is not favourable to a large produce.

WESTERN DOOARS.

When the second edition of this work was printed, this district was unknown as a Tea locality.

My attention was directed to it in 1874; I was the second who planted Tea in it, and I have now completed a garden there.

As regards climate, soil, and lay of land, it is perfect, and I believe it will eventually prove the most paying district in India for Tea.

The Northern Bengal Railway, just opened, gives it great advantages for transport.

Having now discussed each district, all of which, except the Dehra Dhoon, I have seen, I give, in further elucidation, Meteorological Tables. For those not mentioned in the tables I have failed to acquire the necessary information.

My thanks are due to Dr. Coates, at Hazareebaugh, for his kindness in supplying me with much of the data from which the following tables are framed :—

TABLE OF ELEVATION AND TEMPERATURE OF TEA LOCALITIES.

N.B.—The exact temperature of other Tea Districts not being known, I have confined myself to these; but general remarks on the elevation and temperature of other Tea localities will be found elsewhere.

Districts	Place	Elevation in feet	Details	January	February	March	April	May	June	July	August	September	October	November	December	D.J.F.	M.A.M.	J.J.A.	S.O.N.	Year
ASSAM	Goalparah	386	Monthly Temp.	61.7	63.0	72.6	77.6	76.0	80.3	82.1	81.6	80.5	77.5	69.0	64.6	63.1	75.4	81.3	75.6	73.8
			Do. Max.	77.2	87.9	94.0	97.0	91.0	91.0	92.0	91.5	92.0	89.0	84.3	78.3					
			Do. Min.	49.0	48.0	57.2	62.6	67.0	70.0	73.7	73.0	70.1	62.3	50.8	50.0					
	Gowhatty	134	Monthly Temp.	63.6	67.6	74.5	77.4	80.4	81.8	83.0	82.9	82.2	79.2	71.1	65.5	65.6	77.4	82.6	77.5	75.8
	Seebsaugor	370	Monthly Temp.	60.0	64.1	69.3	73.8	78.5	82.4	83.6	83.5	83.1	78.3	69.4	62.4	62.2	73.7	83.2	76.9	74.0
	Debrooghur	396	Monthly Temp.	62.2	63.4	71.3	72.7	77.1	80.7	83.7	81.8	81.0	75.6	67.4	61.0	62.2	73.7	82.1	74.7	73.2
CACHAR	Cachar	76	Monthly Temp.	62.9	66.6	73.4	76.8	80.9	82.2	83.3	81.7	81.2	79.6	70.6	65.4	64.9	77.0	82.4	77.1	75.3
CHITTAGONG	Chittagong	191	Monthly Temp.	68.5	72.3	80.5	83.5	84.5	84.0	82.2	82.3	83.0	81.6	73.7	68.9	69.9	82.8	82.8	79.4	78.7

TABLE OF ELEVATION AND TEMPERATURE OF TEA LOCALITIES—(Continued.)

Districts	Place	Elevation in feet	Details	January	February	March	April	May	June	July	August	September	October	November	December	D.J.F.	M.A.M.	J.J.A.	S.O.N.	Year
DARJEELING	Dar-jeeling	6952	Monthly Temp.	42·2	43·8	52·0	58·7	62·1	63·7	64·9	64·4	63·0	57·3	49·4	44·7	43·5	57·6	64·3	58·4	55·9
			Do. Max.	62·0	66·0	72·0	78·0	79·0	79·0	79·0	75·0	80·0	78·0	63·0	60·0					
			Do. Min.	32·0	28·0	39·0	48·0	48·0	57·0	58·0	59·0	57·0	44·0	38·0	33·0					
CHOTA NAGPORE	Hazaree-baugh	2010	Monthly Temp.	62·7	67·1	73·7	85·6	88·6	83·8	77·8	79·3	77·5	72·6	64·8	61·4	63·7	82·6	80·3	71·6	74·5
			Do. Max.	82·0	91·0	94·0	107·0	100·0	103·0	89·0	88·0	87·0	84·0	78·0	76·0					
			Do. Min.	44·0	46·4	55·0	67·0	72·0	71·0	71·0	73·0	70·0	59·0	52·0	44·0					
NEIL-GHERRIES	Ootaca-mund	7490	Monthly Temp.	51·5	52·8	57·3	60·1	60·8	57·9	55·8	56·1	56·4	55·9	53·9	51·9	52·1	59·4	56·6	55·4	55·9

N.B.—The letters in the columns, between December and the year, refer to months; thus, D. J. F. is December, January, February.
The figures show the average temperature during those months.

TABLE OF LATITUDE, LONGITUDE, AND RAINFALL OF TEA LOCALITIES.

N.B.—The exact rainfalls of other Tea Districts not being known, I have confined myself to these; but general remarks on the rainfall in other Tea localities will be found elsewhere.

Districts	Place	Latitude	Longitude	Details	January	February	March	April	May	June	July	August	September	October	November	December	Total
ASSAM	Goalparah	26° 11′	90° 36′	Average rain, several years	0·42	0·76	1·84	4·85	11·72	23·72	21·33	12·69	10·93	5·61	0·39	0·20	94·44
				Days rain fell in 1869	2	2	4	8	19	24	22	18	15	5	Nil	Nil	119
ASSAM	Gowhatty	26° 5′	91° 43′	Average rain, several years	0·70	1·43	1·48	7·27	10·92	13·29	13·08	11·98	6·82	3·20	0·47	0·12	70·76
				Days rain fell in 1869	2	2	4	8	16	16	9	10	14	2	Nil	1	84
ASSAM	Seebsaugor	27° 2′	94° 39′	Average rain, several years	1·18	2·43	3·77	10·15	11·04	15·56	14·87	13·88	11·13	4·46	1·29	0·69	90·45
				Days rain fell in 1869	11	9	10	13	22	13	19	23	17	8	Nil	2	147
CACHAR	Cachar	24° 48′	92° 43′	Average rain, several years	0·50	3·53	6·09	12·69	16·12	19·55	24·58	16·84	13·90	7·77	7·03	0·79	123·3
				Days rain fell in 1869	2	9	10	16	18	20	18	25	19	8	Nil	Nil	145
CHITTA-GONG	Chittagong	22° 20′	91° 44′	Average rain, several years	0·37	1·62	1·31	5·46	9·42	22·92	22·54	23·04	13·01	5·93	2·30	0·55	108·47
				Days rain fell in 1869	1	7	3	4	14	15	21	25	17	5	Nil	1	113

TABLE OF LATITUDE, LONGITUDE, AND RAINFALL OF TEA LOCALITIES—(Continued).

Districts	Place	Latitude	Longitude	Details	January	February	March	April	May	June	July	August	September	October	November	December	Total
CHITTAGONG	Hill Tracts	?	?	Rain in 1869	Nil	1.90	1.50	12.55	9.00	12.50	18.20	14.30	12.70	5.70	Nil	0.50	88.85
				Days rain fell in 1869	Nil	4	4	7	13	16	22	19	19	4	Nil	1	109
DARJEELING	Darjeeling	27°3'	88°18'	Average rain, several years	0.76	1.60	1.65	3.62	7.01	27.50	29.40	29.09	18.06	6.56	0.20	0.14	129.50
				Days rain fell in 1869	2	3	5	9	17	23	26	22	24	7	1	2	148
	Western Dooars*	?	?	Rain in 1869	0.80	2.00	1.50	6.60	25.30	27.30	46.50	83.50	46.50	9.60	?	2.40	252.00
				Days rain fell in 1869	3	3	5	7	15	19	25	28	22	5	?	?	?
CHOTA NAGPORE	Hazareebaugh	24°0'	85°20'	Average rain, several years	0.42	0.52	0.75	0.42	1.37	10.99	14.63	11.44	6.26	3.51	0.19	0.02	50.52
				Days rain fell in 1869	4	Nil	7	Nil	5	11	24	16	21	9	Nil	1	98

* The rainfall given for the **Western Dooars** cannot be relied on. Perhaps more than the average fell in 1869, but anyhow, I should think 83 inches registered for August is an error. I know the yearly fall there is *not* 252 inches.

I will now endeavour to draw up a tabular statement of the respective advantages of the various Tea districts as regards **climate, labour, lay of** land, soil, facilities of procuring manure and transport.

In importance I regard **them in** the order given. I place labour before soil, because the fact is, in all the provinces suitable and good soil for Tea can be found *somewhere;* and therefore, while soil is all important in selecting a site, it is secondary to labour in deciding on a district. Lay of land comes after labour. When my information on any point is not sure I place a note of interrogation. Where advantages are equal, or nearly so, I give the same number, and the greater the advantage of a district on the point treated in the column the smaller the number. Thus, under the head of Climate, Assam is marked **1**.

As the following table gives no information as to which of all the districts possesses the greatest advantages, all *things considered*, but only gives my opinion of each under each head, and the subject closed in this way would be unsatisfactory, I may state that, in my opinion, the choice should lie between the three first and the last on the list; and my choice would be the last.

Comparative advantages of the Tea Districts in India as regards climate, labour, lay of land, soil, manure, and transport.

Tea Districts	Climate	Labour	Lay of Land	Soil	Manure	Transport	
Assam	1	4	1	1	4	3	
Cachar	2	4	2	2	4	2	Water
Chittagong	3	2	2	2	1	1	carriage
Chittagong Hill Tracts	3	3	3	1	2	1	
Terai below Darjeeling	2	4	1	1	3	5	
Darjeeling	4	3	5	3	3	6	
Hazareebaugh	6	1	1	4	2	4	
Kangra	4	3	1	3	3	9	Land
Dehra Dhoon	5	3	1	3	3	7	carriage
Kumaon	5	3	4	2	3	8	
Neilgherries	4	3	2	2	3	4	
Western Dooars	1	3	1	1	4	1	

CHAPTER IV.

SOIL.

To pronounce as precisely on soil as to climate is not easy. The Tea plant will grow on almost any soil, and will flourish on many. Still there are broad general rules to be laid down in the selection of soils for Tea, which no one can ignore with impunity.

When first I turned my attention to Tea, I collected soils from many gardens, noting in each case how the plants flourished. I then sat down to examine them, never doubting to arrive at some broad practical conclusions. I was sadly disappointed. I found the most opposing soils nourished, apparently, equally good plants. I knew not then much about Tea, and judged of the Tea bushes mostly by the size (a very fallacious test); still, after-experience has convinced me I was more or less right in the conclusion I then came to, that several soils are good for Tea.

Nothing, then, but broad general rules can be laid down on this point, for I defy anyone to select any one soil as the best for Tea, to the exclusion of others.

A light sandy loam is perhaps as good a soil as any *out* of the Himalayas. It ought to be deep, and the more decayed vegetable matter there is lying on its surface the better. If deep enough for the descent of the tap-root, say 3 feet, it matters not much what the subsoil is, otherwise a yellowish red subsoil is an advantage. This subsoil is generally a mixture of clay and sand. Much of Assam, Cachar, and Chittagong is as the above, but, as a rule, it is richest in Assam, poorest in Chittagong.

Where the loam is of a greasy nature (very different to clay), with a mixture of sand in it, it is superior to the above, for it has more body. All good Tea soils must have a fair proportion of sand, and if not otherwise apparent, it may be detected by mixing a little of the soil with spittle and rubbing it on the hand. If the hand be then held up towards the sun, the particles of sand will be seen to glisten.

The soil so common in Kumaon, that is, light rich loam with any amount of decayed vegetable matter on it, and with a ferruginous reddish yellowish subsoil, is, I consider, the finest soil in the world for Tea. The rich decayed vegetable matter is the produce for centuries of oak leaves in the Himalayan forests, and, as all the world knows, oak only grows in temperate climes.

It was long believed that Tea would thrive best on poor soil. The idea was due to the description of Tea soils in China to be found in the first books that treated of Tea. But the fact that Tea, as a rule, is only grown in China on soil which is useless for anything else quite alters the case. If a soil is light and friable enough, it cannot be too rich for Tea.

Ball's book " On the Cultivation and Manufacture of Tea in China" has much on Tea soils, but the opinions the author collected are sadly at variance, and on the whole teach nothing.

In conclusion, I will attempt to point out the qualities in soils in which the Tea plant delights, as also the qualities it abhors.

It loves soils friable, that is, easily divided into all their atoms. This argues a fair proportion of sand, but this should not be in excess, or the soil will be poor. The soil should be porous—imbibing and parting with water freely. The more decayed vegetable matter on its surface the better.

To be avoided are stiff soils of every kind, as also those which when they dry, after rain, cake together and split. Avoid also black-coloured, or even dark-coloured earths. All soils good for the Tea plant are light coloured. If, however, the dark colour arises from decayed vegetation, that is not the colour of the soil, and, as observed, vegetable matter is a great advantage. Judge of colour when soil is dry—for even light-coloured soil looks dark when wet. Soil which will make bricks will not grow Tea; and though I have sometimes seen young plants thrive on stiff soil, I do not believe in any stiff soil as a permanence.

Stones, if not in excess, are advantageous in all soils inclined to be stiff, for they help to keep them open. But then they must not be large, as if so they act as badly as a rocky substratum preventing the descent of the tap-root.

The reason, I take it, why Tea thrives best in light soils is that the spongioles or ends of the feeding roots are very tender, and do not easily penetrate any other.

There is more nourishment in stiffer soils, but for this reason the Tea plant cannot take advantage of it.

If a chosen soil be too stiff, it may be much improved for Tea by mixing sand with it. However, even where sand is procurable near, the expense of this is great. When done, the sand should be mixed with the soil taken out of the holes in which the plants are to be placed (see Transplanting), and it may be done again later by placing sand round the plants and digging it in. All this though is extra labour and very expensive, so none but a good Tea soil should ever be selected, and it is very easily found, for it exists in parts of all the districts discussed.

CHAPTER V.

NATURE OF JUNGLE.

I HAVE not much to say under this head. I have heard many opinions as to the kind of trees and jungle that should exist in contemplated clearances, but I attach little or no weight to them, at all events in Bengal.

In the Himalayas it is somewhat different. There oak trees should be sought for; their existence invariably makes rich soil.* Fir, on the contrary, indicates poor soil. At elevations, however, the desideratum of a warm aspect **interferes,** for the best oak forests are on the colder side. I speak of course of elevations practicable, say three or four thousand feet; above this it is a waste of money to try and cultivate Tea.

In Bengal I do not think the nature of the jungle on land contemplated signifies much. As a rule, the thicker the jungle the richer the soil; but in seeking for a site large trees should not be a *sine quâ non*. Much of the coarse grass land **is very** good, and large trees add enormously to the expense of clearings.† It is not cutting them down which is so expensive, it is cutting them up and getting rid of them by burning, or otherwise, after the former is done.

I have discussed soil fully already, and need only add here that if the knowledge to do so exists, it is better to judge of **soil** from the soil itself than from the vegetation on it, though doubtless a fact that luxuriant vegetation indicates rich soil.

---

* **The** oak tree leaves cause a rich deposit of vegetable matter.
† The Western Dooars are in many parts covered **with** this coarse grass, and nowhere is there better soil.

CHAPTER VI.

WATER AND SANITATION.

THESE may be discussed together and shortly.

Of course adjacent water-carriage is a great advantage for a garden, and it should be obtained, if possible, in selecting a site. The expense of land-carriage, where there is no rail, is great, and Tea cultivation requires all advantages to make it pay well.

But it is water for a garden that particularly concerns us now. It is not easy to find land that can be irrigated (this is discussed elsewhere), but no labour or expense in getting such land would be thrown away. Irrigation, combined with high cultivation in other respects, will give a yield per acre undreamt of.

In no case should a plantation be made except where a running stream is handy. Water is a necessity for seedlings, and a plentiful adjacent supply of it is a great desideratum for the comfort and health of every soul on the garden. We all know how dependent the natives are on water, and it is evident facilities in this respect will conduce much (whether the labour be local or imported) both to get and keep coolies. Norton's tube wells—a cheap and most efficient mode of procuring water—will, I doubt not, be eventually much used on Tea plantations.

It has been observed that, as a rule, a good Tea climate is not a healthy one. There is no getting over the fact, and we can only make the best of it. The house, the factories, and all the buildings should be placed as high as possible, and not very close to each other, both for the sake of health and in the event of fire. The locality should be well drained, and cleanliness be attained in every possible way. Give the coolies good houses, with raised mechans to sleep on, and sprinkle occasionally carbolic acid powder in your own house and those of others.

Sanitation is, however, a large subject. It can be studied elsewhere. General ideas on it, and on the properties of the commonest medicines, are a great advantage to any intending Tea planter.

CHAPTER VII.

LAY OF LAND.

The first idea prevailing about Tea was that it should be planted on slopes. It was thought, and truly, that the plant was impatient of stagnant water, and so it is, but it is not necessary to plant it on slopes in consequence. Pictures of Chinese, suspended by chains (inasmuch as the locality could not be otherwise reached), picking Tea off bushes growing in the crevices of rocks, somewhat helped this notion; and when stated, as it was, that the Tea produced in such places was the finest, and commanded the highest price—which was not true—intending planters in India went crazy in their search for impracticable steeps! Much of the failure in Tea has arisen from this fact, for a great part of many, the whole of some, gardens have been planted on land so steep that the Tea can never last or thrive on it. This is especially the case in parts of the Darjeeling district.

Sloping land is objectionable in the following respects. It cannot be highly cultivated in any way (I hold Tea will only pay with high cultivation), for high cultivation consists in frequent digging, to keep the soil open and get rid of weeds, and liberal manuring. If such soil is dug in the rainy season, it is washed down to the foot of the hill, and if manure is applied at any time of the year, it experiences the same fate when the rain comes. As it cannot be dug, weeds necessarily thrive and diminish the yield by choking the plants.

The choice is therefore of two evils: "low cultivation and weeds," or "high cultivation which bares the roots of the plants in a twelvemonth." **Of the** two, the first *must* be chosen, for if the **latter** were pursued, the plants, getting gradually more and more denuded of soil, would simply topple over in two or three years. But choosing the lesser **evil,** the mischief is not confined to the bad effects of low cultivation. Dig the land as little as you will, the great force of the rains washes down a good deal of **soil.** The plants do not sink as the soil lowers, and the consequence is that all Tea plants on slopes have the lower side bare of earth and the roots exposed. This is more and more the case the steeper the slope. These exposed roots shrivel up as the sun acts on them, the plant languishes and yields **very little leaf.**

Attempts are made **to remedy the mischief by** carrying earth up from below yearly, and placing it under the plant; but the expense of doing **this** is great, and the palliation is only temporary, for the same thing occurs again and again as each rainy season returns.

The mischief is greater on stiff than on sandy soils, for on the former the earth is detached in great pieces and carried down the hill. I know one garden in Chittagong, a large one, where the evil is so great, that the sooner the cultivation is abandoned the better for the owners.

A great many gardens in India, indeed the majority, are on slopes; a few in Assam, the greater number in Cachar, some in Chittagong, and almost all the Himalayan plantations. Such of these as are on *steep* slopes will, I believe, never pay, and instead of improving yearly (as good gardens, highly cultivated, should do even after they have arrived at **full** bearing) such, I fear, will deteriorate year by year.

Plantations on moderate slopes need not fail because of **the slopes.** The evils **slight** slopes entail are **not** great, but the sooner the fact is accepted that sloping cannot vie against flat land for the cultivation of Tea the better.

Where only the lower parts of slopes are planted, the plants do very well. The upper part being jungle the wash is not great, and the plants benefit much by the rich vegetable matter the rain brings down from above. I have often seen very fine plants on the lower part of slopes, where the upper has been left in jungle, and I should not hesitate to plant such portions *if* the slope was moderate.

Where teelah land, in Eastern Bengal, or sloping land in the Himalayas, Chittagong, or elsewhere, has to be adopted, aspect is all-important. A good aspect in one climate is bad in another. In Assam, Cachar, Chittagong, and all warm places, choose the coolest; at high elevations (temperate climes), the warmest.

In the Himalayas, moreover, the warmer aspects are, as a rule, the most fertile; *vice versâ* in warm localities. Many a garden, which would have done very well on the moderate slopes chosen had *only* the proper aspects been planted, has been ruined by planting all sides of teelahs or hills indiscriminately. The southern and western slopes of plantations in warm sites are generally very bare of plants. Not strange they should be so, when the power of the reflected rays of the afternoon sun is considered. Again, in cold climates plants cannot thrive on northern aspects, for their great want in such climes is heat and sunshine. Let the above fault, then, be avoided in both cases, for though doubtless a garden is more handy, and looks better in one piece planted all over without any intervening jungle, even patches of jungle look better, and are decidedly cheaper, than bare cultivated hills.

Of flat land, after what I have written, I need not add much. It is of two kinds, table and valley land; the former is very rare in Tea districts, at least of any extent, which makes it worth while to plant it. There are two gardens in Chittagong on such flat table land, and they are both doing very well. **Table** land cannot be too flat, for the natural drainage is so great no stagnant water can lie.*

Valley land is not good if it is *perfectly* flat. It will then be subject to inundation and stagnant water. There is nothing that kills the plant so surely and quickly as the latter. Even **quite flat valleys** can be made sweet by artificial drainage, **but to do** this **a lower** level, not too far distant, must **exist, and** the danger is not quite removed **then.** Valleys **in which** no water-course exists, and which **slope** towards **the mouth** *alone*, are **to** be avoided, for the **plants near the mouth always get** choked with sand. The **best valleys are** those **with a** gentle slope both ways, one **towards the lowest line of** the valley, **be it** a running water-**course, or a dry** nullah which carries off **rain**, the other **towards** the mouth of **the** valley. Such valleys drain them-**selves, or** at least very little artificial drainage is necessary. A valley **of** this kind, with a running stream through it, **is** *most* valuable for Tea, and **if** the other advantages of **soil** and climate **are present it is** simply a perfect site. Such however are not frequent. If in such valleys, **as** is generally **the** case, **the** slope from the head to the mouth is enough, **the** running stream can be "bunded" (shut up) at a high level, and brought along one side at a sufficient elevation to irrigate **the whole.**

I have never seen but one garden in a valley that fulfils all these conditions exactly. It is in Chittagong; the soil is good, **labour** plentiful, and manure abundant. It ought to do great things, for the possibility of irrigating plants in **the** dry season (which, **as** observed, is very trying in Chitta-**gong**) will give several extra flushes in the year.

Of course in the wet season on such **land** the water **must be** allowed to resume **its** natural course.

* I am now commencing a second garden in the Western Dooars on flat table land, and the site is an exceptionally favourable one.

Narrow valleys are not worth planting. No narrow tracts of land, with jungle on both sides, are worth the expense of cultivation, for the continual encroachment of the jungle gives much extra work. The plants, moreover, in very narrow valleys get half-buried with soil washed down from the adjacent slopes. Narrow valleys are therefore, in any case, better avoided.

To conclude shortly, flat lands can be highly cultivated, steep slopes cannot. Tea pays best (perhaps not at all otherwise) with high cultivation—*ergo*, flat lands are preferable.

CHAPTER VIII.

LAYING OUT A GARDEN.

By this I mean, so dividing it when first made into parts, that later the said parts shall be easily recognised, and separately or differently treated, as they may require it.

The usual custom is to begin at one end of a plantation, and dig it right through to the other. In the same way with the pruning and plucking, and I believe the system is a very bad one. Different portions of gardens require different treatment, inasmuch as they differ in soil, and otherwise. One part of a plantation is much more prolific of weeds than another—how absurd that it should be cleaned no oftener! This is only one exemplification of difference of treatment, but in many ways it is necessary, most of all in plucking leaf.

All parts of a plantation, owing in some places to the different ages of the plants, in others to the variety in the soil and its productive powers, in others to slopes or to aspect, do not yield leaf equally, that is, flush does not follow flush with equal rapidity. In some places (supposing each part to be picked when the flush is ready) seven days' interval will exist between the flushes, in others nine, ten, or twelve; but no attention, as a rule, is paid to this. The pickers have finished the garden at the west end, the east end is again ready, and when done, the middle part will be taken in hand, be it ready or be it not! It may be that the middle part flushes quicker than any other; in this case the flush will be more than mature when it is taken, in fact it will have begun to harden; or it may be the middle part does *not* flush as quickly as the others; in this case it will be picked before it is ready, that is, when the flush is too young, and the yield will consequently be smaller.

I believe the yield of a plantation may be largely increased by attending to this. Every Tea estate should be divided into gardens of, say, about five to ten acres each.* If no natural division exists, small roads to act as such should be made. More than this cannot be done when the plantation is first laid out, but when later the plants yield, any difference between the productive powers of different parts of the same garden should be noted, and these divided off into sections. To do this latter with roads would take up too much space, and small masonry pillars, whitewashed, are the best. Four of these, one at each corner of a section, are enough, and they need not be more than 3 feet high and 1 foot square. Thus each garden may, where necessary, be divided into two sections, which, in a 300-acre estate, partitioned off into thirty gardens, would give about forty to sixty sections. No matter where a section may be, directly the flush on it is ready it should be picked. Where the soil on any one garden is much the same, and observation shows the plants all over it flush equally, it may be left all in one. I only lay down the principle, and I am very certain it works well, the proof of which is that, where I have practised it, some sections during the season give three, four, and five flushes more than others. Had the usual plan of picking from one end to the other been adopted, they would have been all *forced* to give the same number; in other words, the said extra flushes would have been lost,

* A garden I have just finished in the Western Dooars is 300 acres in extent, all on flat land without any breaks in the cultivation, and all divided into sections of 5 acres each. Being in one large block it is not divided into gardens at all, only sections.

and further loss occasioned by some flushes being taken before they were ready, others after a portion of the tender leaf had hardened.

The best plan is simply to number the gardens from 1 upwards, and the sections in each garden the same way. Thus supposing No. 5 garden is divided into three sections, they will be known respectively as 5-1, 5-2, and 5-3. This is the best way for the natives, and I find they soon learn to designate each section. I have a man whose special duty (though he has other work also) it is to see each day which sections are ready to pick the following, and those, and those alone, are picked. Practice soon teaches the number of pickers required for any given number of sections, and that number only are put to the work. If a portion is not completed that day, it is the first taken in hand the next, and if any day on no sections is the flush ready, no leaf is picked the following.

Apart from leaf-picking, the garden and section plan detailed is useful in many ways. Each garden, if not each section which most requires it, is dug, pruned, or manured at the best time, and any spot on the plantation is easily designated. The plan facilitates the measurement of work, and enables correct lists of the flushes gathered to be kept. It is thus seen which gardens yield best, and the worst can, by extra manuring, be brought to equal those.

In short, the advantages are many, too numerous to detail.

Of course all this can be better done on a flat garden than on one planted on slopes, and though it may not be possible to work it out as much in detail on the latter, still a good deal in that way can be done, and I strongly recommend it.

In laying out a plantation keep it all as much together as possible, the more it is in one block the easier it is

LAYING OUT A GARDEN.

supervised, the cheaper it is worked. Still do not, with a view to this, take in any bad land, for bad land will never pay.

Let your lines of Tea plants, as far as practicable, run with geometrical regularity. You will later find, both in measuring work and picking leaf, great advantages therefrom. In gardens where the lines are not regular portions are continually being passed over in leaf-picking, and thereby not only is the present flush from such parts lost, but the following is also retarded.

If your different gardens are so situated that the roads through them, that is from one garden to the other, can be along *the side* of any garden without increasing the length of the road, by all means adopt that route. There is no such good boundary for a garden as a road that is being continually traversed. It will save many rupees by preventing the encroachment of jungle into a garden, and more space is thus also given for plants. It is, however, of no use to do it if a road through the middle of a garden is shorter, as coolies *will* always take the shortest route.

The lines of plants on sloping ground should neither run up and down, nor directly across the slope. If they run up and down, gutters or water-courses will form between the lines, and much additional earth will be washed away thereby. If they run right across the hill the same thing will occur *between the trees in each line*, and the lower side of each plant will have its roots laid very bare. It is on all slopes a choice of evils, but if the lines are laid diagonally across the hill, so that the slope *along the lines* shall be a moderate one, the evil is reduced as far as it can be by any arrangement of the plants. No, I forgot ; there is one other thing. The closer the lines to each other, and the closer the plants in the lines to each other, in short, the more thickly the ground on slopes is planted the less will be the wash, for stems and roots retain the soil in its place, and the more there are the greater the advantage.

Where slopes are steep (though, remember, steep slopes are to be avoided) terracing may be resorted to with advantage, as the washing down of the soil is much checked by it.

On flat land, of course, it does not really signify in which directions the lines run, but such a garden looks best if, when the roads are straight, the lines run at right angles to them.

In laying out a garden, choose a central spot with water handy for your factory, bungalow, and all your buildings; let your Tea-houses be as close to your dwelling-house as possible, so that during the manufacturing time you can be in and out at all hours of the day and night. Much of your success will depend upon this. Let all your buildings be as near to each other as they can, but still far enough apart, that any one building may burn without endangering others. You need not construct any Tea-buildings until the third year.

CHAPTER IX.

VARIETIES OF THE TEA PLANT.

These are many, but they all arise from two species: the China plant, the common Tea-bush in China; and the indigenous plant, first discovered some forty years ago in Assam.

These are quite different species of the same plant. Whether the difference was produced by climate, by soil, or in what way, no one knows, and here we have only to do with the facts that they *do* differ in every respect. A purely indigenous plant or tree (for in its wild state it may more properly be called the latter) grows with one stem or trunk, and runs up to 15 and 18 feet high. It is always found in thick jungle, and would thus appear to like shade. I believe it does when young; but I am quite sure, if the jungle were cleared round an indigenous Tea-tree found in the forest, it would thrive better from that day. The China bush (for it is never more) after the second year has numerous stems, and 6 or 7 feet would seem to be its limit in height. The lowest branches of a China plant are close to the ground, but in a pure cultivated indigenous, from 9 inches to 1 foot above the soil the single stem is clean.

The indigenous grows quicker after the second or third year than the China, if it has not been over-pruned or over-plucked when young. In other words, it flushes quicker, for flushing is growing.

The indigenous does not run so much to wood as the China. Indigenous seedlings require to be watered oftener than China, for the latter do not suffer as quickly from drought. **The indigenous tree** has a leaf of 9 inches long and more. **The leaf of the China** bush never exceeds 4 inches. **The indigenous leaf is a bright pale green, the** China leaf **a dull** dark green colour. The indigenous "**flushes,**" that is, **produces** new tender leaf, much more **copiously** than the **China,** and this in two ways: *first,* the leaves **are** larger, and thus if only even in number exceed in bulk what the China has given; and *secondly,* it flushes oftener. The infusion of Tea made from the indigenous species is far more "rasping" and "pungent" than what the China plant **can give,** and the Tea commands a much higher **price.** The young leaves, from which alone Tea is made, are of a much finer and softer texture in the indigenous than in the China; the former may be compared to satin, the latter to leather. The young leaves of the indigenous, moreover, do not harden so quickly as those of the China; thus, if there is any unavoidable delay in picking a flush, the loss is less with the former. In the fact that unpruned or unpicked plants (for picking is a miniature pruning) give fewer and less succulent young leaves which harden quicker than pruned ones, the two varieties would seem to be alike. The China variety is much more prolific of seed than the indigenous; the former also gives it when younger, and as seed checks leaf, the China is inferior in this as in other respects. The China is by far the hardier plant; it is much easier to rear, and it will grow in widely differing climates, which **the** indigenous will not.

A patch of indigenous with a mature flush on it is a pretty sight. The plants all appear as if crowned with gold (they are truly so if other advantages exist), and are a **great** contrast to the **China variety** if it can also be seen **near.**

I have now, I think, pointed out the leading characteristics of the two original varieties of the Tea plant, and it stands to reason no one would grow the China who could get indigenous. But the truth is, a pure specimen of either is rare. The plants between indigenous and China are called " hybrids." They were in the first instance produced by the inoculation, when close together, of the pollen of one kind into the flower of the other, and the result was a true hybrid, partaking equally of the indigenous and China characteristics; but the process was repeated again and again between the said hybrid and an indigenous or China, and again later between hybrids of different degrees, so that now there are very many varieties of the Tea plant— 100 or even more—and no garden is wholly indigenous or wholly China. So close do the varieties run, no one can draw the line and say where the China becomes a hybrid, the hybrid an indigenous. Though as a rule the young leaves are light green or dark green, as the plant approaches the indigenous or China in its character, there are a certain class of bushes all hybrid, whose young leaves have strong shades of crimson and purple. Some even are quite red, others quite purple. These colours do not last as the leaf hardens, and the matured leaves of these plants do not differ from others. Plants with these coloured leaves are prolific.

The nearer each plant approaches the indigenous, the higher its class and excellence, *ergo* one plantation is composed of a much better class of plants than another. Had China seed never been introduced into India, a very different state of things would have existed now. The cultivation would not have been so large, but far more valuable. The propagation and rearing of the indigenous, as observed, is difficult; the China is much hardier while young. So difficult is it to rear successively the *pure* indigenous, perhaps the best plan, were it all to come over again, would be to propagate a high-class hybrid and distribute it, never allowing any China seed or plants to leave the nursery, which should have **been a Government one**. But we must take things as they are. The Government nurseries in the Himalayas and the Dehra Dhoon (there have never been any elsewhere, and worse sites could not have been chosen) were planted entirely with China seeds, the seedlings distributed all over the country, and thus the mischief was done. The Indian Tea is vastly superior to the Chinese, and commands a much higher price at home, but it is still very inferior to what it would have been, had not Chinese seed been so recklessly imported and distributed over the country.

The home of the indigenous Tea tree is in the deep luxurious jungles of Assam and Cachar.* There it grows into a good-sized tree. I have seen it 20 feet high. These are of no use, except for seed, until they are cut down. When this is done, they throw out many new shoots, covered with young tender leaves, fit for Tea. They are, of course, far too big to transplant, but on some sites where they were numerous, that spot was chosen for the plantation, and some of these are the best gardens in Assam and Cachar.

The indigenous plant and high-class hybrid require a hot moist climate, and will not therefore flourish in any parts of India outside Eastern Bengal. I have tried them in the Himalayas, there the cold kills them. In Dehra Dhoon and Kangra the climate is far too dry; besides, the hot winds in the former, and the cold in the latter, are prejudicial. The Terai under Darjeeling suits them. In Assam, Cachar, and Chittagong, the indigenous and the highest class hybrids will thrive, for the climate of all three is suitable, but perhaps Northern Assam possesses the best climate **of all** for such plants.

* It is a singular fact that none exists in Northern Cachar, that is, on the northern side of the river.

The Himalayan gardens consist entirely of Chinese plants mixed occasionally with a low class of hybrid. They were all formed from the Government Nurseries where nothing but Chinese was reared. Occasional importations of Assam and Cachar seed will account for the sprinkling of low class hybrids which may be found. The same may be said of Dehra Dhoon and Kangra. In some gardens in the Terai below Darjeeling a high class of plant exists. In Assam, Cachar, and Chittagong the plantations vary much, but all have some indigenous and high class hybrids, while many gardens are composed of nothing else.

It is evident, then, that the value of a garden depends much on the class of its plants, and that a wise man will only propagate the best. Only the seed from good varieties should be selected, and gradually all inferior bushes should be rooted out and a good kind substituted. When this shall have been systematically done for a few years on a good garden, which has other advantages, the yield per acre will far exceed anything yet realised or even thought of.

Government action in the matter of Tea has been prejudicial in many ways, but in none more so than when they were doing their best to foster the cultivation by distributing Chinese seed and seedlings gratis. No one can blame here (would the Government were equally free from blame in all Tea matters!), but the mischief is none the less. It will never be possible to undo the harm then done.

The seed of indigenous, hybrid, and Chinese is like in appearance, and cannot be distinguished. Thus, when seed formerly was got from a distance, the purchaser was at the mercy of the vendor.

High cultivation improves the class of a Tea plant. Thus, a purely China bush, if highly cultivated and well manured, will in two or three years assume a hybrid character. High cultivation will therefore improve the class of *all* the plants in a garden; but the cheapest and best plan with low class Chinese plants is to root them out and replace them with others, as will be explained hereafter. Low class seedlings should also be rooted out of nurseries.

I cannot conclude this chapter better than by giving an extract from the "Government Records" alluded to in a previous chapter, and I add a few remarks at foot, as otherwise the reader might be puzzled with some opinions expressed which are so much at variance with the generally received opinions on Tea to-day.

Kinds of Tea Plants cultivated.—"When Government resolved on trying the experiment of cultivating Tea in India, they deputed **Dr. Gordon to** China to acquire information respecting the cultivation and manufacture of Teas, and to procure Tea seeds. Aided by Dr. Gutzlaff he procured a quantity of seeds from the mountains in the Amoy districts. These seeds were sent to the Calcutta Botanical Garden, where they were sown in boxes. On germinating they were sent up the country in boats, some to Assam and some to Gurhmuktesur, and from thence to Kumaon and Gurhwal. From these plants date the commencement of the Tea plantations in the Himalayas.* Tea **was** first made in Kumaon in 1841, and the samples sent to England, and were pronounced to be of good quality, fitted for **the** home markets, and similar to the Oolong Souchong varieties. Thus Messrs. Thompson, of Mincing Lane, report on a sample sent by us to Dr. Royle in 1842: 'The samples of Tea received belong to the **Oolong** Souchong kind, fine-flavoured and strong. This is equal to the superior black Tea generally sent as presents, and better for the most part than the Chinese Tea imported for mercantile purposes.'† By many it was supposed that there were different species of the Tea **plant, and that** the species cultivated in the south districts of China was different from that met with in the north. To solve this mystery, and at the same time procure **the** best varieties of the Tea plant, Mr. Fortune was deputed to China. By him large numbers of Tea

---

* And also the introduction of a bad class of plants.—E. M.

† A single small sample of Tea very carefully made, and with an amount of labour which could never be bestowed on the mass, is little or no criterion. Tea is better made in Kumaon in 1878 than it was in 1842, but Kumaon Tea does not vie in price with Eastern Bengal produce. All the Himalayan Tea is weak, though of a delicate flavour; all Tea grown at high elevation *must* be so.—E. M.

plants were sent from different districts of China celebrated for their Teas, and are now thriving luxuriantly in all the plantations throughout the Kohistan of the North-west Provinces and Punjab. Both green and black Tea plants were sent, the former from Whey Chow, Mooyeen, Chusan, Silver Island, and Tein Tang, near Ningpo, and the latter from Woo-e San, Tein San, and Tsin Gan, in the Woo-e district. But so similar are the green and black Tea plants to each other, and the plants from the Amoy districts, that the most practised eye, when they are mixed together, cannot separate them, showing that they are nothing more than mere varieties of one and the same plant, the changes in the form of the leaf being brought about by cultivation. Moreover, throughout the plantation fifty varieties might easily be pointed out; but they run so into each other as to render it impossible to assign them any trivial character, and the produce of the seed of different varieties does not produce the same varieties only, but several varieties, proving that the changes are entirely owing to cultivation; nor do the plants, cultivated at 6,000 feet in the Himalayas, differ in the least in their varieties from those cultivated at 2,500 feet of altitude in the Dehra Dhoon.

Several varieties.

"That the Assam plant is a marked species is true, it being distinguished by its large membranous and lanceolate leaf, small flower, and upright growth.

Assam species.

"It is a very inferior plant for making Tea, and its leaves are therefore not used.* Though the plants received from the different districts of China do not differ from those first sent to the plantations, it is highly important to know that the Tea plants from well-known green and black Tea districts of China now exist in the plantations, as it is stated that local causes exert a great influence in the quality of the Teas as much as the manufacture does. The expense, therefore, incurred in stocking the Government plantations with the finest kinds and varieties of Tea plants procurable in China, though great, will be amply repaid. From them superior kinds of Tea are produced."

The above extract is a sample of the said "Records." They abound in errors and highly coloured statements, which induced many to embark in Tea on unfavourable sites, and "the red book" (it is bound in a red cover) is not exactly blessed by the majority of the Himalayan planters!

* A little enquiry would have shown this was not true, even when it was written. All Tea planters, brokers, and all interested in Tea, know now (many knew it then) that the "Assam species," viz., the indigenous, makes the most valuable Tea produced.—E. M.

CHAPTER X.

TEA SEED.

THOUGH there is a great difference in Tea plants (see last chapter) the seed of all is the same, and it is therefore impossible to say from what class of plants it has been gathered.

When Tea seed was very valuable (it has sold in the Tea-fever days as high as Rs. 200 and Rs. 300 per maund) it was the object of planters to grow as much as possible.

High class plants do not give much seed, a plantation therefore with much on it should be avoided in purchasing seed.

The Tea flower (the germ of next year's seed) appears in the autumn, and the seed is ripe at the end of the following October or early November.

It takes thus one year to form.

Seed is ripe when the capsule becomes brown, and when breaking the latter the inner brown covering of the seed adheres to the seed and *not* to the capsule.

One capsule contains 1, 2, 3, and sometimes even 4 seeds.

Though the mass ripens at the end of October, some ripen earlier; the capsule splits and the seed falls on the ground. If, therefore, all the seed from a garden is required, it is well to send round boys all October to pick up such seeds.

When the seed is picked at the end of October or early November the mass is still in capsules. It should be laid in the sun for half an hour daily for two or three days until most of the capsules have split. It is then shelled, and the clean seed laid on the floor of any building where it will remain dry. Sunning it *after* shelling is objectionable.

The sooner it is sown after it is shelled the better.

If for any reason it is necessary to keep it, say a fortnight or three weeks before sowing, it is best kept *towards* germinating in layers covered with dry mould. But if to be kept longer leave it on the dry floor as above, taking care it is thinly spread (not more than one seed thick if you have space) and collected together, and re-spread every day to turn it.

For transport to a distance it should be placed in coarse gunny bags only one-third filled. If these are shaken and turned daily during transit a journey of a week will not very materially injure the seed.

For any long journey it is best placed in layers in boxes with thoroughly dry and fine charcoal between the layers, and sheets of paper here and there to prevent the charcoal running to the bottom.

It is scarcely necessary to consider how Tea seed can be utilized when not saleable, for seed prevents leaf, and therefore it should not be grown if there is no market for it. It will, however, make oil, but the price it would fetch for this purpose would not compensate for the diminished yield of leaf it had caused. It is also valuable as manure mixed with cattle-dung, but it would not pay to grow it for this purpose either.

My advice therefore is to allow no more seed on the garden than you require for your own use (even the fullest gardens require some yearly) or than you can sell at a remunerative price.

If the object is to produce a considerable quantity of seed, set apart a piece of the plantation for it, and do not prune it at all. A large number will then be produced on that piece.

If the object is to grow as little seed as possible after the pruning in the cold weather, which destroys the greater part, send round boys to pick off such of the germs as remain.

If this is done ever so carefully, some will escape, enough say to give one maund seed from 10 acres of garden, and this as a rule is enough to fill up vacancies in a good garden.

The following figures regarding seed will be found useful, but remember the higher the class of plant the less durable the seed :—

Seven maunds seed, with capsules, give 4 mds. clean seed.

One maund clean seed (fresh)   = 26,000 seeds.
   ,,   ,,   (ten days old)   = 32,000 ,,
   ,,   ,,   (one month old) = 35,000 ,,

Say therefore, in round numbers, that one maund **Tea** seed = 30,000 seeds.

With good **Tea** seed, sown shortly after it is picked, about 20,000 will germinate.

If you get 8,000 to germinate with seed that has come a long distance, you are lucky.

After a two months' journey 3,000 is probably the outside which will be realised.

My experience, with seed imported into another District from Assam or Cachar, is that more than 4,500 Seedlings cannot be expected from each maund.

CHAPTER XI.

COMPARISON BETWEEN SOWING IN NURSERIES AND IN SITU.

In the one case the seed is placed in nurseries at the close of the year, and the young plants transplanted into the garden at beginning of the following rains.

In the other the seed is (at the same time, viz., close of the year, if you can get it so soon) sown at once in the plantation where the plants are intended to grow.

Each of these plans has its advocates, who don't believe in the other plan at all! The question is which is the better?

Their respective advantages may be shortly summed up as follows:—

NURSERIES.

Advantages.—The seed may be made to germinate early by watering. After it germinates the plants can be watered from time to time as they require it. Artificial shade (a great help to the germination of Tea seed) can be given. The soil can be frequently opened, and the plants in every way better tended in nurseries.

Disadvantages.—The plants lose at least three months' growth when transplanted, and may die. The transplanting necessitates labour at the time of the year it is much wanted for other work. The expense is greater than the other plan, for there are the nurseries to make and the labour of transplanting.

IN SITU.

Advantages.—The plants gain some three months in growth by not being moved. It saves labour at the busy time, viz., early in the rains. It saves all the labour of transplanting, that is, it *saves* labour absolutely, and **gives** labour **when, as stated,** it is much required.

Disadvantages.—If the early rains (that is, rain in December, January, and February) fail, but few seeds germinate. In the case of a new garden, the soil must be kept clean six or seven months before it would be necessary by the nursery plan. No artificial shade can be given.

It will thus be seen that the advocates of both plans have much to urge in their respective favours. Which is better?

The advocates of **each** plan are guided by the climate they have planted Tea **in, and the** truth is simply that the **better** plan **for** one place is **not adapted** to another. Planting *in situ* where it will succeed is **by far** the cheaper and better, and it will do so wherever **there are** certainly **cold** weather and spring rains. Thus (see rain table) it will often succeed in **Assam,** Cachar, Darjeeling, the **Western Dooars,** and perhaps the Terai below Darjeeling. It will **fail** in Chittagong, Dehra Dhoon, Kumaon, Kangra, and Hazareebaugh. In Chittagong, for instance, a garden could never be made by planting *in situ*, or, as it is generally called, at stake.*

In this and other matters adapt your operations to the existing climate.

I will now describe **the** above two methods of sowing seed.

---

* In no climate is the success of it certain, for early rains often fail, and then it is all loss. I would, therefore, in all cases advise nurseries in reserve.

CHAPTER XII.

SOWING SEED IN SITU, ID EST, AT STAKE.

It is named "at stake" because stakes are put along in lines to show where the Tea trees are to be, and the seed is sown at those spots.

The *modus operandi* is very simple. A month before the sowing time (which should be as soon as you can get the seed), at each stake dig a hole at least 9 inches diameter and 12 inches deep, put the soil taken out on the sides, taking care, however, if it be on a slope, to put none *above* the hole. Do not put the soil near enough to the pit to make it likely it will be washed back. Such soil as should be washed in ought to be the new rich surface soil. For this reason the upper side of the hole should be left free on slopes. The pits are made a month beforehand to admit of this, and to allow the action of the air on the open sides to improve the mould.

If lucky enough to have one or two falls of rain during the month, the holes will be more or less filled up with soil eminently calculated to instigate rapid growth. Just before sowing fill up the pit with surrounding *surface* soil. Whether to mix a little manure with it or not is a question. If it is virgin soil, and rich in decayed vegetation, I say no; if not virgin soil, and rather poor, yes; but it must be strictly in moderation—not more, say, than a man can hold in both hands to each hole. In filling up the hole, press the soil down lightly two or three times, or it will all sink later, and your seeds be far too deep.

When the above is all done, there is a perfect spot for

the reception of the seed. The tap-root can readily descend in search of moisture, and the lateral rootlets can spread likewise. They (the latter) will not reach the outer walls of the pit for six months, and will then be strong enough to force their way through.

Now sow the seed. Put in, say, two or three, as the seed is good or bad, six inches apart ; push them into the soft soil one inch, and put up the stake in the centre to mark the spot.

Keep the place clean till following rains, but allow only hand-weeding near the young seedlings, and occasionally open the soil with some light hand-instrument, as a "koorpee," to the depth of half-an-inch.

If all the seeds germinate, and the seedlings escape crickets, and all live, at commencement of the rains leave the best and transplant the others to any vacant spot. You will succeed with some, not with others; but do not be too anxious to take up the spare ones with earth round the roots, and thus endanger the one plant left. That the seedling left be not injured is the *great* point, the others must take their chance.

Some people believe in two, or even three seedlings together, and would thus advise them to be all, or perhaps two, left. I do not approve of the plan, except, perhaps, with Chinese plants. Plant as close as you will in the lines, but give each plant its own home.

There is another mode of planting at stake, which is, I think, better than the above.

Lay the seed in alternate layers of seed and mould in beds. The seeds may be laid *close* to each other, but not *above* each other, with mould, say, two inches thick, above, and then seed again. When they begin to burst, ready to shoot out their roots, examine the seeds, by taking off the soil from each layer, every three or four days. Take out those that *have* burst, and plant with the eye or root side of the seed downwards. Put all that have *not* burst back again. Repeat the operation again and again every second or third day. Be careful and take them up before the root projects—that is, directly the coating has cracked.

By this means only one seed need be put at each stake, for it is certain to germinate, and seed may thus be made to go much further. Great care is, however, necessary in this operation.

CHAPTER XIII.

NURSERIES.

CHOOSE a level site, with, if possible, the command of water at a higher level—anyhow with water handy. Either irrigating or hand-watering for seed beds is a necessity if vigorous and well-developed plants are to be looked for.

The soil should be of the light, friable kind recommended for the **Tea-plant** (see " Soil ") and of the same *nature* as the **soil of the garden, the** ultimate home of the plants. This **latter is all-important, for seedlings** will **never** thrive (pro**bably not live) transplanted into a new** kind of mould, **particularly** a poorer kind.

If possible, the soil **of the** seed beds should be poorer than the soil of the garden—on no account richer. Taking care it is of the same *nature* as the garden soil, choose the poorest you can find. The principle is **well** known **in** England, and it applies equally to India. From poor **to rich** soil plants thrive, but never the other way.

For the above reason, if you manure seed beds, do it very sparingly.

Artificial **shade** for **seed beds is a** necessity; at least very many more seeds will germinate when it is given.

Natural shade over seed beds is *very* bad; for, *firstly*, " the drippings " are highly injurious; and, *secondly*, shade is only required till the plants **are two** or three inches high; after that *any* shade is bad, for plants brought up to the time of **transplanting** in shade are never very hardy.

Seed beds, where water is handy, should not be dug deep. **If** so dug, and the soil is consequently loose a long way down, the tap-root will descend quickly, and will be too long when transplanted. As water can be given when it is necessary, there is no need for the tap-root to go down low in search of moisture.* A long tap-root is generally broken in "lifting" the seedling from the bed.

Seed beds raised, as is the usual custom, above the paths that run between them, are objectionable. They part with moisture too freely. They should, on the contrary, be below the level of the paths, and there is another advantage in this, for the said paths can then be used partly as supports for the artificial shade, and thus do away with the expense of long wooden stakes.

As the seed beds are only required until the beginning of the following rains, there is no possibility of their suffering from excessive moisture. When they are required to remain later, of course this plan of making the beds lower than the paths will not do.

Seed is best sown in drills, six inches apart, and each seed two, or if space can be got, even three inches from its neighbour. This facilitates each seedling being taken up later, with more or less of a ball of earth round the roots—an all-important point (see Transplanting, page 76).

The length of the beds does not signify, but the breadth must not be more than five feet, so that a man on the path on either side can reach to the middle while hand-weeding or opening the soil.

After what has been said no lengthy directions for making the beds are necessary.

Cut down, burn, or carry off all jungle, and then take out all roots, whether grass or other. Now make the surface

---

* In planting "at stake" (see last Chapter) the conditions are different. There the plant is in its permanent home, and the more quickly and deeper the tap-root descends the better, as the plant will then draw moisture from low down when the soil is dry.

level. After this mark off the beds and paths, the latter one foot broad only, with string and pegs. Then raise the path six inches above the spots marked off for the beds. This latter must not be done by earth from the beds, but by earth **from outside** the intended nursery. Next dig and pulverise the soil of the beds to a depth of six or seven inches, **no** more, and level the surface.

All is now ready for the seed. A string, **five feet long,** with a small peg at either end, is given to two men who stand on the path at either side of the bed. Each man has a six-inch measure. The string is laid across the bed, beginning at **one end** and pegged down on either side. A drill is then made along the string about one inch deep, and **this done** the string is, by means of the six-inch measure on either side, removed, and pegged down again in the place for the next drill. Seeds are then sown or placed along the **first** drill made, two **or three inches apart, and** the **earth** filled **in.** This is repeated again and again till the whole bed is sown.

If the character of the seed is doubtful it must be laid in thicker, but with good seed two-and-a-half to three inches is the best distance.

The sowing finished the artificial shade has to be given. Along the paths, at five feet apart, put in forked stakes, two feet long—viz., six inches into the path, and eighteen inches above it. **Connect these with one** another by poles laid in the forks; now lay other (but thinner) poles attached to the first poles at either end *across* and above the bed; and again across these latter, that is along *the length* of the beds, split bamboos, and then bind the whole framework here and **there.** The said framework **made will then** be two feet above the beds—viz., eighteen inches of stake support, and the six-inch raised paths. The eighteen inches of opening all round, under the frame, that **is,** between **the** frame and the path, allows the necessary air to circulate; while the expense, danger from high winds, and the objectionable entrance of the sun at the sides, all of which high artificial shade is subject to, are avoided by this low frame-work.

Mats are the best to cover the frame-work. In case of accidental or incendiary fire they are not so objectionable as grass, for they burn less and slower, but mats are expensive. Any coarse grass (freed from seed) will answer, and it should be laid on as thin as will suffice to give shade.

The beds may be watered, if there is no rain, a fortnight after the seed is sown, and from time to time during the dry season, whenever the soil at a depth of three or four inches shows no moisture.

The soil should also be kept free of weeds, and after the plants are three or four inches high, the spaces between the drills should be slightly stirred every now and then.

After the seed has germinated, and the seedlings have, say, four leaves on them, the artificial shade should be taken away. But it must be done gradually, taking off portions of the grass first, so that the young seedlings may by degrees be inured to the hot sun.

Though cultivation, as described, by watering and opening the soil at times is well, these should not be done much, or the seedlings will be too large when the time comes to transplant them. Large seedlings do not, as a rule, thrive as well as moderate-sized ones, after being transplanted.

Among the many very absurd mistakes made in the cultivation of the Tea plant, none exceeds the ridiculous way Tea seed used to be sown in the Government plantations in the North-western Himalayas. The seed was sown in drills, as I have advised, but in six linear inches of the drills, where it is right to put two, or at most three, seeds, perhaps thirty were placed! I do not exaggerate; the drill, six inches deep, was filled with them. Many and

F

many lacs of seed, **in those days** worth many thousand rupees, were thus sacrificed. Private planters in the Himalayas, taught by the Government method, once did the same. **I believe** the absurd practice is exploded now.

Seed cannot be sown too soon after being picked. It is ripe early in November, so the beds should be **all** ready by November, and **if the seed has not far to come it can** thus be sown early **that month.**

To each maund there are in round numbers 30,000 seeds, (see page 56). The number of plants it will take to fill **an** acre depends, of course, on the distances they are set apart (see page 72), but having decided this point, also the area **to be planted,** and consequently **the** number of maunds of **seeds to** be sown (see page 56), **the** following table will be found useful in calculating the size of nursery required :—

*Table showing the size of nursery required for **one** maund and ten maunds seed, the drills being 6 inches apart, and **each** seed 3 inches or 2 inches **from its** neighbour.*

Distance each seed is set apart in the drill.	Area in sq. inches each seed will occupy.	Area, in sq. feet, of beds without paths required for each md.	Area, including paths required for each md.	Size of nursery, including the paths to take in for 10 mds.
3 inches . .	18	3.763	4,513 sq. feet or 501 sq. yards.	100 yards by 50 yards.
2 inches . .	12	2,500	2,995 sq. feet or 332 sq. yards.	100 yards by 33 yards.

If nurseries **for more than** ten maunds are required, then allow 100 yards to **be the** breadth, and **for** each extra ten maunds add respectively for 3 or 2 inches (see **1st** column) **50** or 33 yards to the **length.** Thus fifty maunds will require nurseries **100** yards by 250 yards, or 100 yards by 165 yards, according as it is decided to plant the seed 3 inches or 2 inches apart in the lines.

CHAPTER XIV.

MANURE.

An idea existed formerly—got, I believe, from stray Chinamen, who I don't think knew much about Tea in any way—that manure, though it increased the yield, spoilt the flavour of Tea. The idea is opposed to all agricultural knowledge, for high cultivation, which in no case can be carried out to perfection without manure, much improves the strength and flavour of all edibles, the product of mother-earth.

My first experience of manure to the Tea plant was obtained in the Chittagong district from a small garden close to the station, which has been for some years highly manured. I was struck with the frequency and abundance of the flushes and the strength and flavour of the Tea. My high opinion of the Tea was later borne out by the Calcutta brokers. I allude to the "Pioneer" garden, close to the Chittagong station. During the best Tea months flush succeeded flush at intervals of less than a week, while eight to ten maunds (640 to 800 lbs.) was the yearly yield per acre! The soil was very sandy and poor.

After-experience showed me that manuring nearly doubles the yield of plants, and that so far from injuring the flavour of Tea it improves it, while it adds greatly to the strength.

I shall therefore beg the question that manure *is* an advantage. If any planter doubts, let him try it, and his doubts will soon be solved.

Any manure is better than none, but I believe one of the best manures for the Tea plant (always excepting night-soil and the excrements of birds, which cannot be procured) is cattle manure. It is not heating, like horse-dung, and may be applied in large quantities without any risk. The fresher it is applied, in my opinion, the better, for **it has** then far **more power.** If mixed with any vegetable refuse, the bulk being increased, **it** will go further, but I **do not** think it **is** intrinsically any the better for it.

There are several chemical manures advertised for Tea plants. "Money and Ponder's Chemical Manure," lately patented by Mr. Ponder and myself, is said to have been very successful on several gardens. It is manufactured by Mr. J. Thompson, Kooshtea, Bengal, who will supply all details.

All garden refuse should be regarded as manure and buried between the plants. I allude to the prunings of the bushes and the weeds at all times from the land. To carry these off the ground, **as** I have sometimes seen done, is simply taking off so much strength from the **soil.** The greener, too, all this is buried the better.

When it is considered how much is taken from the Tea plant, it is evident the soil will be exhausted, sooner or later, if no means are adopted to repair the waste. Where manure cannot be got the waste must be made up, as far as possible, by returning all other growth to the soil. But manure *should* be got if possible, for it will double the yield **of a garden; and highly** concentrated chemical manures will, I am sure, **be** eventually much used on Tea gardens.

The best way to apply it, if enough manure is procurable, **is** round each plant; not close to the stem (the rootlets by which the plant feeds are not there) but about **1** foot from **it.** Dig a round trench with a *kodalee,* about 9 inches wide **and 6** inches deep, at the above distance from the stem, lay in the manure, and replace the soil at top. If the plants are young the trench should be narrower, shallower, and 6 inches, instead of 1 foot, from the stems.

MANURE.

If enough manure is not procurable for this (the best) plan, the most must be done with what can be got, as follows:—If the plants are full grown, and there is say 4 feet between the lines, dig a trench down the centre and lay in the manure. The plants will then be manured on two sides. If the plants are young lay the manure *near* them on two sides, if possible, but failing that even on one side. The principle is to lay the manure at the distance the feeding rootlets are, and the older the plant the greater distance these are from its stem.

As to the quantity of cattle manure. Say for plants four years old and upwards (if younger, less will be an equivalent) one maund to 20 trees is a moderate dose, one maund to 15 trees a good dose, and one maund to 10 trees highly liberal manuring, and as much as the plants can take up.

Say in round numbers each acre contains 2,500 plants (4 by 4—a usual distance—gives 2,722 plants, as shown at page 72), and say the manure is procurable at three annas a maund.*

The following table shows the expense of each degree of manuring, viz., 10, 15, and 20 trees per maund :—

Table showing the possible cost and result of manuring with cattle manure.

Rate of Manuring	Maunds of manure per acre at 2,500 plants per acre	Cost of manure at 3 annas per maund N.B.—Ans. omitted	Probable extra yield of Tea per acre	Value of extra yield of Tea at Rs. 50 per maund	Profit by manuring per acre	Deducting the probable cost of putting in the manure, the following profit is shown per acre
	Mds	Rs.	Mds.	Rs.	Rs.	Rs.
One md. to 10 plants	250	47	2½	125	78	70
One md. to 15 plants	166	31	2	100	69	62
One md. to 20 plants	125	23	1½	75	52	46

* It is brought and placed between the lines, in one garden in the Chittagong district, for one to two annas a maund!

It is not too much to calculate that this will add respectively 1½, 2, and 2½ maunds of Tea per acre to the yield, and I have carried this out in the table and shown the results.

I quite believe the results shown will be obtained by manuring, and I base my opinion on practice not theory.

N.B.—I have deducted Rs. 8 for the first, Rs. 7 for the second, and Rs. 6 for the third, as the probable cost of putting in the manure, as it may have to be carried from the factory to the garden. If purchased after being placed between the lines (and if manure is bought of adjacent villagers they will so place it), the cost would be less.

The above table, of course, only applies to localities where cattle manure can be purchased at 3 annas per maund, including carriage to the factory.

The value of the extra yield of Tea is estimated at only Rs. 50 per maund in the above table, because the leaf which will give one maund of Tea is worth no more, as follows:—

	Rs.	A.	P.
Probable price obtainable for one maund or 80 lbs. Tea in Calcutta, at 14 annas a lb. all round (a fair calculation, one year with the other, if it is well manufactured)	70	0	0
Deduct cost, manufacture, packing, transport, and broker's charges as set out in the chapter on "cost manufacture," page 162	16	9	0
Value of leaf which will make one maund Tea	53	7	0

But I prefer estimating it at Rs. 50 only, to be on the safe side.

CHAPTER XV.

DISTANCES APART TO PLANT TEA BUSHES.

WHEN the idea existed, which it did once, that ploughs could be used to cultivate a garden between the lines, these latter, with this object, were placed unnecessarily wide apart.

All distances may be seen in different gardens, viz., 6 × 6, 6 × 3, 6 × 4, 5 × 4, 5 × 5, 4 × 3, &c., &c.

The plough idea has nowhere been found to answer, and is exploded.* Still, even for hand labour to cultivate, and for facilities in picking leaf, it is necessary there should be room enough one way to pass along. Cultivation here means digging, and space enough for this must be left between the lines. Giving so much, what is then the principle that should guide us? Clearly, with a view to the largest yield obtainable, to place as many plants on the land as it will bear.

Four or $4\frac{1}{2}$ feet are, I think, the best distances between the lines.

They give space enough for air to cultivate, and to pass along, even when the trees are full grown.

Where manure is obtainable and the soil can be kept up to a rich state by yearly applications, a garden can scarcely be planted too close.

I see no objection to trees touching each other in the lines.

On considerable slopes, to prevent the wash of soil, the plants should be placed as close as possible, say $3\frac{1}{2}$ feet between and 2 feet in the lines.

---

* Land *before* it is planted can be cultivated with ploughs. My manager is using them largely in the Western Dooars, the land being there all flat. He uses English ploughs, bought of Ransomes and Sims, Ipswich, with bullocks, and often an elephant. He finds the latter the best. After ploughing he uses English harrows.

A closely planted garden will grow less weeds than a widely planted one, and will consequently be cheaper to work.

As the expenditure on a garden is in direct proportion to the area, and the yield in direct proportion to the number of plants (always supposing there is power enough in the soil to support them), it follows that a closely planted garden *must* be very much more profitable than the reverse.

Hybrid plants grow to a larger size than Chinese, and should therefore have more room.

The following is a useful table :—

Table showing the Plants to an Acre, and the Area one lakh of seedlings will cover, at the distances named.

Distances in feet	Square ft. to each plant	Plants in one acre	The area in acres one lakh of seedlings will cover	Remarks
6 by 6	36	1,210	82½	Too wide for any plants.
6 " 5	30	1,452	69	
6½ " 4	26	1,675	59¾	
5 " 5	25	1,742	57½	
6 " 4	24	1,815	55	
6 " 3½	21	2,074	48	For Hybrids, but still I think too wide.
5 " 4	20	2,178	45½	
6 " 3	18	2,420	41¼	Good distances for Hybrids.
4 " 4	16	2,722	36¾	
5 " 3	15	2,904	34½	
4 " 3	12	3,630	27½	Chinese for early return.
3½ " 3½	12¼	3,555	28	Chinese.
3½ " 3	10½	4,148	24	
6 " 3¼	19½	2,233	44¾	Hybrid.
5 " 3¼	16¼	2,726	36¾	Chinese.
5 " 3½	17½	2,489	40	
3½ " 2	7	6,223	16	Best distance for Chinese on steep slopes.

On flat lands I advise—

Hybrid, if high-class . 4 × 3½ or 4½ × 4
Chinese . . . . 3 × 3

All the following equal one acre :—

4 roods. 4,840 square yards.
160 poles. 43,560 " feet.

CHAPTER XVI.

MAKING A GARDEN.

I HAVE not very much to say on this head, as most of the operations entailed are treated separately. Still a few directions on primary matters are required.

Having selected a site and made arrangements for the Tea seed required for the first year's planting, you should commence operations early in October, either by constructing the nursery, or clearing land on the proposed site of the garden, as you may decide which mode of planting, viz., "nurseries," or "sowing at stake," to adopt.*

If the latter, you should begin to cut the jungle somewhat earlier, but it is no use beginning to do this before the middle of September in any case, for before that the jungle would spring up again so soon that it would be labour lost.

Before you do *anything* decide how much you will cultivate the first year, and make your arrangements for seed accordingly. Here let me advise you in no case to attempt more than 100 acres. If you do 100 really well the first year you will have done *very* well. Remember you have also buildings (though few) to construct, and trying to do too much you may simply fail in all.

Previous to October you should have made yourself thoroughly acquainted with all your land, so that you can then fix with knowledge on the best sites for your buildings, nursery, and Tea plantation.

You will find much on these matters in other chapters which should be read carefully.

These respective sites having been fixed upon, and sup-

* In no case trust to the latter alone.

posing you are going to plant in both ways, from nurseries and *in situ*, construct the nurseries as advised under that head, page 62, and also cut the jungle on the intended garden site.

There is not much to say about cutting jungle. Cut all the brushwood first near the ground, and the big trees later, so that when they fall they may lie on the underwood. In the portion you intend to plant at stake you will not have time to cut down the big trees, and had better simply " ring " them. If this is properly done, that is, if the ring is broad enough and deep enough (less than one foot broad and five inches deep for large trees is not safe), they will certainly die in a twelvemonth, and will not give objectionable shade more than half that time. In the part to be planted " at stake " you must burn all the cut jungle by the end of October, and it will be well, if you have labour enough, to send men up the big trees to cut off the branches beforehand, so that they will more or less burn with the rest. Doing this, and piling up the underwood to be burnt round the base of the big trees, will cause earlier death, and diminish the objectionable shade.

Having burnt the jungle, that is, as much as will burn, and carried off the rest from the parts to be planted at stake, dig out all the small roots, and that done, dig the whole some 4 or 5 inches deep. Then stake it off with small bamboo stakes 18 inches long, showing where the Tea trees are to be (see page 72 as to the best distances), and then make your holes and plant your seed at each stake as directed at page 59.

See the way it is recommended to stake land as regards its lay at pages 45 and 46.

You will probably not have the ground ready before the end of November (do not attempt more than you can do to that date), and then take care and keep the seed, as directed at page 55, until it is sown.

For the part to be planted from nurseries the following June you have plenty of time. Nowhere have I, or anyone, seen large vigorous Tea plants under trees. It is therefore evident trees are hurtful, and no more should be left in a garden than are required for the labourers to sit under occasionally, and to collect leaf under before it is taken to the Teahouse. The trees that are left should be those on the sides of roads. One to every two or three acres is ample. After therefore cutting down all the low jungle, cut down all but the said few trees (it is cheaper in the end than ringing them), and then cut off and cut up all the branches into sizes that will burn readily. Cut up the large trunks also into lengths, for all that will not burn must be carried off later. Leave all so lying until February, then choose a day with a high wind and fire it from the windward side. It may burn some days. Then collect all unburnt into heaps, and fire again and again until nothing more will burn. Now take out all roots, big and small, and when well dry, stack all these, and what was left before, and fire again and again. The land should now be tolerably clear, and can be dug at once. The roads should be marked off before this, for they are better not dug.

Now stake the land at the distances determined on, and a month before the rains, or even more, if you are so far advanced, make holes for the young seedlings at each stake, precisely like those recommended for "planting at stake," page 59. Only, if possible, these should be a little larger each way than there advised, say 10 inches diameter and 15 inches deep.

Read carefully the direction as to those pits, and follow them out here. Much of the success of your planting depends on these holes.

At the first commencement of the rains transplant, as directed under that head in the next chapter.

Any large heavy trunks, which cannot be easily carried off the land, may be placed longways between the lines, but the less of dead timber you leave lying about the gardens the better.

CHAPTER XVII.

TRANSPLANTING.

IF the pits for the plants have been all prepared, as directed at pages 59 and 75, this operation is simple enough.

A fortnight or so before it commences tip all the seedlings in the nursery. Take off only the closed leaf at the head of each young plant (see a leaf diagram, page 104), so that the bud at the base of the next leaf be not injured. Doing this will make the seedlings hardier and enable them earlier to recover the transplanting.

On the day you intend to take up the seedlings from any bed, if you have water enough at command, flood the bed. This, as you take up each seedling, will cause the soil, being moist, to adhere better to the roots.

The difference between young plants transplanted with a ball of earth round the roots, and those moved with their roots bare, is no less than three months' growth, if even it does not make the difference between life and death.

Proceed thus to ensure the former. At one short end of the bed, the lowest if it is on a slope, dig close to the first row of seedlings a trench so deep that its base shall be lower than the lowest end of the tap-roots. Then with a five or six-pronged steel fork (this is better than a spade, for it does not cut the rootlets) put in between the first and second row, and pressed down with the foot to its head, force carefully so much of the row down into the trench. Then with the hand take up each seedling separately, helping the soil with a very light pressure (so light that it shall not change the lateral direction of any of the rootlets) to adhere, and place it in a low basket sloping. Do this again and again, till two baskets are full, when they will be carried, banghy fashion, to the garden.

When the first row is finished clear away the loose soil, so that a similar trench to the first shall be formed, and then proceed as above with the second row, and so on.

No further directions for lifting the seedlings out of the nurseries are required.

All is ready for their reception in the garden if the directions at pages 59 and 75 have been followed out. The work now to be detailed must be done by careful men well superintended.

In the soft soil of the lately filled up pit, described at page 59, a hole is made either with the hand or a narrow kodalee (the former, if the soil has not settled much, will suffice), large enough and deep enough to take in the seedling with all the earth attached to it. The seedling is then put in and the soil filled in and round it, which completes the operation.

The manner, though, in which this is done is of great consequence. Four things are all important:—(1) That the tap-root shall not be turned up at the end because the hole is too shallow. (2) That any rootlets projecting outside the attached earth shall be laid in the hole, and shall preserve, when the soil is filled in, their lateral direction. (3) That the collar of the plant (the spot where the stem entered the earth in the nursery) shall be, when the pit is filled up, about $1\frac{1}{2}$ inch higher than the surface of the surrounding earth. (4) That in filling in the hole the soil is pressed down enough to make it unlikely to sink later, but not enough to "cake" the mould.

The following is the consequence of failure in these four points:—

1. Probably death, in any case very much retarded

growth. I have planted some seedlings so purposely, the majority died; those that lived recovered very slowly, and digging them up later the tap-root was found to have gone down after all by assuming the shape of the letter S, the growth downwards being from the head of the letter.

2. Rootlets, turned away from their lateral direction, interfere with other rootlets, and though they eventually grow right if the plant lives, they retard it.

3. Fill in as you may (unless you "cake" the soil, which induces worse evils) the plant sinks a little; thus, if not placed a little high, it will eventually be too deep. If on the other hand placed too high, the rootlets and collar will be exposed, which is an evil.

4. Unless this is attended to the plant will sink too much and the collar be buried, likewise an evil, which it takes the young seedling some time to recover.

Only first teaching and then practice will enable either European or Native to plant well. This is how it should be done.

Take the seedling in the left hand, holding it by the stem just above the collar; then take the very end of the tap-root between the second and third fingers of the right hand, and thus put it down into the hole (you thus insure the tap-root being straight). Now judge exactly the height of the collar that it be as directed. Rest the left arm then on the ground to keep the plant steady, release the tap-root, and fill up the hole about one-third, pressing the soil lightly. The plant will then be fixed, and you can employ both hands to fill up the remainder, and keep the rootlets in a lateral position. Press the soil lightly as you do so, and when all is filled up press it down a little harder round the stem of the plant.

All the transplanting should be finished as early in the rains as possible. A seedling, planted in the first fifteen days of June, is worth two planted in July, and after the latter month it is generally a case of seedlings and labour lost.

Days with heavy rain are not good to plant in. Those with showers or light drizzling rain are best. When there is very heavy rain the soil "cakes" much. Fine days, if the ground is wet, and if more rain may soon be looked for, are good, better though if cloudy than sunny.

Where much planting has to be done, of necessity planting must be carried on daily, for, as observed, it *must* all be finished by end of July at latest.

In case of a sunny break in the weather, stop planting after the second day, for early rain to young transplants is a necessity.

In making a garden too much care cannot be given to the way seedlings are placed in their homes.

Just before sending the third edition to press, I saw in the *Indian Tea Gazette* some details of " new transplanting and transporting tools," patented by Mr. Jeben. I hope these will prove a success, for such are much wanted, and if they will do all it is said they can do, a great boon will have been conferred by Mr. Jeben on the Tea industry.

Mr. J. W. Mountjoy, of Pandawbrang, Arracan, writes as follows regarding these tools :—

" The Transplanter has, in working, proved to be a complete success. Almost all the remaining seedlings have been transplanted by the aid of your instrument, without the slightest injury to their roots or check to their growth. The fact is, the young plants do not know that they have been transplanted, and now that sunshine has succeeded the late very heavy rains, new and vigorous growth is ' bursting out ' from all the seedlings that were transplanted by means of your Transplanter. No manager of a Tea or Coffee plantation, who had once seen this instrument at work, would ever again be likely to recur to transplanting by hand, and not a single seedling should die when removed from the nursery and carried to its place of ultimate growth by means of your Transplanter. Your transplanting apparatus is better than baskets, and has moreover the great recommendation of being **very** economical. Your Transplanter will, with **moderate** care, last ·**for** many years, and **combines** thorough economy **with** thorough efficiency."

I am glad to give the above extract, for I look on the invention, if successful, as a most important one.

CHAPTER XVIII.

CULTIVATION OF MADE GARDENS.

As manuring, which is part of this, is treated separately, we have here only to consider the best means of stirring the soil to give air to the roots of the plants, and to keep down weeds, which, if allowed, injure the yield vastly.

Unless when plants are full blown and in full bearing (and not even then unless they are planted close) it is not only not necessary, but a waste of labour and money, to open the soil all over the garden with a view of stimulating or cultivating the plants. Much money has been wasted in this way: for instance, in a garden planted 6 by 6 or 6 by 5, and the plants but two years old, I have seen the whole dug many times in the year. The roots of the said plants did not protrude at that age more than 1 foot or so, what good could they possibly derive from the extra space dug?

The soil *over* the rootlets of Tea plants cannot be stirred too often. The oftener it is done the oftener the trees flush, and when young the more vigorously will they grow. What is the best way to do it?

I believe simply by digging *round* each plant. I go to show why this is, I believe, the best.

Putting aside the waste incurred in digging a whole garden when not necessary, the way the soil is then dug near the plants is, I think, objectionable. The ground is dug in a straight line *up to the plant*, and in doing so, if the digging is deep, roots are very apt to be cut. Again, when the work is task-work, the men shirk as much as possible digging close up to the stems under the branches, and thus the soil over much of the roots, is not stirred at all. This is not easy to detect, for you must look under the branches of each tree to see how the work has been done.

In "digging round plants" the men should *follow* the kodalee round the tree, and *the position of the blade in the same line as the roots* makes any injury very unlikely. Even if tasked, as when the work is examined, it is *only* round the plants, it is more readily perceived if the ground has not been stirred close up to the stems.

I therefore prefer digging round plants, with the view of cultivating them, to digging the whole garden. I believe the object is better attained. That it is much cheaper is evident.

The annulus, or space to be dug round, beginning 9 inches from the stem, varies with the age of the plant. Up to two years one kodalee in width will do, and after that say 2 feet.

The draw-hoe of 8 inches wide is a better tool for the above than the kodalee, especially as it is work well suited to boys, and the "draw-hoe" is a lighter tool.

Till plants from seed at stake are a year old, and till seedlings from nurseries are the same age, calculating in the latter case from the transplanting, no kodalee or even draw-hoe should come near them. The soil round for 6 inches should be slightly opened once a month or so, but it should be done with the "koorpee."

We have now discussed the cultivation of the plants. The above often done, say once a month, if possible, during the season, with judicious pruning and liberal manuring, constitutes high cultivation. Did weeds not grow there would be no need to do more, but weeds *do* grow, and must not be allowed. The richer the soil the more weeds, the more manure you apply the more weeds also.

Weeds choke the plant and diminish the yield. Weeds

take from the soil, and from manure, when given, the strength you want for your constantly recurring flushes. If, therefore, you have a large crop of weeds you have a small yield of Tea.

How to stop this? There is one golden rule, " never let them get ahead of you." This, it is true, argues ample labour; but unless you *have* ample labour for the area you cultivate, better let your money lie in the Bank and not grow Tea. Reduce your area until you *can* keep ahead of your weeds, for keep ahead you must if you wish for success.

The secret of keeping ahead of weeds is to destroy them when young, to do this again and again, as often as they come up, never allowing them to bear seed. The kodalee, an excellent digging tool, is not good for this: you want a lighter instrument, which can go over more ground and will not open the soil in the dry season to any depth. The Dutch hoe, the widest procurable in the blade, with a long lithe handle of 6 feet, is perfect for this.

With weeds at the height fit for a Dutch hoe, viz., 3 or 4 inches, and not numerous (which they will not be if you have "kept ahead"), a man will easily do 45 square nulls, *id est*, 720 square yards. He would not do more than 30 nulls with a kodalee.

The Dutch hoe must be well known. It is used for weeding drives and walks in England.

To conclude shortly, for "hoeing and weeding" I recommend as follows:—

Dig the whole garden thrice in the year, viz., spring, rains, and autumn. Bury all weeds as you dig in trenches between the lines.

In the intervals use the Dutch hoe as often as weeds appear.

Cultivate the plants by digging round them once a month if possible.

Do all this and you will find your garden is kept clean and well cultivated, at far less cost than you incurred for cultivation when it was choked with weeds for months together, while your yield will **be at** the same time much increased.

If you keep your garden thus clean, **and do** not allow the weeds to get ahead of you, the following table shows **about** the cost of each cultivation **operation each** time you do it :—

Detail of work	Headman at 4½ annas	Men at 3½ annas	Women at 3 annas	Boys at 2½ annas	Total cost			Say in Rs.
Digging the whole surface.	¾	12	5	..	2	13	6	3
Digging round plants	½	..	4	5	1	13	9	2
Dutch hoeing or weeding .	½	4	..	..	1	14	3	2

If weeds get ahead **the cost** in **each case** will be nearly double **the** above.

The following table, which is as near the mark as any such estimate can be, will be found useful. It will also be made use of when calculating the cost of making a garden in Chapter XXIX., pages 164, 165, and 166.

Table showing the cost per annum of keeping up at its best **100** *acres of* Tea *from the year it is planted until* the sixth year inclusive.

Year	Rate per acre per annum	Per 100 acres	Remarks
	Rs.	Rs.	
First .	50	5,000	The year the seed is sown at stake
Second .	60	6,000	
Third .	70	7,000	
Fourth .	80	8,000	
Fifth .	90	**9,000**	
Sixth .	100	**10,000**	The plants should be large plants now, but they will not be at full bearing until the eighth year.

The above rates in the case of a 300-acre garden making will include *everything* but buildings.

The rates are progressive, because the expenditure on the following increases, or should increase, yearly.

1. Manager's pay (say every second year).
2. Assistant (first entertained, say third year).
3. Cost and wear of tools.
4. Cost of pruning.
5. Cost of cultivation.
6. Cost of manure.
7. General expenses.

No cost for Tea manufacture is included in the above, as this is estimated for separately. See table at pages 160, 161, and 162.

Keeping up high cultivation in every way and manuring liberally, a made garden in full bearing can be kept up to its highest producing powers (including the pay of the manager, establishment, and everything else) for Rs. 100 per acre per annum.

An acre of Tea may, I am aware, be kept up in a manner for Rs. 50 or so yearly, but the profit on such a plantation must be nil.

On the contrary, with the above expenditure per acre, on a good and favourably located garden, the profit will be very large. See table at page 172.

It is with Tea as with all other cultivation. It has been proved in England, and in all other countries where really high cultivation is followed out, that the higher the system followed the greater the profit.

CHAPTER XIX.

PRUNING.

It is stated elsewhere at length (page 102) *why* I conceive pruning to be necessary for the Tea plant. Whether I am right or not, the fact is certain that without pruning very little leaf is produced.

Pruning must be done in the cold weather when the plant is hybernating, that is to say, when the sap is down. The sooner *after* the sap goes down it is done the better, for the sooner the tree will then flush in the spring.

There have been many theories about pruning Tea bushes, but none, I think, worth much *practically*, for the simple reason that it is impossible to prune 250,000 plants (the number in a 100-acre garden, at 2,500 to the acre)* with the care and system a gardener prunes a favourite fruit tree. The operation *must* be a coarse one, done by ignorant men, in large numbers at one time, who can in a measure be more or less taught, and the nearer they do right the better: still, really careful and scientific pruning can never be carried out on a Tea plantation.

The time to do it, too, is very limited. It cannot be begun before the trees have done flushing, say, at the earliest, middle of November, or continued, if early flushes and a large yield next season is looked for, beyond end of January, at the latest. Thus at the most two months and a half is all the time given.

I shall confine myself therefore to giving such directions as will be practically useful.

* In a 500-acre garden the number is 1,250,000, which *ought* all to be pruned in two months!

The best instrument is the common "pruning knife." It cuts far cleaner than the "shears," besides which the natives very seldom use the latter well. What is called in England a "hedge-bill" is useful to trim the outsides of the trees. If required it must be got from England, as I do not think it is procurable in Calcutta. Whatever instruments are used should be kept **very sharp,** and for this **purpose,** besides sharpening them every morning on the **grinding** stone, each **pruner** should be provided with a small **pocket** "hone."

The theory, and it is correct, is in pruning, to cut near above a bud or branch, but not near enough to injure them. **The** cut should be quite clean and sloping upwards, so that nothing can lodge on it. This theory can be, and must be, strictly carried out in cutting the thick stems and branches, but it is quite impossible to do it with the slender branches or twigs of the tree.

Prune so as **to cause** lateral growth. A Tea plant should never be allowed to **exceed, say,** 4 feet in height, **but the** wider it is the better.

Prune off all lower branches tending downwards,* for the plant should, if possible, **be clean underneath to a** height of, say, 6 inches. This clean stem high class plants have naturally, not so the Chinese, or the Chinese cast of hybrid.

Plants should be more or less pruned out in the centre. **In the following** spring young wood is then formed in the heart of the tree, and it is only young wood and shoots that give leaf.

Plants, if above **two** years old (see foot note next page), exceeding 2½ feet in height at the end of the season (and all **plants of any age will) may be** pruned down to 20 inches,

---

* The best plan with the lowest branches is to *pull* them off, with a sharp downward action, as then they will not grow again.

but the thick wood must be pruned down to varying heights several inches lower.

Small plants must naturally be more lightly pruned.

The best plan is, I think, to have two gangs:

The first to go ahead and cut out the thick wood (here judgment is necessary, so let them be the best men) to varying heights, from about 11 to 18 inches. The second gang to follow, each with a rod 20 inches long, to cut down all the light wood left to that level.

All plants, how **low or** how young soever they may be, must be pruned somewhat.* The lower their stature and the less their age the less pruning they require.

Of **the** two extremes, at least with the Tea plant, it is probably better to over than to under-prune. The treatment of the plants, with reference to the leaf to be taken in the spring, must **be a good** deal regulated by **the** way, or rather the extent, **to** which **they have been** pruned. On this point see page 103.

The cost of pruning depends on whether it is high or low, and whether **the** plants **are** large, middling, or small. The greatest cost is about Rs. 6, the least about **Rs.** 3 per acre.

Let all prunings be buried between the lines of plants, if possible, before the leaves have even withered. They make **capital** manure, but much of the virtue escapes if they are allowed to lie on the ground any time before they are buried.

---

* But not before the end of 18 months after transplanting, as the object at first is to get a long tap-root to draw moisture from low down, and this is best attained by allowing the plant to grow as it will. I look on this as all-important. I care not how high a plant may grow, for 18 months I would in **no** way interfere with its growth.

CHAPTER XX.

WHITE ANTS, CRICKETS, AND BLIGHT.

These insects (for blight, too, is said to be an insect) are very destructive to the Tea plants. The cricket, however, only injures it when quite young, so we will consider that little pest first.

When Tea seed germinates, and the young seedling is 2 or 3 inches high, the cricket delights to cut the stem and carry, or try to carry, the two or three green leaves attached to the upper part into its hole. Even after seedlings are planted out, if the stems are slender, it cuts them. To the young seedlings, in nurseries or planted " at stake," they often do great harm, killing in some places one-third or so.

It is much easier to prevent their ravages in nurseries than in this latter case, simply because the spot in which they must be sought and destroyed is circumscribed in the one, almost unlimited in the other.

Only one thing can be done. Employ boys (they soon get clever enough at the work) to hunt for their holes and dig them out. The holes are minute, but run down a long way. The only plan to follow them is to put in a thin pliable stick and remove the soil along it. On getting to the bottom of the stick, if it is not the bottom of the hole, you repeat the operation till you do get to the bottom, and there you will generally find the cricket.

Early in the morning they can be often found and caught outside their holes. The boys employed should be paid for them by the number they catch. They can be placed alive and brought to the factory in a hollow bamboo, and then killed in some merciful way.

When once a Tea plant has got a stem as thick as a thick pencil no cricket can hurt it.

They are much worse in some places than others, and in my experience I have found them worse on **low lands**.

The white ant is a much more formidable enemy **than the cricket**. They *do* (as all planters know) attack and destroy living bushes.* Whether they first attack some small dead portion or not is a question, but practically it does not signify the least, for if they do they manage to find such in about one-third of the trees in a garden. Beginning with the minute dead part they kill ahead of them as they go, and will, eventually, in many cases, if left alone, kill the largest trees.

They have a formidable enemy in the small black ant which exists in myriads, and kills the white ant whenever the latter is not protected by the earthen tunnels he constructs. In many places so great is the pest that, did this small black ant not exist, I believe no **Tea** Garden could stand.

From the close of the rains to the cold weather is the worst time for white ants, and the time the planter should guard particularly against their ravages. At that time if he **examines his trees** closely he will very likely find white ants on a quarter of the whole.

Digging round the plant where they are disturbs their runs and does much good. At the same time they should be brushed off any **part** of the tree they have attacked, and the tree should be well shaken.

All this, however, only does temporary good, for they often are found as thick as ever on the plant a week later.

Tobacco water is beneficial, but in wet weather it is soon washed off.

---

* A long controversy on this point lately took place in the papers; that is to say, the point discussed was, whether white ants do or do not attack living tea trees.

Kerosene oil is *very* efficient. A little is put round the stem, but it is expensive. The next best thing I know is the earth oil (petroleum) from Burmah, and this is cheap enough. It is thick, but used from a bottle it gets heated by the sun and is then quite limpid.

When white ants are found on a tree, a little with a small brush is put on the part they have attacked. They are also well shaken off, and a ring of oil is placed round the stem. My experience is that they will not attack that tree again for a long time. I was at first fearful that both it and the kerosene (the one, I believe, is only a manufacture of the other) would injure the trees, but both are safe. I strongly recommend others to try it, if they doubt, on a small spot only in the first instance.

Whatever is used, or whatever is done, white ants must not be left to work their will in the autumn. All the trees should then be examined once at least, and once again, if possible, the following spring.

Blight (a serious matter, I hear, in Cachar) I know but little of. I do not remember hearing anything about it when I was there, now some fourteen years ago. It is rare in the Chittagong district, but I have seen one or two trees attacked with it. Under its influence the young leaves get covered with brown spots and shrivel. It is most destructive to the yield of a garden.

From one or two experiments made I believe pruning off all the diseased branches, and scraping back the soil for a space of 2 feet round the stem, so as almost to lay the roots bare, will be found beneficial, but I do not speak with certainty.

All the Himalayan gardens are free from these three pests detailed, except that occasionally a few crickets have been seen.

CHAPTER XXI.

FILLING UP VACANCIES.

So difficult is this to do, that I have heard several planters declare they would attempt it no further, but, on the contrary, accept the vacancies in their gardens as an unavoidable evil.

That it is difficult I, too, can certify. Seedlings put into **vacant** spots year after year die, either in the rains they **are planted or in** the following spring. If, however, a few yards off a fresh piece of land is taken in and planted, the plants live. What is the reason? It can be nothing connected with the soil, for on adjacent spots they live and die.

It puzzled me a long time, but I *believe* I can now explain it. *First*, seedlings planted in vacant spots in a garden are never *safe*. When in the rains there are many weeds in the gardens, and it is being dug, the young seedlings are not observed, are either dug up, or injured so by the soil being dug close to them, that they shortly after die. This is, I believe, the *principal* cause of the failure, and it may be **in a great** measure, if not entirely, obviated by putting, *first*, a high stake on either side of the seedling, and taking care it remains there all through the rains. *Secondly*, as an additional precaution, and **a very** necessary one, before any such land is dug, send **round boys** with "koorpies" to clean **away the jungle** round **the young plants, and at** the same **time** open the soil slightly over their roots. Doing this "cultivates" them, and the plants being apparent, with the **newly-stirred** vacant **spaces** round them, **are** seen by the **diggers,** and are not likely **to** be damaged.

The second cause of failure I attribute to the old plants on either side of the young seedling, taking to themselves all the moisture there may be in the soil during any drought. The young seedling, whose tap-root at the time is not a long one (for it is in the spring of the year following the year of planting that this occurs), is dependent for life entirely on the small amount of moisture that exists in the soil, at that insignificant depth (say 8 inches). But on two sides of the said seedling's tap-root, and in fact surrounding it, if the neighbouring Tea bushes are full grown, are the feeding rootlets of the big plants, sucking up all the moisture attainable (the necessities of *all* plants being then great), and leaving none for the poor young seedling, which consequently dies in the unequal contest.

This last evil (in climates where there is a deficiency of spring rains, and, in fact, more or less in all Tea localities, for in none is there as much rain as the plants require in the spring) there is no means of avoiding as long as seedlings, after transplanting, *lose time*, the effect of the transplanting, and thus fail to attain a good depth before the said dry season.

In fact, unless something is devised, I believe with many, trying to fill up vacancies is a loss of time and money.

The pits to plant in, advised at page 59, should of course be made in these vacant spots, for they help much towards the early descent of the tap-root. Still they can scarcely avail sufficiently to avoid the evil, if the plant is lying inert, as is generally the case for two or three months after planting; this delay being, moreover, in the rains, the best growing time.

If we can devise any means to avoid this delayed growth in the young seedling after it is transplanted, then the tap-root, before the drought of next spring, will have descended low enough to gather moisture for itself; that is, from *lower* depth than the greater number of the rootlets of the neighbouring big plants traverse. Could this be done, and if the means above detailed are resorted to, to prevent the young plants being injured when the gardens are dug, I see **no** reason why vacancies should not be successfully filled up. Then might be seen, what nowhere can be seen **now, a** Tea garden full of plants, that is, with *no* vacancies.

When it is considered that many gardens in all the districts have 30 or even 40 per cent. vacancies, none less than say 12 **per cent.,** we may strike a fair average **and** roughly compute the vacancies in Tea gardens throughout the country at 20 per cent. In other words, the yield of Tea from India, with the *same* expenditure now incurred, would be one-fifth more were plantations full!

I have shown how the first evil can be obviated. I *think* **the** following will obviate the second.

Get earthen pots made $7\frac{1}{2}$ inches diameter at the head and $7\frac{1}{2}$ inches deep, like the commonest flower pots, only these should be nearly as wide at the bottom as at the top. A circular hole, 2 inches diameter, must be left in the bottom. Fill these with mould of the same *nature* as the soil of the garden where the vacancies exist. Put two or three seeds in each, all near the centre, and not more than half an inch below the surface. Place these pots, so filled, near water, and beneath artificial shade, as described in Chapter XIII.

When **the** seeds have germinated, and the seedlings have two or three leaves, **so that** you can judge which is the best class of seedlings in each pot,[*] root out all but one, **the best** one. Now **remove the shade** gradually, water **from** time to time, and let the seedlings grow in the pots **till** the rains. Having, before the rains, made the holes at the vacancies as before described, after the first

---

[*] By " best class" I mean the most indigenous class.

fall carry the pots to the garden and place each one near a hole.

Then plant as follows. **Stand the** pot on the brink of the hole, having previously with a hammer **broken the** bottom. Then crack the sides also gently, and deposit pot and all in the hole at the proper depth. If not enough broken, the sides of the pot **may** now be **further** detached, nay, even partially removed. Now fill up with earth to the top. Pieces of **the** pot left in the hole will do no harm; but it, the pot, must be sufficiently broken at the bottom to allow of the free descent of the tap-root, **as also enough** broken at the sides to allow of the free spreading of the rootlets.

If all this **has been** carefully done, so that the mould in the pot shall not have been shaken free of the rootlets, the seedlings will not even *know* it has been transplanted. Its growth will not be delayed for **a** day, instead of two or three months; and by the time the dry season comes, the tap-root will have descended far enough to imbibe moisture.

Another plan to effect the same object. Instead of pots, **use** coarse **bamboo** open wicker-work baskets. The split bamboo forming the said wicker-work about half an inch wide, the interstices about one quarter of an inch square. Let the diameter of **the basket be the** same at top and bottom, viz., 9 **inches;** the depth of the basket 10 inches.

When the seedlings in the nursery are large enough to enable **you to select a** good class of plant, transplant one into each basket previously filled with soil.* This being done when the plants are very young, and there being *then* no difficulty in taking them up with earth attached to their short tap-roots and rootlets, **they** will scarcely be thrown back at all. Being near water they can also be well tended. Put basket and all **into** the vacant hole at the beginning of the rains, and fill up as directed for the pots. **The** interstices will allow the feeding

* Mind again this be of the same nature as the garden soil.

rootlets to **pass** through, besides the basket rots quickly under **ground, so** quickly **it cannot** impede the plant.

Seed is not sown at once in the baskets as in the pots, because **the** baskets would not **last** so long. Even putting the seedling in it during (say) February, the basket, with the occasional watering necessary, will, more or less, have rotted before it is put into the hole.

I have concluded a contract for ten thousand pots and five thousand baskets at half an anna each for both kinds. Two pice, to ensure the filling up of a vacancy, is not a large outlay.

Since writing the above I have had experience of both the above plans. The pot system is far the better, and answers very well.* I am now trying to improve this still further by making the pots a little larger, and placing a thin inner lining of tin inside each about half an inch from the sides. This space is first filled with sand, then the pot is filled with mould, and the tin pulled out. The same tin will therefore do for any number of pots. The seed is then put in.

I think by this plan if, when about to plant, the mould in the pot is well wetted, that it, with the seedling, can be turned out whole in one piece, and then put in the hole *without* the pot.

The same pots would then answer year after year, and the expense would be quite nominal.

If well done, the seedling in this, as in the former case, would not even *know* it had been transplanted.†

---

* The baskets are too frail; being often wetted, they fall to pieces before the planting time.

† It may be that the transplanting and transporting tools invented by Mr. Jeben (see page 79) will solve the difficulty of filling up vacancies.

CHAPTER XXII.

FLUSHING AND NUMBER OF FLUSHES.

THE Tea plant is said to flush when it throws out new shoots and leaves. The young leaves thus produced are the only ones fit to make Tea, and the yield of a plantation depends therefore entirely on the frequency and abundance of the flushes.

The way a flush is formed is fully explained under the head of "leaf picking" (pages 103, 104, and 107).

The number of flushes in different plantations varies enormously, owing, *first*, to climate; *secondly*, to soil; *thirdly*, to the pruning adopted; *fourthly*, to the degree of cultivation given; and *fifthly*, though not least, to the presence or absence of manure.

How to secure all these advantages to their fullest extent is shown under those heads, and we have here only to consider what is a low, a medium, and a high rate of flushing per season.

In doing this we must speak of elevated (as Himalayan) gardens separately. The cool climate of heights makes it impossible for Tea to flush there as on the plains.

Speaking generally of elevated gardens (the higher they are the shorter the period, and *vice versâ*), seven months may be considered as the average producing period, viz., from beginning of April to end of October, and during that time twelve to fifteen flushes may be obtained, which, I believe, with high cultivation and liberal manuring, can be increased to eighteen.

In all localities, with favourable Tea climates, the plants

flush both for a longer period and oftener. Speaking generally also, in this case, of the five best localities, viz., Assam, Cachar, Chittagong, the Terai below Darjeeling, and the Western Dooars (for even in these districts many advantages exist in one garden which do not in another), the following is an approximation to the flushing periods :—

Upper Assam.—February 25th to November 15th.
Lower Assam.—February 20th to November 20th.
Cachar.—February 20th to November 20th.
Chittagong.—March 10th to December 20th.
Terai below Darjeeling and Western Dooars.—March 1st to November 20th.

The opening period is a little late in Upper Assam on account of the cold, and closes a little earlier for the same reason.

Lower Assam and Cachar are much alike.

The opening in Chittagong is later than in the two just mentioned from want of early rains, but the season continues longer on account of the low latitude and consequent deferred cold weather.

Roughly, then, rather more than nine months may be assumed as the flushing period for these districts. The next point is how *often* do gardens in these localities flush in that time.

Not very many planters can say, certainly, how often their gardens have flushed in a season, because they are picked so irregularly, and no account of the different flushes kept. Enquiring on this point, when I was in Cachar some thirteen years ago, 9 to 24 were the minimum and maximum numbers given me at different gardens, showing how little was really known about it.

Such knowledge as I have on the subject is mostly derived from carefully kept records of my own garden in the Chittagong district. The plantation is all worked in sections, in the way described previously, and the dates given in the table below are the days each flush was finished (that is, the picking was finished) during the seasons 1869 and 1870; 1869 being carried up to the end of the season, 1870 up to the date I wrote the first edition of this Essay.

In the table it will be observed there is a great difference between the two years. The section for which the dates are given was planted from seed beds in the month of June, 1866. In 1869 it was therefore only three years old. This will partly account for the first flush occurring a month earlier in 1870, as it was then a year older; but fortunate early rains in 1870 had also much to do with it.

Flushes	1869 Dates	Interval in days	1870 Dates	Interval in days
1	March 22	..	February 22	..
2	May 6	44	March 30	35
3	,, 29	23	April 13	10
4	June 11	12	,, 25	12
5	,, 23	12	May 5	9
6	July 5	11	,, 14	9
7	,, 17	12	,, 25	11
8	,, 31	14	June 4	9
9	August 10	9	,, 12	8
10	,, 21	11	,, 22	10
11	Sept. 2	11	July 1	8
12	,, 12	10	,, 8	7
13	,, 25	13	,, 16	8
14	October 9	13	,, 25	9
15	,, 22	13	August 2	7
16	Nov. 2	10	,, 11	9
17	,, 11	9	,, 21	10
18	,, 19	8	,, 29	8
19	Dec. 4	14	Sept. 7	8
20	..	..	,, 18	11
21	..	..	,, 27	9
22	..	..	October 5	7
Average intervals between Flushes.		Nearly 14 days.	..	Very little over 10 days.

In 1869 there was no flush between March 22nd and May 6th, a period of 44 days; and in 1870, none between

February 22nd and March 30th, a period of 35 days, a very long time in both cases, which is entirely accounted for by the dry weather prevailing at Chittagong in the spring (see under head of Climate), for in Cachar, Assam, and the Western Dooars two or three flushes would have occurred in that time.

There were 19 flushes in all in 1869, and 22 in 1870, up to the time I wrote, so there were probably in all 27 in the latter year.

In the table I give the intervals between each flush. It shows an average of 14 days in 1869 to 10 days in 1870; the difference is due to the increased age of the plants, and the liberal manuring given in the cold weather 1869-70.

Such a result as is shown for 1870, and the probable result of 27 flushes to the end of that season, could not be obtained without high cultivation and liberal manuring. The land in question had been manured every year since it was planted, but an extra dose was given in the cold weather of 1869-70. The ground was therefore very rich.

I think, therefore, 25 flushes in the season may be looked for on gardens in good Tea climates, when high cultivation and liberal manuring are resorted to. Where manure cannot be obtained, I think, even if in other respects the land is highly cultivated, more than 22 flushes will not be obtained. Where neither manure nor high cultivation is given, above 18 flushes will not be got.

It seems to be a general idea with planters (see diagram, page 104) that when a flush is picked the succeeding flush, at an interval of say seven to ten days, consists of shoots from the axis of the leaf down to which the previous flush was picked. Thus in the diagram, supposing the shoot to be picked down to the black line above 2, the idea is the next flush will be a shoot springing from the same place, viz., the axis of leaf *d*. But it is *not* so. In the above case it will take a whole month, after the said shoot has been picked, before the new shoot from the base of the leaf d is ready to take, probably six weeks in Himalayan gardens.

'Tis true the flushes in favourable Tea climates follow at about seven to ten days from each other, but these are *other* shoots. The replacement of the actual shoot taken is a whole month in developing. I have carefully watched this, and am sure I am right.

With similar treatment, gardens in Cachar, Assam, and the Western Dooars would probably give two or three more flushes in the season than Chittagong, because there the spring rains are much more abundant; and I am very certain that, if the day ever comes that manure in large quantities is procurable in those districts and is applied, the yield on those gardens will be very large.*

The difference between very small and very large profits is represented by 18 and 25 flushes, so I strongly advise all planters to cultivate highly, and to get all the manure they possibly can. If even procured at a high figure, it (the manure) will pay hand over hand.

* Where new gardens are made on rich virgin soil, to manure them at all for the first few years is, I think, unnecessary. But the richest soils on Tea gardens get exhausted in time, and manure should be applied *before* this point is arrived at.

CHAPTER XXIII.

LEAF PICKING.

THE first consideration is how to get the largest quantity of leaf without injuring the trees.

To a certain extent, it is true that the more a Tea bush is pruned and picked the more it will yield. It appears as if Nature were always trying to repair the violence done to the tree by giving new mouths or leaves to breathe with in place of those taken away. I may exemplify my meaning in another way. A Tea bush which has as many leaves on it as *it requires* will throw out tardily new shoots, and their number will be small. In other words, a plant which is not pruned, and from which the young leaves are not taken, grows gradually large and bushy, and then gives up flushing altogether. It has all the leaves it *requires*, and it has no necessity to throw out more.

If, however, Nature is too much tried, that is, if too much violence is done to her, she sulks and will exert herself no more. Up to this point, therefore, it is well to urge her. How can we know when we have reached it?

Only general rules can be laid down. Experience is the great *desideratum* on this and many other subjects connected with Tea.*

If the plant can always be kept in such a state that the foliage, without being *very much so*, is still less than Nature requires, I conceive the object will be attained.

The greatest violence is done to the plant when it is

---

* See foot-note, page 86, which shows that for 18 months after transplanting, young bushes should not be pruned or picked at all.

pruned, and reason would seem to argue that when this violence is repairing, that is, when the first shoots in the spring show themselves, and until new mouths (or leaves) in sufficient quantities exist, until then but little leaf should be picked.

Fortunately, moreover, while in the interests of the plant this is the best plan, it also is the mode by which the largest yield of leaf will be secured in the season. I go to show this.

The ordinary size of a good full-grown Tea plant, at the end of the season, is, say, 3½ or 4 feet high, and 5 feet diameter. It is pruned down, say, to a height of 2 feet, with a diameter of 3 feet. It is then little more than wooden stems and branches, and to anyone ignorant of the *modus operandi* in Tea gardens, it would appear as if a plantation so pruned has been ruined. The tree remains so during all its hybernating period, that is, during the time it is resting and the sap is down (this period is longer or shorter, as the climate is a warm or cold one, and it is always during the coldest season), but on the return of spring new shoots start out from the woody stems and branches in the following way:—At the axis or base of each leaf is a bud, the germ of future branches, these develop little by little, until a new shoot is formed of, say, five or six leaves, with a closed bud at top. Then if it be not picked the said bud at top hardens. At the axis or base of each of the said five or six leaves are other buds, and the next step is for one, two, or three of these to develop in the same way and form new shoots. The original shoot grows thicker and higher until it becomes a wooden branch or stem. The same process, in their turn, is repeated with the new shoots. A diagram (see next page) will make my meaning clear. We here have a shoot fully developed, of six leaves, counting the close leaf a at top as one, viz., the leaves a, b, c, d, e, f. The shoot has started and developed from what was originally a bud at K, at the axis or base of the leaf H. In the same way as formerly at K a bud existed, which has now formed the complete shoot or flush K a, so at the base of the leaves c, d, e, f, exist buds

1, 2, 3, 4, from which later new shoots would spring. These again would all have buds at the base of the leaves, destined to form further shoots, which again would be the parents of others, and so on to the end of the season, or until the tree is pruned.

It will readily be seen the increase is tremendous. It is only limited by the power of the soil to fling out new shoots, and the *necessities* of the plant, for, as I have explained, when as much foliage exists as the plant requires, but few new shoots are produced.

Now supposing the shoot in the diagram to be (with perhaps another not shown at L) the first on the branch I I in the spring (the said branch having been cut off or pruned at the upper I). It is then evident the said shoot is destined to be the parent and producer of all the very numerous branches and innumerable shoots into which the plant will extend in that direction. It is, in other words, the goose which will lay all the future eggs. If, eager to begin Tea making early, the planter nips it off, the extension on that part of the tree is thrown back many weeks. It may be taken off at 1, 2, or 3 (the back lines drawn show the proper way to pick leaf); the least damage will be done if it is taken off at 1, the most at 3.

The said shoot K a is the first effort of Nature to repair the violence done to the tree by pruning. It is the germ of many other branches and shoots, and it ought *never* to be taken. I have, I hope, made so much plain.

There is, however, another consideration. Any shoot, left to fully develop and harden, does not throw out new shoots from the existing buds 1, 2, 3, 4 so quickly as one checked in its upward growth by nipping off its head. For instance, supposing the shoot under consideration *not* to be the first of the season, but on the contrary to be a shoot when the plant has developed sufficiently to make picking safe, if taken off at 2, then the new growth from 2, 3, 4 will be much quicker than it would be had the whole shoot been left intact.

Our object then with *first* shoots should be to secure this advantage without destroying any buds, and this we can do by taking off simply the closed leaf at the top *a*. This must be done so as not to injure the bud at the base of the second leaf *b* (I have not numbered it, for there is no room in the diagram to do so), and we shall thus leave all the buds on the shoot intact.

Again here the interests of the plant, and profit to the planter, go hand in hand. The closed bud *a* in this case will be found very valuable. I go to show this.

The value of Tea is increased when it shows " Pekoe tips." Only the leaves *a b* make these. They are covered with a fine silky whitish down, and, if manufactured in a particular way, make literally white or very pale yellow Tea,* which, mixed with ordinary **black** Tea, show as "Pekoe tips." **In** ordinary leaf-picking these two leaves are taken with all **the** others, **but** unfortunately, when manufactured with them, they **lose this white or pale** yellow **colour,** and come **out as black as** all the other Tea.

As the season goes on, this is less and less the case, till towards the end nearly all the *a b* leaves show orange-coloured in the manufactured Tea. Still they are not *white* (the best colour) **as** they can be made when treated separately. No means have yet been devised to separate them *before* manufacture from the other leaf, and though sometimes picked separate, the plan has serious objections (see next page). In the case, however, of the first two or three **flushes the** welfare of the plants demands that no more should be taken, and though the quantity obtained will be small, **it** will, if carefully manufactured so as to make "white Pekoe tips," add one or two annas a lb. to **the** value, **when** mixed with it, of one hundred times its own weight of black Tea!

More will be found under this head in the **Tea** manufacturing part. I now beg the question that the said downy leaves taken alone are very valuable.

In detailing the mode of picking I advocate, it would be tedious **to** go minutely into the reasons for each and everything. I have said enough to explain a good deal, but will add anything of importance. Of the latter are the following.

Tea can be made **of** the young succulent leaves only. The younger and more succulent the leaf the better Tea it makes. Thus *a* will make more valuable Tea than *b*, *b* than *c*, **and so** on; *e* is the lowest leaf to make Tea from, for though a very coarse kind can be made from *f*, it does not pay to take it. The stalk also makes good Tea, as far as it is really succulent, that is, down to the black line just above 2.

* I mean manufactured Tea. The infusion is called liquor.

The leaves are named as follows from the Teas it is supposed they would make:—

        a.—Flowery Pekoe.
        b.—Orange Pekoe.
        c.—Pekoe.
        d.—Souchong, 1st.
        e.—   ,,   2nd.
        f.—Congou.

Mixed together ... *a, b, c*—Pekoe.
                       a, b, c, d, e—Pekoe Souchong.

If there be another leaf below *f*, and it be taken, it is named, and would make Bohea.

Each of these leaves was at first a flowery Pekoe leaf (*a*), it then became *b*, then *c*, and so on.

That is to say, as the shoot developed, and a new flowery Pekoe leaf was born, each of the leaves below assumed the next lowest grade.

Could the leaves fit to make each kind of Tea it is proposed to make be picked and kept separate, and each be manufactured in the way most suitable to its age, and the Tea to be produced, the very best of every kind could easily be manufactured. But this cannot be; the price of Tea will not allow it, and the labour to do it would moreover fail. It has been attempted again and again to do it, partly to the extent of taking the Pekoe leaves *a, b, c* separate from the others (for the manufacture best suited to these upper leaves is not suited to the lower), but it has been as often abandoned, and I doubt if it is now practised anywhere. I am sure it will never pay to do it.

Picking leaf is a coarse operation. It is performed by 80 or 100 women and children together, and it is impossible to follow each, and see it is done the best way. They must be taught, checked, and punished if they do wrong, and then it will be done more or less right; but perfection is not attainable.

I advise the following plan in picking. Please refer to the diagram :—

If the garden has been severely pruned (as it ought to be) take only the bud *a* for *two* flushes; then for *two* more nip the stalk above 1, taking the upper part of leaf *c*, as shown (done with one motion of the fingers). But from the fifth flush take off the shoot at the line above 2, and by a separate motion of the fingers take off the part of leaf *e* where the black line is drawn. By this plan, when the rains begin, the trees will show a large picking surface, for plenty of buds will have been preserved for new growth. After the month of August you may pick lower if you like, as you cannot hurt the trees. For instance, you may nip the stalk and upper part of leaf *e* together, and separately the upper part of *f*.

The principle of picking is to leave the bud at the axis of the leaf down to which you pick intact.

Some planters pick all through the season at the line above 1, and take the *d* and perhaps the *e* leaf separately. I do not like the plan, for though it will make strong Teas, the yield will be small. Moreover, the plants will form so much foliage; they will not flush well; and again, they will grow so high that boys who pick will not readily reach the top.

Shortly, the principle I advocate is to prune severely, so that the plant in self-defence *must* throw out many new shoots; to be sparing and tender with these until the violence done to the tree is in a measure, but not quite, repaired; then, till September, to pick so much that the wants of the plant in foliage are never quite attained; and after September to take all you can get.

I believe this principle (for the detailed directions given may be varied, as for instance when trees have *not* been heavily pruned) will give the largest yield of leaf, and will certainly not injure the plants.

CHAPTER XXIV.

MANUFACTURE. MECHANICAL CONTRIVANCES.

To manufacture your leaf into good Tea is certainly one of the first conditions for success. It will avail little to have a good productive garden if you make inferior Tea. The difference of price between well and ill-manufactured Tea is great, say 4 as. or 6d. a lb., and this alone will, during a season, represent a large profit or none.

Fortunately for Tea enterprise, the more manufacture is studied the more does it appear that to make good Tea is a very simple process. The many operations or processes formerly considered necessary are now much reduced on all gardens. As there was then, that is formerly, so there is now, no *one* routine recognized by all, or even by the majority; still simplicity in manufacture is more and more making its way everywhere; and as the real fact is that to make the best Tea, but very few, and very simple, processes are necessary, it is only a question of time ere the fact shall be universally recognised and followed out.

For instance, panning the "roll" * was formerly universally practised. Some panned once, some twice, some even three times! But, to-day, pans are not used in most gardens at all!! Other processes, or rather in most cases the repetition of them, have been also either discarded or abridged. But a short statement of manufacture in old

---

* In describing manufacture I shall call the leaf brought in "Leaf," until it enters on the rolling process; from that time until the drying over charcoal is concluded, "Roll;" and after that, "Tea."

days, and the simplest mode of manufacture, will best illustrate my meaning :—

Days	One and a common old plan			One plan to-day by which the best Tea can be made		
	Number of operations	Detail	Days	Number of operations	Detail
1st	1	Withering.	1st	1	Withering.
	2	1st Rolling.		2	Rolling.
	3	2nd ,,		3	Fermenting.
	4	Fermenting.	2nd	4	Sunning (if sun).
	5	1st Panning.		5	Firing (Dholing).
2nd	6	3rd Rolling.			
	7	2nd Panning.			
	8	4th Rolling.			
	9	Sunning.			
	10	1st Firing (Dholing).			
	11	Cooling and crisping.			
3rd	12	2nd Firing (Dholing).			
3	12	Total days and operations.	2	5	Total days and operations.

So much for simplicity, and I affirm that no more than the five operations detailed are necessary. I shall try to show this further on.

In studying Tea manufacture I first tried, in order to get reliable data to go on, to ascertain the effect of each and every operation, and not only that, but the effect on the made Tea of each operation exaggerated and diminished. It would be tedious, and of no use, to set out in detail all the experiments I conducted, the results only I will try to give.

I began at the beginning. Why wither at all? I made Tea (following out in each case all the other processes detailed in the old plan) of 1st, totally unwithered leaves; 2nd, of leaves but little withered; 3rd, of leaves medium-withered; and 4th, of **leaves** over-withered.

I arrived at the following results :—Unwithered or under-withered leaves break in the rolling and give out large quantities of a light green coloured juice during the same process. The Tea is much broken and of a reddish grey colour. The liquor is very pale in colour, cloudy, weak, soft, and tasteless.

Over-withered leaf on the other hand takes a good twist in the rolling, gives out but little juice, which is of a thick kind, and of reddish yellow colour. The tea is well twisted, "chubby" in appearance, and blacker than ordinary. The liquor of an ordinary depth of colour, clear, with a mawkish taste.

The medium-withered leaves make good Tea, but I found the withering should be rather in excess of what is generally done to ensure strength. I will show later to what extent I think leaf should be withered.

The next point was rolling. I knew some planters rolled the leaf hard, others lightly. That is, some rolled with force till much juice was expressed, others with a light hand, allowing little or no juice to be pressed out. Which was the better?

After many experiments I arrived at the following:— Hard rolling gives darker coloured and stronger liquor than light rolling. Hard rolling destroys Pekoe tips,[*] inasmuch as the juice expressed stains them black.

Light rolled Tea has therefore many more Pekoe tips than hard rolled.

Hard rolled Tea is somewhat blacker than light rolled.

In all, therefore, but the point of Pekoe tips hard rolling is better.

The next question was, what is the advantage of repeated rolling? I rolled twice, panning once between, *vide* old plan, and found the Tea as well made and as strong as that rolled three or four times. I then decided to roll *no*

---

[*] Pekoe tips are the whitish or orange-coloured ends that may be seen in Pekoe Tea. See pages 105, 106, and 116.

more than **twice.** The second time was, I *then* thought, **necessary, as** I found the **leaf of** the roll opened in the pan, and a second rolling was **requisite to twist** it again.

But what did panning **do?** I heard pans had been discontinued in some gardens. **In** what way was panning an advantage? I made Tea, fermenting it between the two rollings, but *not* panning it, and it was **equally** good. I tried again and again, but never could detect that panning **caused any** difference to either the Tea, the liquor, or the **out-turn.*** In short, though I never found panning did any **harm,** I equally found it never did any good. Its use is, in fact, simply barren of *all* results.

I therefore dispensed with it. Having done so, why roll **the second** time at all? I experimented, and found the second rolling as barren of results **as** the panning.

I had now got rid of operations 3, 5, 6, 7, and 8 in the old plan. The next was No. 9—" sunning." I made Tea with and without it, and found as follows:—

Sunning between **the fermenting and firing processes has** no effect whatever on the liquor or the out-turn, but it makes the Tea rather blacker, and as it drives off much of the moisture in the roll, the firing process after it is shorter **and** does not consume so much charcoal. What little effect therefore it has is good (for if not continued too long, **it does not make the Tea too** black) and it is economical. I therefore decided on retaining it.†

Next came **the operations 10,** 11, and 12, viz., " first firing, cooling and **crisping, and second** firing." Where **these are** done (and they **are done in** some gardens now) **the usual** thing is to *half-fire* the roll the same afternoon and

---

* The out-turn consists of the Tea leaves after infusion.

† **At the** end of the season, however, sunning **has more than** the above effect. It then makes the Tea "Chubby" in form, of a reddish colour, and improves the strength **of the** liquor.

evening it is made, then allow it to "cool and crisp" all night, and finish the firing next day. I tried this plan, and also the plan I have now adopted, of doing the whole firing at one time the same evening. I tried the experiment again and again, and always found the Tea, the liquor, and the out-turn were the same in both cases. In short, that the three operations did no more and no less than the one. As the three entail extra labour and extra expense in charcoal I abandoned them.

I thus reduced the twelve operations detailed to five, and naturally by so doing much decreased the cost of manufacturing Tea. I in no way lay claim to having devised this simplicity myself. Part had been done by others before I even turned my attention to it, and I have done no more than help with many to make the manufacture of Tea a simple process.

I was now convinced that (though I had still much to learn regarding the said five processes) success was comprised therein, and that to multiply them could not avail.

The next consideration is—What are the qualities desired in Tea to enable it to command a good price at the public auctions either in Calcutta or London? The brokers in these cases judge of the Tea first, value it, and give their report and valuation to intending purchasers and sellers. From what appearances and qualities do they judge?

They judge from three things, *first*, the Tea; *secondly*, the liquor; *thirdly*, the out-turn.

The Tea.—The colour should be black, but not a dead black, rather a greyish black with a gloss on it. No red leaf should be mixed with it, it should be all one colour. The Tea should be regular: that is, each leaf should be about the same length, and should have a uniform close twist, in all but "broken Teas." (These latter are called "broken" *because* the leaf is more or less open and broken.) The Tea

I

should also be regular of *its kind*, that is, if Pekoe all Pekoe, if Congou all Congou; for any stray leaves in a Tea of another kind, if even of a *better* kind or class, will reduce its value. In the higher class of Teas, viz., Pekoes and broken Pekoes, the more Pekoe tips that are present the higher, in consequence, will its price be.

The Liquor.—In taste this should be strong, rasping, and pungent, with, in the case of Pekoes, a "Pekoe flavour." There are other words used in the trade to particularise certain tastes, but the words themselves would teach nothing. Tea tasting cannot be learnt from books. *If* the liquor is well flavoured, as a rule, the darker it is in the cup the better. But to judge of Teas by the colour of the liquor alone is impossible, for some high-class Teas have naturally a very pale liquor.

The Out-turn.—A good out-turn is generally indicative of a good Tea. It should be all, or nearly all, one colour. No black (burnt) leaves should appear in it. A greenish tinge in some of the leaves is not objectionable, and is generally indicative of pungent liquor, but the prevailing colour should be that of a bright new penny.

Every planter should be more or less of a Tea-taster, and should taste his Teas daily. After a time (particularly if he gets other Teas to taste against his own) he will learn to recognise, at all events, a good as against a bad Tea, a strong as against a weak Tea, &c. No Tea should be put away with the rest until it has been tasted. It may be burnt or have other defects, not apparent till infused, and one day's bad Tea will bring down considerably the value of a whole bin of good Tea.

The fancy, amongst brokers and dealers, for "Pekoe tips," in all Pekoe Teas, constitutes the *one* great difficulty in Tea manufacture. If the leaves which give "Pekoe tips" (see page 106) are separated from the other leaves, and manufactured separately and differently, that is rolled *very* little and *very* lightly, not allowed to ferment at all, but sunned at once after rolling, and, if there is sun enough, finished in the sun, otherwise by a very light and gradual heat—best placed *above* the drawers in the Dhole-house; if this is done, I say, these will come out perfect " Pekoe tips " of a white colour, which is the best.

If *not* separated from the other leaf, but manufactured with it, the sap from the other leaves, expressed in the rolling, stains these said leaves, which are covered with a fine white silk down, and makes them black like all the rest of the Tea; the whole of which is then valued lower *because* **there are no " Pekoe tips."**

Now, in the latter case the " Pekoe tips " are there all the same, only they don't *show*. The Tea is really just as good, in fact a shade *better*, with black than with white or orange tips,* but it does not sell so well, and as we cannot argue the brokers or dealers into a rational view of the case, we must humour their fancy (they are virtually our masters) and give them the Pekoe tips—*if we can*.

How are we to do it? **The plan of picking these small leaves separately, in order to manufacture them separately, does not answer; it is too expensive; it diminishes the yield of a garden, and labour for it fails. All this is shown at pages** 107 and 130. Is there any other way?

It may be done during some periods of the season when there is not leaf enough on the garden to employ all the leaf-pickers, **by setting** a number of them to separate the said two leaves from the others *after* the whole leaf is brought to the factory. This is expensive, but it pays when there is labour to do it, for then the Teas can be made very showy **and** rich with white Pekoe tips.

* It is better, because the " tips " having been hard-rolled give stronger liquor.

An ingenious planter, a Mr. McMeekin, in Cachar, invented a rolling table with the object of separating the said leaves. **It is constructed of** battens, and while rolling the leaf on it, many of the small leaves fall through. The said table is now well known in Cachar, and is in use in several gardens. I have tried it and find that **it in a** great measure answers **its** object, but the objection to it is that the **leaf** *must* be rolled lightly, and lightly-rolled leaf, as **observed**, does not make strong Tea.

The Pekoe tips may be, in a great measure, preserved by rolling *all* the leaf lightly on a common table. But then again the Tea is weak, and the plan will not give so many Pekoe tips as McMeekin's table.

In short, in the present state of our knowledge, except by the hand process (a tedious and expensive one for separating the leaf), strong Teas and Pekoe tips are incompatible.

The difficulty is just where it was, and will so remain until dealers give up asking for Pekoe tips (not a likely thing), or till a machine is invented to separate quickly and cheaply the two said small leaves from the others *after* they have been all picked together. That such a machine is possible I am certain, and the inventor would confer a boon on the Tea interest far beyond the inventor of any other machine, for all the other processes *can* be done by hand **without much** expense, this cannot.

I may here notice such machines and contrivances as exist for cheapening the manufacture of Tea, or rather such as I know of.

Rolling-machines have for their object the doing away with hand labour entirely for rolling the leaf. Kinmond's rolling-machine is first on the list, for it is the best yet invented.*

---

* It *was* the best, but is superseded by a new rolling-machine (Jackson's) I have seen quite lately.

Note to Third Edition.—Jackson's rolling-machine, **by** a late Calcutta

Kinmond's consists of two circular wooden discs, the upper one moving on the lower, which is stationary, with an eccentric motion. The adjacent faces of the said discs are made rough by steps in the wood, cut in lines diverging from the centre to the circumference, and over these rough faces is nailed coarse canvas.

The leaf is placed between the discs and rolled by the motion described. The lower disc is arranged by means of weights running over pulleys, so that it shall press against the upper with any force desired.

The motive power, as designed by the inventor, is either manual, animal, or steam.

Mr. Kinmond showed me this machine, just after he had invented it, at the Assam Company's Plantations in Assam, and I have since seen it working by manual and steam power. With the former it is quite useless, for by no arrangement can sufficient or regular force enough be applied. With the latter it does very well, and on a large garden which will render the outlay for the machine and engine justifiable (the former is, for such a simple machine, very expensive), it may probably eventually prove an economy.

Not having seen it under animal power, I can give no positive opinion as to how it would answer, but I see no reason why it should not do well. I believe wind or water power might, on suitable sites, be easily applied to it, and they would certainly be the cheapest of any.

Another rolling-machine was invented by a Mr. Gibbon, and a good deal used in Cachar. I have never seen it.

Kinmond's is, I believe, the best rolling-machine yet

legal decision, is declared to be **simply Kinmond's**, with alterations. As Jackson is now prohibited from selling his machines, I presume the two inventors will come to some understanding as to the alterations, which are most certainly improvements.

invented (though it is fair to state I know no other except by report), but I do not believe in any Tea rolling-machine superseding *entirely* the necessity of hand-rolling.* A rolling-machine may be, and is, very useful to roll the leaves partly, that is, to break the cells, and bring the leaf into that soft *mashy* state that very little hand labour will finish it. No rolling-machine yet invented can, I think, do more than this, and it is, I think, doubtful if any will ever be invented that will do more. Machines do not give the nice final twist which is obtained by the hand. I was told lately that most of the gardens in Cachar that had machines had dropped them and gone back to hand-rolling. I cannot help thinking this is a mistake. They should use both, the hand-rolling for the final part alone. Very few rolling-men would then suffice, with the aid of the machine, to manufacture a large quantity of leaf.

I only know of one other Tea rolling-machine, which is Nelson's. It does not profess to do more than *prepare* the green leaf for rolling, which, as stated above, is, I think, all that any machine will ever do. I have never seen it working, but it appears simple, being nothing more than a **mangle**. The leaf is placed in bags, and then compressed under rollers attached to a box, weighted with stones. The prospectus states, it will prepare 80 lbs. green leaf in fifteen minutes, and that one man can then finish as much of such prepared leaf in three minutes as would occupy him twelve minutes if the same had not been prepared. I see nothing unlikely in this. The machine, though inferior to Kinmond's **in** its arrangement, *ought* to be cheap enough to bring it within the reach of all.†

---

* **I had** not seen Jackson's machine when I thought as **above**.

† Unfortunately it is not. It is advertised at Rs. 300, with a yearly royalty of Rs. 50 the first year and 20 after. The royalty should be dropped, and the machine sold for Rs. 150, which would give the inventor a good **profit**.

I have already spoken of one of McMeekin's inventions. His chest-of-drawers for firing Tea is, I think, superior to his batten table. It is now so well known, and in such general use, that I shall describe it very shortly. It is nothing more than a low chest-of-drawers, or trays fitted in a frame one above the other, the bottom of each tray being fine iron wire, so that the heat of the charcoal, in the masonry receptacle over which it is placed, ascends through all the drawers and thus dries or fires a large quantity of "roll" at the same time. By the old plan, a single wicker sieve was inserted inside a bamboo frame called a "dhole," which was placed over a charcoal fire made in a hole in the ground. On the sieve the roll was placed, and all the heat, after passing through this *one* sieve, was wasted. Mr. McMeekin's idea was to economise this heat by passing it through several drawers.

Most planters use these drawers, and there is no doubt in the space saved, and the economy of heat: it is a great step in advance over the old barbarous method, where not only was the heat wasted after passing through *one* sieve, but a great deal was lost through the basket work of the "dhole" itself.

Still I do not advocate four, still less five drawers one above the other. I think the steam ascending from the lower drawers must, more or less, injure the roll in the upper ones. I confine myself to two, and even then in the top tray leave a small circular space vacant by which the steam from the lower drawer can escape. I utilize the heat that escapes, partially, by placing "dhallas" in tiers above, with roll in them. These are supported by iron rods let into the wall, and are useful not only for partly drying the roll, but also for withering leaf when there is no sun.

Some planters have proposed to do away with charcoal altogether under McMeekin's drawers, supplying its place

by hot air. The first point in considering this invention is the question whether the fumes of charcoal, as some assert, *are* necessary to make **good T**ea. If they are *not* necessary (that is, if they produce no chemical effect on the Tea, and therefore heat from wood devoid of smoke would do as well) **there can** be no doubt such heat would be cheaper, and more under command, by this or some other plan. Are then the fumes of charcoal necessary?

I do not know that anyone can answer the query. I certainly cannot, for I have never made Tea with any other agent than charcoal, and I have never met with more than one planter who had. He said the Tea was not good. Still it would, I think, require very careful and prolonged experiments to establish the fact either way. Speaking theoretically, as it *appears*, the only effect of charcoal is to drive all the moisture out of the roll and thus make it Tea, I cannot but believe other heat would do as well. It is, however, a question that only experience can solve.*

I have now (four years since the above was written, and at the time I am preparing the second edition of this essay) been for some time employed on experiments with a view **to settle** the above question. Whether I shall be able to devise a simple apparatus to effect the manufacture of Tea without charcoal is doubtful, but I can, I think, now safely affirm that the fumes of charcoal are *not* necessary to make Tea. On this point I am myself quite satisfied. The advantages of making Tea with any fuel (wood, coal, or anything else) would **be** numerous :—

1.—Economy.
2.—Absence of charcoal fumes.
3.—Less chance of fire in Tea Houses.
4.—Probably reduced temperature in Factories.

* Note to 3rd edition.—It is a question no longer. Many besides myself have now proved that charcoal fumes are in no way necessary.

5.—Great saving of labour.

6.—Saving of fuel—for it takes much wood to make a given weight of charcoal.

In addition to all the above, the wholesale destruction of forests that now takes place in all Tea Districts, in order to supply the charcoal for Tea, would be much lessened.*

I have seen a machine advertised for packing Tea, that is to say, for so pressing it down that a large quantity shall go into a **chest**. I have never seen the machine, and so cannot say how it works, but I do not think such a machine at all necessary. By the mode of packing, described at page 150, **as much** Tea as a chest **will** hold *with safety* can be put **into it**. **If more were forced in, the** chest would probably come to pieces in transit.

I see a sifting machine is now being advertised—" Jackson's sifting machine." I have seen drawings of it, but not the machine itself. In the one respect, that it is much larger than anything used hitherto, it is more likely to succeed.

There is a machine for sifting and fanning Tea at one and the same time. I know not who invented it. **It is a** simple winnowing machine with sieves placed **in front of the** fan. By means of a rod and crank **attached to the axle of** the revolving fan the sieves are made to shake from side to side when **the** fanners are turned. The Tea is put into the upper sieve, a coarse one, and passing successively through finer ones, is thus sorted into different Teas. The open leaf at the same time is blown out by the fan.

I purchased one, but I do not find it does the work well. Sifting Tea is a nice process, and I did not find it sorted the Teas with any nicety. I have taken out the sieves, and **use** it now only for fanning, which it does very well, though **no** better than an apparatus which could be constructed at one-third the cost.

* See this subject further discussed **in the** Addenda.

I do not believe in *any* present or future machine for sifting Tea, inasmuch as it is an operation which, to be well **done,** has to be continually varied. More will be said on this head further on.

I have now detailed shortly all the Tea machines or contrivances I know, or have heard of, and I think there is plenty of room yet for inventors.* The machine, as before observed, most to be desired is one to separate the small Pekoe leaves from the others, ere the rolling of the leaf is commenced. If such a machine existed, it would much increase the value of all Indian Teas, and if the Agricultural and Horticultural Society are inclined to offer a prize for any machine, it should be this.

At the point where the separation should take place, the stalk is much tenderer than elsewhere, and this led me to think a blow or concussion on the mass of green leaf might effect the object. I attached a bow by the centre to an immovable board, placed at right angles to the plane of a table (like the back of a dressing table), and then, causing leaf to drop from above, subjected it to sharp strokes from the string of the bow. It effected the object partially, for many Pekoe ends were detached, but it bruised and cut the other leaf too much also. I believe a revolving barrel, with blunt but thin narrow iron plates inside, which would strike the leaf placed within, as the barrel was turned, would perhaps answer. I give the above idea for what it is worth, for any inventive genius **to** improve on.

As it is impossible, as far as I can see, to construct any machine which should *cut* the stalk *only* in the right place, *ergo*, I believe some arrangement which would take advantage of the fact, that the stalk is tenderer there than elsewhere, is the only one that could answer.

* I now believe Jackson's rolling-machine, previously alluded to, will finish the rolling entirely.

Now to return to the manufacture of Tea. I will consider each of the five operations detailed, which I believe are all that are necessary to make good Tea, separately.

Withering.—There are several tests to show when leaf is withered. Fresh leaf squeezed in the hand, held near the ear, crackles, but no sound should be heard from withered leaf. Again, fresh leaf, pressed together in the palm of the hand, when released, springs back to nearly its original bulk, but withered leaf, in like circumstances, retains the shape into which it has been pressed. The stalk of withered leaf will bend double without breaking, but fresh leaf stalks, if bent very little, break. Practice, though, soon gives a test superior to all these, viz., the feel of the leaf. Properly withered leaves are like old rags to lay hold of, and no further test, after a time, than the feel of the leaf is necessary.

The agents for withering leaf are sun, light, heat, and air. Of these the most powerful is sun, for it combines all the others with it. Light is a powerful agent, for if some leaf be placed in a partially dark room, and some in a well-lighted verandah, the latter will wither in half the time the former will take. If light and moderate ventilation be present, heat is a rapid accessory to rapid withering.

There is often great difficulty in withering leaf in the rain. It *can* be withered in Tea pans, but "the out-turn" is then more or less injured, for after infusion the out-turn comes out green instead of the proper "new penny" colour. Withering in dholes is also objectionable for the same reason, though if the heat is moderate the green effect is less. It is further a long and tedious operation.

Space and light are the great wants for withering leaf in wet weather. Bamboo mechans, tier above tier, should be constructed in every available space. Large frames, covered with wire mesh, may also be made (by means of weights running over pulleys) to run up to the roof of any Tea building. The leaf withers well in such frames, for heat ascends, and much heat is given out by dholes.

It signifies not though where leaf is spread as long as there is space and light. Houses made of iron and glass would be far the best for withering leaf, for, if well ventilated, all the necessary agents for withering, detailed in the last page, would be present. I do not doubt the day will come when these will be used, for properly withered leaf is a necessity for good Tea.*

In dry weather, when leaf comes in from the garden, spread it thinly anywhere and turn it once early in the night. It will generally be withered and ready to roll next morning. If not quite ready, then put it outside in the sun. Half an hour's sunning will probably finish it.

In wet weather, if there is any sun when it comes in, or any time that day, take advantage of the sun to wither the leaf *partly*, so much that, with the after withering all night under cover, it will be ready next morning. If not ready next morning, put it out in the sun, if there is any, till it is ready.

In very wet and cloudy weather, when there is no sun and continual rain, so that the leaf *cannot* be put outside (for remember that outside, when there is no sun, the light alone will wither it), artificial withering of some kind must be resorted to. I have mentioned the only means I know of for doing this.

As properly withered leaf is an important point in making good Tea, it is well worth while to keep one or two men, according to the quantity of leaf, for that work alone. They soon learn the best way to do it, and if made answerable the leaf is properly ready for the rollers, the

---

* Note to 3rd edition—I am now sending out the glass necessary for a glass withering house to be erected on the garden just finished in the Western Dooars.

object is generally attained. In this and every thing else in Tea manufacture, give different men different departments, and make them answerable. Much trouble to the manager, who should supervise all, and much loss to the proprietor from bad Tea, will then be avoided.

Rolling.—This is a simple operation enough when the men have got the knack of it. Some planters advocate a circular motion of the hands when rolling, under the impression it gives the leaf a better twist. Some like rolling it forward, but bringing it back without letting it turn during the backward motion. I believe in neither way, for it appears to me to be rolled no better, or no worse, by these plans than by the ordinary and quicker mode of simply rolling it *any way*. The forward and backward motion is the simplest and quickest, and the way all rollers adopt, who are given a certain quantity of leaf (say 30 lbs. a fair amount) to roll for their day's work. In this ordinary rolling the ball in the hand, 'tis true, does not turn much in the backward motion, for 'tis more or less *pulled* back, but whether it turns or not does not, I believe, signify the least.

Rolling in hot pans was formerly extensively practised. It is not much done now. I have tried the plan, but **found no** advantage in it.

Rolling on coarse mats, placed on the floor, might be seen also. **When** I visited the Assam Company's gardens near Nazerah, in Assam, I saw it done there. It is **a great** mistake. The coarse bamboo mat breaks the leaf sadly, and much of the sap or juice from the leaf, which adds much to the strength of the Tea, runs through the coarse mat, and is lost.

One and the principal reason why Indian Tea is stronger than Chinese is that in India the sap or juice is generally retained, while in China it is, strange to say, purposely wasted!

A strong immovable smooth table, with the planks of which it is formed well joined together, so that no apertures exist for the juice of the leaf to run through, is the best thing to roll on. If covered with a fine seetul pattie mat, **nailed** down over the edges of the table, a still greater security is given against the loss of any sap, and I believe the slightly rough surface of the mat enables the leaf to roll better. An edging of wood one inch above the surface of the table should be screwed on to the edges over the mat, if there is one, to prevent leaf falling off.

The leaf is rolled by a line of men on each side of such a table ($4\frac{1}{2}$ feet is a good width for it) passing up from man to man, from the bottom of the table to the top. The passage of each handful of roll from man to man is regulated by the man at the end, who, when the roll in his hand is ready (that is, rolled enough), forms it into a tight compressed ball (a truncated shape is the most convenient) and puts it away on an adjacent stand. When he does this, the roll each man has passes up one step.

The roll is ready to make up into a ball, when it is in a soft *mashy* state, and when in the act of rolling it gives out juice freely. None of this juice must be lost, it must be **mopped up** into the roll, again and again in its passage up the table, and finally into the ball, when made up.

There will be some coarse leaves in the roll which cannot be twisted. These, if left, would give much red leaf in the Tea. They should be picked out by, say, the third or fourth man from the head of the table, for it is only when the leaf has been partly rolled that they show. The man who picks out the coarse leaf should not roll at all. He should spread the roll, and pick out as much as he can, between the time of receiving and passing it on. In no case allow roll to accumulate by him, for if so kept it hardens and dries, and gives **extra** work to the last rollers to bring it into the mashy state again. Besides which I rather think, any such lengthened stoppage in the rolling helps to destroy Pekoe ends, and is certainly injurious to the perfect after-fermentation, inasmuch as it (the fermentation) partly takes place then.

This finishes the rolling process. **Each man** as stated can do 30 lbs., but there is further work for him to be now described.

Fermenting.—The balls accumulated are allowed to stand until fermented. I look on this being done to the right extent and no more, as perhaps the most important point in the whole manufacture.

Some planters collect the roll after rolling in a basket, and there let it ferment, instead of making it up into balls for that purpose as described. I much prefer the ball system for the following reasons:—When a quantity is put into a basket together and allowed to ferment a certain time, what was put in first is naturally more fermented than what was put in last, the former probably over, the latter under-done. The balls, on the contrary, can be each taken in succession *in the order they were laid on the table,* and thus each receive the same amount of fermentation. I think further the twist in the leaf is better preserved by the ball plan, and also that a large quantity in a basket is apt to ferment too much in the centre.

It is impossible to describe, so that practical use shall be made of it, *when* the balls are sufficiently fermented. The outside of the ball is no good criterion. It varies much in colour, affected by the extent the leaf was withered.* You must judge by the inside.

---

* The more the leaf is withered the thicker in consistency and the smaller in quantity the juice that exudes, as also the yellower in colour. Further, the more the leaf is withered the darker the outside of the balls. Bright rusty red is the colour produced with moderately withered leaf; very dark greenish red with much withered leaf.

Perhaps as good a rule as any is that half the twisted leaves inside shall be a rusty red, half of them green. Practice alone, however, will enable you to pronounce when the balls are properly fermented. There is no time to be fixed for it. The process is quicker in warm than cool weather.

The fermentation should be stopped in *each* ball just at the right time. Great exactitude in this is all-important, and therefore, as I say, the balls should be taken in rotation as they were laid down.

The fermentation is stopped by breaking up the ball. The roll is spread out *very* thin, and at the same time any remaining coarse leaves are picked out.

This concludes the fermenting process.

Sunning.—The roll is then without *any* delay put out in the sun, spread *very* thin on dhallas or mats. When it has become blackish in colour it is collected and re-spread, so that the whole of it shall be affected by the sun. With bright sunshine, an hour or even less suns it sufficiently. It is then at once placed in the dholes, which must be all ready to receive it.

If the weather is wet, it must, *directly* the balls are broken up, and the coarse leaf is picked out, be sent to the dholes. This is the only plan in wet weather, but the best Tea is made in fine weather.

Firing or Dholing.—In the case of wet weather, unless you have very many dholes, fresh roll will come in long before the first is finished. The only plan in this case is to half do it. Half-fired the roll does not injure with *any* delay, but even half an hour's delay, between breaking up the balls and commencing to drive off the moisture, is hurtful.

In any but wet weather necessitating it the roll can be fired at one time, that is, not removed from the drawer until it has become Tea.

The roll in each drawer must be shaken up and re-spread two or three times, in the process of firing. The drawer must be taken off the fire to do this, or some of the roll would fall through into the fire, and the smoke thus engendered would be hurtful. If the lowest drawer is made to slide in and out a framework covered with zinc should be made to run into a groove below it, and this zinc protector should be always run in before the lower drawer is moved. This is part of Mr. McMeekin's invention, and is very necessary to prevent roll from the lowest drawer falling into the fire when it (the lower drawer) is moved.

The roll remains in the drawers, subject to the heat of the charcoal below, until it is quite dry and crisp. Any piece then taken between the fingers should break with the slightest attempt to bend it.

The manufacture is now completed. The roll has become Tea.

All the above operations should be carefully conducted, but I believe the secret of good Tea consists simply in, *first*, stopping the fermentation at the right moment; and, *secondly*, in commencing to drive off the moisture immediately after.

I do not say that the manufacture here detailed may not be improved upon later, but I do say that in the results of economy, strong liquor, and well twisted leaf, its results are very satisfactory, and not surpassed by any other mode at present in vogue. I do not pretend that it will give Teas rich in Pekoe tips. To attain this, light rolling as shown must be resorted to, but just as far as Pekoe tips are procured so far must strength be sacrificed. Until the small Pekoe leaves can be detached and manufactured separately, this must always be the case.

From the Tea made as described by sifting and sorting, all the ordinary black Teas of commerce, as detailed at page 137, can be produced, excepting "Flowery Pekoe."

To make Flowery Pekoe the closed bud and the one open leaf of the shoot are alone taken, and these are manufactured alone. It does not, as a rule, pay to make this Tea at all, though it fetches a long price. It does not pay for the following reasons:—

1. After the head of the flush is taken the pickers that follow do not readily recognise the remainder of the shoot, and consequently omit to pick many of them. A heavy loss in the yield is thus entailed.

2. The after Teas, made without these small leaves, are very inferior, as they are much weaker, and totally devoid of Pekoe tips.

3. The labour, and *ergo* the expense of picking the flush, is double.

The manufacture of Flowery Pekoe is simple enough. When the two leaves from each shoot of which it is made are collected they are exposed to the sun, spread out very thin, until they have well shrivelled. They are then placed over small and slow charcoal fires, and so roasted very slowly. If the above is well done, the Pekoe tips (and there is little else) come out a whitish orange colour. The whiter they are the better. If the leaf is rolled *very lightly* **by** the hand *before* sunning, the liquor will be darker and stronger, but the colour of the tips will not be so good.

Flowery Pekoe is quite a fancy Tea, and for the reasons given above it can never pay to make it.

Green Tea.

The pans for this should be 2ft. 9in. diameter and 11in. in depth. They should be thick pans, which will not, therefore, cool quickly. Many are required for this manufacture, four or five for every maund of Tea to be made daily. They should be set up in a sloping position, and the arrangement of the fireplaces such that the wood to burn under them can be put in through apertures leading into the verandah. One chimney will **do** for every two pans, and it should be built high so as to give a good draught, **for** hot fires are necessary.

Flat-bladed sticks are used to stir both the leaf and the **Tea** in the pans, **for the hand cannot bear the heat.**

The men when working the Tea in the pans should have high stools to sit on, for it is **a nine hours'** job.

The bags in which "the roll" is placed at night should be made of No. 3 canvas, 2 feet long and 1 foot broad.

I will now detail the manufacture.

To make Green Tea the leaf must be brought in twice in the day. What comes in at one o'clock is partly made **the** same day. The evening leaf is left till the following morning, laying it thick (say 6 inches), so that it will *not* wither. But if the one o'clock or the evening leaf comes in wet, they must both be dried, the former *before* being put **into the pans, the latter** *before* **being laid out for the** night.

The manufacture thus begins twice daily, viz., morning **and one o'clock,** but "**the roll**" of both these **is** treated together up to the time "the roll" **is ready to place in the bags.**

The **leaf having no moisture in it is placed** first in hot pans, **at a temperature of say** 160°, and stirred with sticks for about seven minutes, until it becomes moist and sticky It is then too hot to hold in the hand.

It **is then rolled for two or** three minutes **on a table** until **it gets a** little **twisted.**

Then lay it out on dhallas in the sun (say 2 inches thick) **for about** three hours, **and** roll it thrice during that time, always in the sun. It **is ready** to roll each time when " the **roll**" has become blackish on the surface. It is not rolled more than three minutes each time, and then spread out **as** before. If you put on a proper number of men to do this **they do each** dhalla in succession, and when they have done the last, "the roll" in the first dhalla will be blackish on the surface again, and ready to roll again.

When three rollings are done, the roll should have a good twist on it.

It is then placed in the pans, at the same heat as before, and worked with sticks as before for two or three minutes, until it becomes too hot to hold.

It is then stuffed, as tight as it *can* be stuffed, into the bags described above, putting as much into each bag as you can possibly get it to hold. The mouth is then tied up and the bag beaten with a flat heavy stick to consolidate the mass inside, and so it is left for the night.

Next morning it is taken out of the bags, and worked with the flat sticks as before in the pans for nine hours without intermission. The temperature 160° at first down to 120° at the last.

During and owing **to this** last process the green colour is produced.* It is worked quicker and quicker as the hours pass.

The following are the kinds of Tea into which it is best sorted:—

1. Ends
2. Young Hyson
3. Hyson
4. **Gunpowder**
5. **Dust**
6. Imperial

The relative value is in the order in which they are numbered.

The sorting of Green Tea is a nicer operation, and takes twice as long as sorting Black Tea.

If there are pans enough, and the work is well arranged, there should be no night-work with Green Tea, for all

---

* Much Green Tea is coloured, but none from India has been so treated.

should be over by 5 P.M.; whereas with Black Tea night-work is generally a necessity.

The price obtained for Green Tea is more dependent on its *appearance* than in the case of Black.

It is not easy to make Black and Green Tea in the same factory.

Green Tea, if well made, pays much better than Black Tea; and, as before observed, I think all gardens with Chinese plants should adopt the manufacture.* When once the building is fitted for it, and the routine established, the Green Tea manufacture is always preferred by those who have tried both.

The Hybrid plant makes the best Black, the Chinese the best Green Tea.

* Note to Third Edition.—Since this was written Green Teas have gone down considerably in value. They are still much used in America, but in Great Britain there is but little demand for them.

CHAPTER XXV.

SIFTING AND SORTING.

SIFTING is a very important item in the manufacture of Tea. Careful and judicious sifting, as contrasted with the reverse, may make a difference of two or three annas a lb. in the sale of Teas.

I was shown some **Tea** quite lately which, as regards "liquor," was valued by the brokers at **Re.** 1-3 per lb., but the "Tea" at only 14 annas! This was entirely owing to faulty sifting and sorting.

I don't believe in *any* machine for Tea sifting, simply because it is not a regular process.* For example, you cannot say that, to make Pekoe, you must first use one sieve, then another, and so on. The sizes of sieves to be used, and the order in which they are to be used, will vary continually, as both are decided by varying causes, viz., the comparative fineness or coarseness of the Tea made daily, the greater or less presence of red leaf in it, and (because Tea varies much during the season, and gets coarse towards the end) by the time of the year. These points all necessitate changes in the sizes, and the order of the sieves.

'Tis true sieves might be changed in a machine as required, but the only machine that could even pretend to save labour would be one in which all the sieves were arranged one below the other, and thus the Tea would fall through each alternately, the motion being common to all. But this won't do for Tea sifting. Judgment must be used

* We have yet to see what Jackson's machine can do.

to decide *the length of time* each sieve is to be shaken; further, with *how much motion* it shall be shaken, &c., &c. But this is simply impossible with any machine, though all necessary to sift Tea well.

The cost of Tea sifting by hand (see page 161) is not eight annas *per maund*, including picking out red leaf, which *must* be hand-work. Good and bad sifting will affect the value three annas per lb. or Rs. 15 per maund!

With all parts of Tea manufacture it is well to employ the same men continually in each department, but above all, perhaps, should this be done in Tea sifting. A good sifter is a valuable man. He knows each kind of Tea by name; he knows what sieves to use, and the order in which to use them for each Tea; what the effect a larger or smaller mesh will have on each kind, &c., &c. In fact, he knows much more of the *practical* part of sifting than his master can, though the latter is, probably, a better judge how far the Teas are perfect when made.

Tea sieves are of two kinds, both round. One made of brass wire, with wooden sides, $3\frac{1}{2}$ inches high, the other cane, with bamboo sides, $1\frac{1}{4}$ inches high only. The latter are called "Chinese sieves," and though the brass ones are used in many places, there is no possible comparison between them, for the labour required in the use of the brass ones is much greater, and the results, as regards well sorted Tea, much better with the Chinese.

Both kinds are numbered according to the number of orifices in one linear inch. Thus a No. 6 sieve has six orifices to the inch in both; but in the brass kind, a No. 6 has six orifices *including* the wire; in the Chinese kind, the cane between each aperture is *not* included in the measure. Thus the orifice in a No. 6 Chinese sieve is exactly 1-6th of an inch square, but somewhat less in a brass sieve.

As I well know brass sieves cannot remain in favour after the others have been only once tried, I shall confine my directions to the Chinese kind.*

I practise, and I advise, Tea to be sifted daily. The Tea made one day, sifted the day after, and in fact stored away in the bins ready sifted. I find it is more carefully done this way, for by the other plan a larger quantity being done at once by several men, they cannot, from want of practice, be expert. But by the daily plan one, two, or three men, as necessary, can always be kept on the work, and consequently they learn and do it well.

To sift the following, Chinese sieves are required; and if daily sifting is resorted to, they will be found ample for any ordinary-sized garden:—

4 of No. 4	9 of No. 9
6 of No. 6	9 of No. 10
6 of No. 7	6 of No. 12
4 of No. 16.	

Previous to sifting all red leaf should be picked out of the Tea. This, as stated under the head of "Manufacture," should be done twice before the "roll" is fired; but towards the end of the season especially, some will still remain in the made Tea, and this must be carefully separated.

From what I have said it is evident that no rules can be laid down as to what sieves to employ to get out certain Teas. Only practice can teach this.

Further, practice can only enable you to judge in a Tea broker's point of view of different classes of Tea. This essay would, however, be incomplete did it not contain a description of these. Such a description has been ably given by Mr. J. H. Haworth in his "Information and

---

* Even to break Tea on them it is a mistake to use brass sieves. Tea is best broken by a wooden roller, heavily weighed with lead, run in. The glaze or gloss on Tea is thus preserved.

Advice for the Tea Planter from the English Market" (*Journal, A. & H. Society of India, Vol. XIV.*), and, as his knowledge on the subject is far in advance of mine, and consequently more to the point than any description I could give, I will close this chapter with the following extract from his valuable pamphlet, and **trust he will excuse my doing so**:—

Of the Different Classes of Tea.

Teas are arranged in various classes according to the size, make, and colour of the leaf. I treat first and principally of the Black descriptions, as Green Teas are manufactured in only a few of the Tea-growing districts of India.

The following classes come under the name of Black Tea:—

Flowery Pekoe.
Orange Pekoe.
Pekoe.
Pekoe Souchong.
Souchong.
Congou.
Bohea.

The various broken kinds, viz.:—
Broken Pekoe.
Pekoe Dust.
Broken Mixed Tea.
Broken Souchong.
Broken Leaf.
Fannings.
Dust.

We occasionally meet with other names, but **they are generally original**, and ought not to be encouraged, as a few **simple** terms like **the above are** sufficiently comprehensive to describe all classes manufactured.

Perhaps before entering into a detailed description of **the various** classes it will be well to explain the term "Pekoe" (pronounced Pek-oh), which as we see occurs in so many of the names above quoted. It is said to be derived from the Chinese words "Pak Ho," which are said to signify white down. The raw material constituting Pekoe when manufactured is the young bud just shooting forth, or the young leaf just expanded, which on minute examination will be found to be covered with a whitish velvety down. On firing these young leaves, the down simply undergoes a slight change in colour to grey or greyish yellow, sometimes as far as a yellowish orange tint.

When the prepared Tea consists entirely of greyish or greenish greyish Pekoe, with no or very little dark leaf mixed, it is called Flowery Pekoe.

Flowery Pekoe is picked from the shrub entirely separate from the other descriptions of Tea, only the buds and young leaves being taken. In the preparation it is not subjected so severely to the action of heat as the other classes of Tea, and generally preserves a uniform greenish grey or silvery grey tint. Its strength in liquor is very great, flavour more approaching that of Green Teas, but infinitely superior, having the strength and astringency, without the bitterness, of the green descriptions. The liquor is pale, similar to that of Green Tea, and the infused leaf is of a uniform green hue. In many instances, where too much heat has been employed, we find dark leaves intermixed, and the prevailing colour, green, is sprinkled with leaves of a salmony brown tinge, which is the proper colour for the out-turn of any other ordinary black leaf Tea. A very common mistake is to call an ordinary Pekoe, that may contain an extra amount of Pekoe ends, Flowery Pekoe. When this class of Tea is strong and of Flowery Pekoe flavour, it is called by the trade a Pekoe of Flowery Pekoe kind. In England Flowery Pekoe sells, as a rule, from 4s. 6d. to 6s. 6d. per lb. One parcel has sold as high as 7s. 6d.

By many people the expediency of making Flowery Pekoe is much doubted. The true Flowery Pekoe leaf is the one undeveloped bud at the end of each twig. To pick this alone, without any ordinary Pekoe leaves, involves a great deal of trouble and expense, and I think though the Flowery Pekoe be very valuable, that the account would hardly balance when we consider the deterioration of the Pekoe by the abstraction of the young leaves.

The ordinary Pekoe is a Tea of blackish or greyish blackish aspect, but dotted over with greyish or yellowish leaves which, on close inspection, will be found to possess the downy appearance which gives the name to Pekoe. In general we do not find the whole leaf covered with down, but only part of it, which in its growth has been developed later than the other parts. These are called by the trade " Pekoe ends " when very small Pekoe tips. A Pekoe is generally of good to fine flavour, and very strong, and its liquor dark. Its value is from 2s. 9d. to 3s. 8d. per lb.

When the Pekoe ends are of yellowish or orange hue, and the leaf is very small and even, the Tea is called Orange Pekoe. In flavour it is much the same as an ordinary Pekoe, and many growers do not separate the two varieties, but send them away in the finished state mixed together. Its value is from 2*d*. to 4*d*. per lb. more than Pekoe.

The term Pekoe Souchong is generally applied to a Pekoe that is deficient in Pekoe ends, or to a bold, Souchong class leaf with a few ends mixed. We often meet with it applied to an unassorted Tea, including perhaps Souchong, Congou, a few Pekoe ends, and some broken leafs. Prices range from 2*s*. 3*d*. to 2*s*. 10*d*.

The name of Broken Pekoe indicates at once what class of Tea it is, namely, Pekoe which has been broken in the manipulation or otherwise. It possesses the strength and fine flavour of a full leaf of Pekoe, being therefore only inferior to it in point of leaf. In value it is very little inferior to Pekoe, sometimes as valuable, or even more so, as owing to the frangibility of the tender Pekoe ends, they are sometimes broken off in very large quantity, thus adding to the value of the broken Tea, though at the same time deteriorating the Pekoe. Prices from 2*s*. 6*d*. to 3*s*. 4*d*.

Pekoe dust is still smaller broken, so small in fact as actually to resemble dust. It is of great strength, though often not pure in flavour, as frequently any dust or sweepings from other Tea is mixed with it to make the lot larger. The price of Pekoe dust may range from 1*s*. 6*d*. to 2*s*. 8*d*.

A Tea only slightly broken is often called by the planter Pekoe Dust; again an Orange Pekoe is often called Broken Pekoe, and the converse. A knowledge of the signification of these and other terms would teach the grower to be very careful in marking his Teas, as the nomenclature influences to a great extent the sale in the home market.

Having described the finer Teas, we now come to the consideration of the classes of Tea which form the bulk of the manufacture of a garden.

Souchong may be taken as the medium quality, and when experience and skilled labour are employed in the manufacture as the bulk of the produce of an estate. The qualifications for being comprehended under this term are just simply an even, straight, or slightly curved leaf, in length varying say from ½ inch to 1½ inch. It has not the deep strength of Pekoe, but is generally of good flavour and of fair strength. The prices of Souchong are from 1*s*. 10*d*. to 2*s*. 8*d*.

Congou comes next. It may be either a leaf of Souchong kind, but too large to come under that class, or though of smallish-sized leaf, too unevenly made, or too much curled (so as to resemble little balls) to be so classified. The flavour is much the same as that of Souchong, but the Tea has not so much strength. Some of the lower and large leaf kinds may be only worth perhaps from 1s. 3d. to 1s. 6d., whereas the finer qualities sell as high as 2s. to 2s. 3d. per lb.

Bohea is again **lower than a** Congou. It may be either of too large a leaf to be called Congou, or, as is generally the case, it may **consist** principally of old leaf, which on being fired does not attain the greyish blackish colour which is so desirable for all the black leaf kinds except Flowery Pekoe, but remains of a brownish or even pale yellowish hue. It has scarcely any strength, and is generally of coarse flavour, sometimes not, but is never of much value unless of *Namuna* kind (a term which will be described hereafter). We may quote prices at from 3d. to 1s. 2d. per lb.

We now come to the broken descriptions of these middle and lower classes of Tea.

Broken Mixed Tea is, as its name imports, a mixture of the various **kinds of** Tea broken. It may have a very wide range, include some of the lower classes or approach Broken Pekoe in character and value, but the kind usually thus named is a Tea worth from 1s. 8d. to 2s. 6d., generally of a blackish aspect, and containing a few Pekoe ends.

The term Broken Souchong is commonly and appropriately applied to a Tea which, though broken, has some approach to a full leaf, and that of the even Souchong character. Its value may vary, say from 1s. 6d. to 2s. 2d.

Broken leaf is a term of great comprehensiveness, but generally is used to signify a Tea worth from 8d. to 1s. 1d. per lb. It may be of a brownish, brownish blackish, or blackish colour. Its strength is seldom great, but its flavour may be fair or good, but in the lower **qualities it is generally** poor, thin, or coarse. It would be better to employ this term only as a general name of Broken Tea, and not to use it to signify any particular class, as it is very indefinite.

Fannings is similar in colour and class of leaf to broken leaf as described above; in value also much the same, perhaps on the average a little lower. I suppose, in most cases, the mode of its separation from the other classes of Tea is, as its name implies, by fanning.

Dust is a very small broken Tea, so small, in fact, as to approach the minuteness of actual dust. It is often very coarse, or "earthy" in flavour, owing perhaps to sweepings and dust having become mixed with it. Its value is from 6d. to 1s. 6d. In any Tea of this class worth more than these quotations, a few Pekoe ends or tips will generally be found, which **bring it under the name of Pekoe Dust.**

We will now look at Black Teas in a body, and point out what **is** desirable and what is objectionable in them.

We have seen that all Teas which **contain** Pekoe fetch higher prices than others, consequently we infer that Pekoe is a desideratum. If we glance at the descriptions of the various classes of Tea which have been given above, we shall find that it is an element of strength and good flavour. I do not mean to say that any Pekoe is stronger or of better flavour than any Tea which does not contain Pekoe, **as** the soil, the climate, the cultivation, the manufacture, and various other causes, may influence the strength and flavour of different Teas; but, **as a rule, in Teas that** are produced under the same circumstances, the classes containing Pekoe are stronger **and of better** flavour than those without it.

There is another class of Tea which I have not yet described that possesses very great strength and very fine flavour. This is the class known as the "Namuna" kind. All readers of these pages who have been connected with **India** any time will recognise the word,* though they may not quite see how it comes to occupy the position in which we consider it. It is said that its first application in this manner arose from a planter having sent to England some sample boxes of Tea with the ticket "namuna" on them. These Teas happened **to be** of the peculiar description which **now goes by that name, and which I** proceed to describe. The London brokers have always since then applied the name "namuna" to this class **of** Tea. The leaf may have, perhaps, the ordinary greyish blackish aspect, with generally a greenish **tinge. In** the pot it **produces a** very pale liquor, but on tasting it **its quality** belies the poor thin appearance of the infusion. It is very strong, **stronger by** far than ordinary Pekoe; in flavour, say, about half-way between a Flowery Pekoe and a Green Tea, quite distinct from **the Flowery** Pekoe flavour, possessing somewhat of the rasping bitterness of the Green Tea class with the flavour a little refined. The out-turn is generally green, sometimes has some brownish leaves mixed. **Any** of the black leaf Teas may be of **this Class,** from **the** Pekoe to the lowest dust, and all throughout the scale, if the

---

* I need hardly remark that **the** Hindustani word *Namuna* (pronounced *Nemoona*) means *sample*.

flavour be **distinct** and pure, may have their value enhanced from 4d. to 10d. per lb.

Similar in every respect, except **one**, is the Oolong kind. The **one** wanting quality **is the** strength, sometimes, by-the-bye, the flavour **is** a little different. It may have the greenish, greyish blackish leaf (though generally the green leaves are distinct from black ones, the **Tea** thus being composed of greyish blackish leaves with a few green ones intermixed), always has the pale liquor, generally the greenish infused leaf; but sometimes it is sadly intermingled with black leaves, as it is a Tea whose flavour is frequently burnt out, though its weakness and green appearance are no doubt often caused by deficient firing. Teas of this kind on the average sell below the ordinarily-flavoured Teas **of** the same class of leaf.

In Teas of ordinary flavour the following rules hold good:—The **darker the liquor the stronger** the Tea, and the nearer the approach **of the colour of the infused leaf to a uniform** salmony brown, the purer the flavour. **Whenever we see** any black leaves mixed with it (the out-turn) the Tea has been over-fired, and we may either expect to find the strength burnt out of it, or else to find it marred by having a burnt or smoky flavour incorporated with it. When you **come** across an altogether black or dirty brown out-turn, you may be certain of pale liquor containing little or no strength and no flavour to speak of, unless sometimes it be sour. This is a quality which I shall now touch upon, and regret that I cannot with any certainty give any **reliable** information whereby the planter may guard against this greatest of faults. It may have various grades,—slightly sourish, **sourish, and** sour, depreciating the value of the Tea, say, from 3d. to 1s. 6d. per lb. **The** flavour of a sour Tea is hardly capable of description. **It is not so** acid as sour milk, in fact, not acid at all, rather a sweet flavour than otherwise being blended with the sourness. It is extremely unpleasant in its more developed grades, and cannot be easily understood **except by** actual tasting. To the uninitiated this fault is only perceptible in **the more strongly** marked instances, but to one of the trade the least tendency to it not only condemns the parcel at once, but also causes him to suspect any other lots made at the same or any other time by the same grower, and it is a curious but **unaccountable** fact that **some two** or three gardens (or growers?) almost always produce Teas having this fault. I will not cite all the different explanations **that** have been offered on this subject; I will simply quote the one which seems to have gained most ground, and leave those more competent than myself to express any opinion on the subject. The cause assigned to which I refer is that the Tea leaf after being picked is allowed to remain too long in the raw state before being fired, during which time it undergoes a process of fermentation; some then say that this causes sourness, while others maintain that the fermentation is absolutely necessary for the production of a Black Tea. The fact that we never meet with sourness in a Green Tea, one feature in the preparation of which being that it is fired almost immediately on being gathered, goes to corroborate this view.

Burntness I have already referred to. As I said before, **it may either destroy the strength and** flavour altogether, or sometimes, without destroying **the** strength, add an unpleasant burnt flavour to it. **When the Tea has** the **flavour of** smoke about it, **it is called smoky or smoky burnt.** By being **burnt, a Tea may** be deteriorated in value, say **from 2d. to 1s.** per lb. **The symptoms of** burntness are **a** dead black **leaf (as** opposed **to the greatly-desired** greyish, blackish colour) having a burnt smell which often entirely neutralises the natural aroma of the Tea. In looking over a broker's character of a parcel of Teas, you may occasionally meet with the terms "fresh burnt," "brisk **burnt,**" or "malty burnt." These phrases do not carry a condemnatory meaning with them. The meaning of the word burnt, as used here, would be better expressed by the term **"fired."** The term "malty" means of full rich flavour, perhaps from the aroma of this class of Tea resembling somewhat that of malt. Teas of the three above descriptions, you **may** have noticed, **often fetch very good prices.** The **meaning** of the word "full," applied to a liquor, is hardly appreciable except by tasting. It does not signify strength or flavour, but is opposed **to thinness.** A Green Tea may be strong or of good flavour, **but its liquor is never full.** Fulness is generally characterised by a dark liquor. The quality known as "body" in a wine is somewhat akin **to** fulness in a Tea. We speak of a "full" leaf Tea in contradistinction to a broken leaf. "Chaffy" is generally used in connection with Bohea and other brown leaf classes of Tea. A light (in weight) brown, open or flat leaf, **in fact,** one resembling chaff, **would be called** chaffy. **The** lower classes of **Tea,** especially the **dusts, are** often described as "earthy" in flavour. By this a coarse low flavour is understood, perhaps often caused by the admixture of real **dust.**

When the make of a Tea is spoken of as a "well made," "fairly made," &c., leaf, the effect of the manipulation or rolling is referred to. We may have a "well made even," or a "well made mixed large **and small," leaf.** We may have a "straight" or "curled," or, as the latter is generally expressed when applied to a large leaf Tea, "twisted" leaf. It may be "flattish made," indicating that though the leaf is not open it wears a flattish aspect, or it may be open, which betrays a want of sufficient or skilful manipulation. A "wiry" leaf is small, perfectly rolled, and very thin (in diameter), generally rather curled, so as in fact to resemble small pieces of bent wire. It will be seen at once that only the finer Teas can have a wiry leaf, principally the Orange Pekoes and Pekoes. Sometimes we meet with a fine Souchong that may be thus described.

Green Teas.

As in the North-west Provinces Green Teas form the bulk of the produce, it will be well to give a short description of them, though the tenor of my remarks below will show the general opinion as to the desirability of making them.*

Gunpowder is the **most** valuable description, its price ranging from 2s. 8d. to 3s. 8d. per lb. Instead of possessing the long and thin finished leaf, which is the desideratum of Black Teas, it is rolled into little balls more or less round, varying from one-eighth to one-quarter of an inch in diameter. Sometimes it is not altogether composed of round leaf, but has some long leaf mixed.

When the Tea is of the shape of Gunpowder, but is larger than the **size** above quoted, it is called Imperial. Prices of Imperial are from 10d. to 2s. 6d.

Amongst Green **Teas Hyson may be** taken as the parallel of Souchong of the black leaf descriptions. Undoubtedly there is often much young Pekoe leaf in it, but all chance of *discriminating* it in the finished leaf is done away with by the change in colour. Hysons sell from 1s. 2d. to 3s. 6d.

---

* I think I need hardly pause to correct the popular error that the Green **and** Black Teas are made from two different species of plant. Most of my readers will know that they are both made from the same leaf, the difference **lying only in** the manufacture.

SORTING.

Young Hyson is smaller than Hyson, occasionally slightly broken. It fetches from 7d. to 2s. 6d.

Hyson skin consists of the bold broken leaf of Hyson and Young Hyson. A small broken Green Tea is seldom sent on the home market. The reason of this is obvious. When we consider that Hyson skin only fetches from 7d. to 1s., it is apparent that anything approaching a dust would give very little chance of a profit. I have seen one or two parcels, too much broken to come under the title of Hyson skin, sell at 3d. to 6d. per lb. in London. It would be well if some of the Indian planters would take a lesson from the Chinese, and not send home their very low Teas, black or green, as they are very difficult of sale in London, and in many cases cannot pay the cost of packing and shipping. The Chinese make a great quantity of their broken Teas into Brick Tea, and send it into the Central Provinces of Asia, where it meets with a ready sale. I do not see why this should not be done by the Indian growers. There is a large consumption of Tea on the other side of the Himalayas, not very far from Darjeeling and Assam. I hear also that in the neighbourhood of the growing districts, especially in the North-west Provinces, the natives are beginning to consume largely, and will pay 8 as. to 1 rupee for a Tea that could not possibly fetch more than 1s. to 1s. 6d. per lb. in England. Whether the natives of India, as a whole, do or do not take to drinking Tea will have a material effect on the future prospects of the article.

Before dropping the subject of Green Teas, I will say a word or two as to the expediency of making Green Tea. I have questioned several experienced people on the subject, but none can tell me their especial object in manufacturing their leaf into Green Tea. One gentleman told me that he thought it was because their Tea-makers (Chinamen) knew better how to make greens than blacks. I have carefully examined the leaf of several of the North-west Green Teas, and, noticing their English sale prices, consider that they would have sold on the average at least 3d. per lb. higher had they been made into Black Tea. The best way to test this would be to have a Green and a Black Tea made from the same leaf, and then to value the one against the other. I regret that I have never had the opportunity of doing this. We notice that the largest and most experienced producers never make Green Tea.*

* Note to Third Edition.—As previously stated in foot-note page 133, Green Teas are now but little used in Great Britain.

I must not pass over Caper without a short description. It is **a Tea which is made** in large quantity in China, though I have only seen one parcel of Indian growth. It forms a link between the black and green descriptions. The colour of the leaf is a very dark green; in form it is similar to a gunpowder, Imperial, or round leaf Congou. The liquor is pale, and the out-turn green; flavour perhaps nearer to that of a green than of a Black Tea.

CHAPTER XXVI.

BOXES. PACKING.

By far the best Tea boxes are the teak ones made at Rangoon. The wood is impervious to insects of all kinds, even white ants. Sawn by machinery the pieces sent to compose each box are very regular. The plank is half inch, and each chest made up measures inside 23 by 18 by $18\frac{1}{2}$ inches, and necessarily outside 24 by 19 by $19\frac{1}{2}$ inches. The inner cubical contents are 7,659 cubic inches, and this suffices for above one maund of fine, and under a maund of coarse Tea.

Each box is composed of fourteen pieces—viz., for the two long sides three each, for the two short sides two each, two for the bottom, and two for the lid. By the arrangement of three pieces in the long sides, and two only in the short sides, the centre piece of each long side is attached to *both* the short end pieces, and thus great strength in the box is ensured, there being no place where it can possibly separate at the joints.

These boxes are not made to "dovetail." Each piece (and they are sawn with mathematical regularity as to length, breadth, and thickness) must be nailed to its neighbour. The best nails for this are the kind called "French Pins," $1\frac{3}{4}$ inches long.

The wood is sold at Rangoon in bundles, and could be landed in Calcutta for about Re. 1-8 or 1-12 per box. The boxes need not be made up till shortly before they are wanted, and in this form, of compact bundles of short pieces, are very convenient for transport and stowage.

Of course in many districts these boxes are not procurable, and local ones must be made. If so, use hard wood, and make your boxes *about* the size given above, for small boxes add much to the cost of freight.

Let the planks be ⅝ inch thick, for ½ inch, that is, ⅜ inch boards are not strong enough, except they are of teak or any other very good wood.

Take care the joints of the several pieces composing the sides and ends do *not* coincide at the corners, for if they do the box is very apt to come asunder.

The best way to arrange the pieces is as described above in the Rangoon boxes.

"A form" must be made on which the inner leaden case shall be constructed, that is, a well-made smooth box, to fit *exactly* into the box you pack in. It must be some 3 inches higher than the interior of the original box, and have bars running across inside, for handles to lift it up, and let the lead case slip off it, after it (the lead case) is finished.

Solder your lead case, over your form, in the way to waste least lead. In the Rangoon boxes described, two large, two small sheets,* and one piece, 22 by 9 inches (let in between the two large sheets) suffices, and there is little or no waste.

The lead case ready, hold up the form by the inner rods, and let the case slide off. Put it at once into the packing-box, taking care no nails protrude inside, or anything else which will hurt it, and thus prepare all the boxes for the break of Tea you are about to pack.

One great advantage the Rangoon boxes, and in fact all machine-sawn boxes, have is their equal, or nearly equal, weight. Purchasers of Teas, at the public auctions, require "the tare" of boxes to be as near the same weight as possible. If the tares differ, say more than half-a-pound,

---

* **Large** lead is 37 by 22 inches; small lead, 25 by 19 inches.

the Tea will be depreciated in value.* It is well there should be about the same weight of Tea in all the boxes that contain any one kind, but this is not essential, which equality in tares is.

Your boxes all ready and lined with lead, choose a fine day for packing. Do this whether you finally dry the Tea in the sun or over the dholes; for even in the latter case it is well to avoid a damp day.

But before you pack you must bulk. That is, you must mix all the Tea, of any one kind, so intimately together that samples taken out of any number of chests shall agree exactly. This can be done by turning out all the Tea on a large cloth placed on the floor, and turning it over and over. No two days' Teas are exactly alike, and you have perhaps a month's Teas to pack; it is therefore necessary to mix them well.

Though I know many planters think the fumes of charcoal necessary and beneficial for the last drying, I do not. I have tried both sun and charcoal, and no difference was perceptible. The former costs nothing, is more commodious, and I always apply it when possible. The sun cannot burn the Teas; the charcoal, if the heat is too great, may.

Whether you use sun or charcoal, put the Tea hot into the boxes. The *only* object of the final drying is to drive off the moisture, which the Tea will certainly, in a more or less degree, have imbibed since its manufacture. Even the large zinc-lined bins which should be fitted up in all Tea stores, and in which the Tea is placed after manufacture, will not entirely prevent damp, so in all cases a final drying is necessary.

* Note to Third Edition.—This matter of equal tares is very important. If they differ more than half-a-pound all the Tea is turned out and re-weighed in London, which is a great loss in many ways.

Keep it in the sun, or over the charcoal, until it is hot **throughout, hot** enough to ensure all the moisture having been driven off. Then put into the box enough to about **one-quarter** fill it. **Now let two men** rock the box, over a half-inch round iron bar, placed on the ground, until the Tea has well settled. Then place a piece of carpet over the Tea, the exact size of **the** box, and let a man stand inside and press **it** down **a** minute or two with his feet. Now fill up nearly another quarter, and press it again over the carpet as before. Repeat this, putting less and less into the box each time, as you near the top, until it is quite **full, but do not** rock it at all the last two or three times, **only press it with the feet** as described. No patent screw press, or anything else, will pack the Tea better or more closely than this **plan,** and when **the** men are practised **at it,** you will find **there** will **not be a** difference of more than two or three lbs. in the Teas of any **one** kind put into the boxes.*

The box full, **just even** with the top, and well pressed down to the last, lay over the Tea a piece of the silver paper, which is found inserted between each sheet in the lead boxes. This prevents any solder or resin getting on the Tea when soldering the top. Now fit on the lead sheet **top, solder,** and nail on the wooden lid.

Weight of Tea in each box.—The boxes ready lined, with a lead cover loose, must be **all** weighed *before* the Tea is packed, and again *after* they are filled and soldered down, but *before* the wooden lid is put on. The difference of these weights, minus the weight of the little solder used in fastening **down the top lead (for** which allow say one pound to give a margin also), will be **the net weight of Tea** in each **box.**

---

* **It is not** essential that the same quantity of Tea shall be in each box.

Thin iron hooping, put round both ends of the boxes, much increases their strength, and is not expensive.*

Stamp each box on its lid and on one end.† Use for this zinc plates, with the necessary marks cut out in them. A brush run over these with the colouring matter does the work well and quickly.

Let the stamp comprise the kind of Tea, the plantation or owner's mark, the number of the box, and the year; for instance—

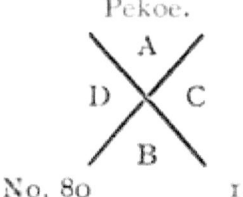

No. 80   1871

The invoice you send with the break must give for each box the number, the gross weight, the tare, the net Tea, and the kind of Tea, with a declaration at foot that the Teas of each kind have been respectively well bulked and mixed together before packing.

Remember the larger the quantity of Tea, of any one kind, to be sold at one auction, the higher the price it will probably fetch. Sell, if possible, twenty or thirty chests of one kind of Tea at the same time, for small quantities as a rule sell below large, both in Calcutta and London.

Equality of tares is the most important point to attend to in packing Teas. It may be difficult, but with machine-sawn boxes, nearly the same weight, any difference must be made up with extra hooping, lead, solder, or nails. Anyhow it *must* be done, so that no tares shall differ more than half-a-pound (see foot-note page 149).

---

* This should, except the lid part, be put on the boxes before the Tea is packed.

† The object of stamping the end, as well as the lid, is that when the boxes are piled one above the other the mark can be read.

CHAPTER XXVII.

MANAGEMENT.   ACCOUNTS.   FORMS.

SYSTEM and order, a good memory, a good temper, firmness, attention to details, agricultural knowledge, industry, all these, combined with a thorough knowledge of Tea cultivation and Tea manufacture, are the requisites for the successful management of a Tea plantation.

To find men with *all* these qualities is, I allow, not very easy, still they do exist, and such a one must be had if success in Tea is looked for.

Before the work is given out each day, the manager should decide exactly what is most required, and apply it to that. He should write down, when distributing the men, the works, and the number employed on each. This paper he should carry in his pocket, and he can then verify the men at work at each or any place when he visits it during the day.

The writer, the moonshee, and the jemadar (if there is one), should write similar papers when the coolies are mustered in the morning, and the manager should detail to each of these men which work they are particularly responsible for. This should also be shown in the " Morning Paper."

Each of the above men then measures out the work to the coolies; visits it once or oftener in the day, and measures all that remains undone at night. A daily report of the work is kept, written by the writer in the evening.

The two forms given below are those I have adopted. The latter is suited to local labour paid daily, but it can easily be altered to suit either local labour paid monthly or imported coolies.

This is the **Morning Paper**.

Work to be done on				188	
Detail	No. of Garden	In whose charge	Headman on the Work	Probable number	Actual number
Total Coolies					

The column of "Probable numbers" is given so that before it is known exactly how many men will be present for work they can be divided in the most likely way.

Each headman (called "Mate," "Mangee," &c., in different districts) is best designated by a letter or number. In neither form would there be room to put in names at length.

The form below written in the evening is made into a book for each month. The advantages of it for after reference are great, and it can of course be altered to suit the kind of labour employed on any garden.

Work on   for   188   .

Detail of Work	No. of Garden	Mangees	Chupp			Coolies	Measurement and Remarks
							As.
Total at Work.							× 3 =
Command							× 2½ =
Sick							× 2 =
Absent							× 1½ =
Total							× 1 =

Picking Leaf =
Making Tea =
Tea Sorting =
Cut =
Total =

The following is the **plan** I recommend for the leaf-picking and the Tea accounts.

The leaf of each picker is best measured in the field, and, as loads are collected, brought to the factory by one or two men throughout the day. It entails a loss of time, and further a depreciation in the leaf, if it is kept long in a close mass in one basket, which is the case when each picker brings his or her leaf to the factory twice a day. The pickers are paid so much per basket, holding in any case $2\frac{1}{2}$ lbs. I find the most convenient plan is to give the mangee in charge of the pickers tickets of any kind for this, which tickets are changed for money in the evening. As each load of leaf comes in through the day it is weighed, and this gives a check on the tickets given by the mangee or mate. This is the meaning of the two columns in the form below, "tickets by leaf" and "tickets paid."

In the form the first column of "leaf results" shows the condition of the leaf when picked, whether wet (W) or dry (D). Unless this were noted the proper amount of Teas the leaf *ought* to make could not be known, and there would be no check against theft, which is carried on to a great extent in many gardens.

As explained previously, only the sections ready in each garden are picked. The sections are not entered in the form, only the number of the garden. The flushes now noted are the 20th, in some the 21st, or 22nd in others.

The Tea is calculated from the leaf. It should be 25 per cent. if the leaf is picked dry, and 22 per cent. if picked wet. As each load comes in a memorandum is made as to whether it is dry or wet, and the figures in the column "Tea should be" are thus found.

The Tea is weighed the morning after it is made and entered in the column "Tea made." The percentage it bears to the leaf is then calculated and entered in the account column.

After sifting the whole is weighed again, and the result entered in the column "Tea after sifting." Doing this is very important, for it checks theft. Directly after it is weighed this second time it is put in the bins in the store.

Daily Leaf and Tea Account.

Date	Tea Results					Leaf Results						
	Tea should be	Tea made	Per cent.	Tea after it is sifted	State of leaf	Tickets		Number of Garden	Flushes			Total leaf
						By leaf	Paid		20	21	22	
October Sunday, 1st	,,	,,	,,	,,	220 W 600 D	410	360	3 5 7 8	,, 310 112 ,,	170 ,, ,, ,,	,, ,, ,, 228	820
Monday, 2nd	198	200	24	199	D	462	440	3 9	,, 410	515 ,,	,, ,,	925
Tuesday, 3rd	231	230	25	233	W	200	180	1 2 3	430 ,, ,,	,, ,, 210	,, 160 ,,	800
Wednesday, 4th												
Thursday, 5th												
Friday, 6th												
Saturday, 7th												
Total for the week	,,	Mds. lbs. 1632										

If this system is carried out, no Tea (exceeding a pound or so) can be stolen without its being at once missed, and the importance of this cannot be exaggerated. Tea proprietors do not guess *how* much is lost in this way. Maunds upon maunds might be stolen in many gardens, and unless the theft were accidentally discovered there is nothing in the Tea accounts to show it to the manager.

I have suppositiously filled up the three first days of the form. The 820 lbs. leaf picked on Sunday is made into Tea on Monday. The 198 is written down Sunday evening. On Tuesday morning, when the Tea is weighed and found to be 200 lbs., that is entered in the Monday line, as also the percentage. On Tuesday evening, after it is sifted and made into different Teas, it is weighed again and found to be 199 lbs., and so entered.

In dry weather after sifting, owing to dust flying off, it is always a little less. In wet weather, on the contrary, it increases in weight. In the Tuesday line where "W" shows it was a wet day and the Tea 230 lbs. before sifting it, is 233 afterwards. This is owing to moisture imbibed, and it is the only objection to sifting daily, whatever the weather. The advantages of the plan, though, are so great, as explained, that I put up with this, and practically I do not find it detrimental. Of course, as previously explained, all moisture is driven off before the Tea is *packed*. However, to make all quite safe, after a very wet damp day, the Teas might be re-dried for a few minutes over charcoal before being put into their respective bins. I do not do this myself though, and do not think it necessary.

I hope now I have made the above form plain. It is in a book, and each page will hold one week. The total of the Tea made in the week is added up and shown at foot, and that amount is then transferred to the credit side of the Tea store account. Thus (see both forms) 16 maunds 32 lbs. is credited.

The form given on the next page is also kept in a book, and the total of right-hand side subtracted from the left gives at any time the quantity of Tea in store.

Tea Store Account.

RECEIPTS					EXPENDITURE				
Week ending on Saturday	Tea made in week		Total		Date	No. of Invoice	To whom	Tea in each Invoice		Total	
	Mds.	lbs.	Mds.	lbs.				Mds.	lbs.	Mds.	lbs.
Brought over October	..	..	405	8	Brought over October			..	..	351	14
7th	16	32				3	15	40	15		
14th	15	0			,,	20	16	33	10		
21st	17	10								73	25
28th	14	40	63	2							
Carried over .					Carried over .						

Regarding accounts between the manager and his employers, I think **they** should be of the simplest kind. If a man *can* be trusted he *should* be trusted ; if he cannot, no **system of accounts will restrain** him, and he should be **kicked out. A simple** account current, furnished monthly, **showing under few heads the** receipts and expenditure, is all **that can be** required. It is not by *any* papers received from **a manager** that an opinion can be expressed **as** to how he does his work, and how **the** plantation progresses. A competent person visiting **the** garden can **easily** ascertain, and in default of this, and combined with this, the only true test is the balance sheet at the end of each season.

Shortly, it is not by the form, the nicety, the detail of accounts between manager and employer, that success is ensured or even forwarded. It is, as far as accounts are concerned, by the forms and *system* the manager adopts as between him and his subordinates, and these he should be able to show are good to the employer, or anyone deputed by him to visit the garden.

The profit shown yearly, whether it is large or small, all things considered, is, however, the only true ultimate test.

CHAPTER XXVIII.

COST OF MANUFACTURE, PACKING, TRANSPORT, ETC.

These are as follow:—They will vary more or less according to the district, rate of wages, &c., but in the form the tables are given, if not suitable to any case, they can easily be made so.

I have added sorting, packing, freight to Calcutta, and broker's charges in Calcutta, to the cost, so that all is included from the moment the green leaf is picked off the trees till the hammer falls at the public auction.

Table cost of Manufacture, Sorting, Packing, Transport to Calcutta, and Broker's Charges for each maund of Tea.

Manufacture.	Rs.	As.	P.	Rs.	As.	P.
1 head man with the pickers, say	0	4	0			
320 lbs. green leaf picked, at 1 pice per lb.*	5	0	0			
1 man withering above leaf, at say 4 annas	0	4	0			
¼ share head man in rolling house	0	2	0			
10⅔ men rolling above, at 30 lbs. leaf per man, and say 4 annas per man	2	10	8			
¼ boy clearing out ashes of Dhole house, at say 2 annas	0	0	6			
¼ share head man in Dhole house	0	2	0			
Carried over				8	7	2

* In practice the basket in which the leaf is measured being made to hold 2½ lbs., for which a ticket is given, representing 2 pice, the leaf to make a maund of Tea does not really cost so much.

COST OF MANUFACTURE.

	Rs.	As.	P.	Rs.	As.	P.
Brought forward	8	7	2			
1 man firing "Dhole work" say	0	4	0			
¾ maund charcoal for Dhole work, at 8 annas	0	6	0			
Lights for night work, viz., turning green leaf and dholing, say	0	4	0			
Wear and tear of dhallas, baskets, picking baskets, fuel for artificial withering, &c.	0	1	10			
				9	7	0

Sifting and Sorting.

	Rs.	As.	P.	Rs.	As.	P.
1½ boys to pick out red leaf, at say 2 annas	0	3	0			
1 sifting man, at say 4 annas	0	4	0			
Wear and tear of sieves, say	0	0	3			
				0	7	3

Packing.

	Rs.	As.	P.	Rs.	As.	P.
1 box	1	13	0			
4 sheets lead, viz., 2 large and 2 small	1	6	6			
Labour of lining box with lead, solder, closing lead, closing wooden box, stamping, and cost of nails	0	0	9			
Labour of drying previous to packing, whether in sun, or over dholes, including charcoal, if the latter are used	0	0	9			
Labour of filling the box, shaking it well, and pressing down the Tea (2 men)	0	0	6			
				3	5	6

Transport.

	Rs.	As.	P.	Rs.	As.	P.
Freight to Calcutta for one maund Tea, say	1	12	0			
				1	12	0

	Rs. As. P.	Rs. As. P.
Brought forward . .		14 15 9

Broker's Charges in Calcutta.

Landing, lotting, and advertising per chest	0 14 0	
Brokerage at 1 per cent. on the amount sale, say Rs. 70 for the maund .	0 11 3	
		1 9 3
Total for one maund of Tea*		16 9 0

N.B.—If more than two maunds Tea are made per day, some of the items under head of " Manufacture " would be a little less. See page 70, where it will be seen that each maund of Tea is worth to the manufacturer (after deducting all costs) Rs. 50.

* After experience has shown me this amount, when any quantity of Tea is made, is too high—Rs. 12 to 13 would be nearer the mark.

CHAPTER XXIX.

COST OF MAKING A 300-ACRE TEA GARDEN.

IN the following estimate 100 acres are supposed to be planted the first year, 100 acres the second, and 100 acres the third.

To elucidate a table I shall draw up in the next chapter showing the probable receipts and expenditure on such a garden for a series of years, I shall suppose this plantation to be begun in 1875, and number the years accordingly.

The expenditure would truly, in the supposed case, begin in the latter part of 1874, but it is more convenient to regard it as commencing 1st January, 1875.

I estimate all new cultivation as planted "at stake," that is, the seed sown *in situ*. Nurseries are only to fill up vacancies.

I shall not pretend in this to go into minute details, such as are given at page 84, for it is simply impossible to do so. The cost of making a plantation must vary greatly, being determined by climate, available labour and its rates, lay of land, nature of jungle to clear, &c., &c. In this estimate only round numbers can be dealt with. The prices I assume are average ones, neither suited to very heavy jungle, and very expensive labour, or the reverse :—

	1st year (1875).	Rs.	Rs.
Purchase 700 acres land, at Rs. 8 per acre	.	5,600	
40 maunds seed, at Rs. 70*	. . .	2,800	
	Carried over Rs. .	8,400	

* The cost for seed, nurseries, and transplanting increases each year as the area over which vacancies may exist enlarges.

Brought forward Rs. .	8,400	
Nurseries for vacancies and labour transplanting*	200	
First temporary buildings. . . .	1,000	
All expenditure to plant 100 acres, at Rs. 80 per acre†	8,000	
Cultivating the said 100 acres first year, at Rs. 50 per acre‡	5,000	
		22,600

2nd year (1876).

60 maunds seed, at Rs. 70* . . .	4,200	
Nurseries and labour transplanting* . .	300	
Repairs, buildings and some new ones still of a temporary nature . . .	500	
All expenditure to plant the second 100 acres, at Rs. 70 per acre† . .	7,000	
Cultivating first 100 acres, at Rs. 60, second 100 acres, at Rs. 50 per acre‡	11,000	
		23,000

3rd year (1877).

70 maunds seeds, at Rs. 70* . . .	4,900	
Nurseries and labour transplanting* . .	400	
Buildings for Tea manufacture (temporary) and repairs to buildings . . .	3,000	
		8,300
Carried over . .		53,900

* See note * p. 163.

† The expenditure for planting the 100 acres each year includes cutting and clearing jungle, removing **roots**, digging, staking, pitting, **and** sowing the seed. In fact *all* expenditure including part of the pay of Manager and Establishment. The rate per acre *decreases* each year, because each year **there** is more expenditure of other kinds, which helps to pay for the Manager **and Establishment.**

‡ **The** reason why the rate for cultivation on **the** 100 **acres** planted each of the three first years increases each year is given in the table and remarks at pages 84 and 85.

COST OF MAKING A GARDEN.

Brought forward Rs.		53,900
All expenditure to plant the third 100 acres, at Rs. 60 per acre *	6,000	
Cultivating first 100 acres, at Rs. 70, second at Rs. 60, third at Rs. 50 per acre †	18,000	
		24,000
Interest on first year's outlay, two and a half years, second year's outlay, one and a half years, third year's outlay half year, at Rs. 5 per cent. per annum		5,357
Total expense to make the 300-acre garden		83,257

The garden is now made at a cost, including interest on all outlay of Rs. 83,257, and I am very confident that a good 300-acre garden can, as set out, be made for that sum. The rates assumed are so liberal that a fair margin is allowed for bad seed or any other misfortune.

4th year (1878).

20 maunds seed, at Rs. 70 ‡	1,400	
Nurseries and labour transplanting ‡	500	
Repairs, buildings §	500	
Cultivating first 100 acres, at Rs. 80, second at Rs. 70, third at Rs. 60 per acre ‖	21,000	
		23,400

* See note ┼, p. 164. † See note ‡, p. 164.

‡ The seed to be bought is now less each year, as it is produced on the garden, and after the fifth year no more has to be purchased. From the fourth, and all subsequent years, nurseries for vacancies are calculated at Rs. 500, which is enough, as the garden has been previously yearly replenished. This expenditure will be continual as long as the garden lasts, for there will always be some vacancies to replace.

§ Rupees 500 is a fair sum to estimate for ordinary annual repairs to buildings, and it will be required as long as the garden lasts. A temporary Factory was made in 1877, and a permanent building is now allowed for in 1881. Permanent Manager's and Assistant's houses are also allowed for in 1882. The garden can afford this now, for the profits are large. (See table at page 172.)

‖ For the rates assumed here see page 84.

5th year (1879).

10 maunds seeds, at Rs. 70*	700	
Nurseries and labour transplanting* .	500	
Repairs, buildings †	500	
Cultivating first 100 acres, at Rs. 90, second at Rs. 80, third at Rs. 70 per acre ‡ .	24,000	
		25,700

6th year (1880).

Nurseries and labour transplanting* .	500	
Repairs buildings †	500	
Cultivating first 100 acres, at Rs. 100, second at Rs. 90, third at Rs. 80 per acre ‡ . . . - . .	27,000	
		28,000

7th year (1881).

Nurseries and labour **transplanting*** .	500	
Building a permanent Tea **Factory and Tea** Store and repairs to building† . .	12,500	
Cultivating first 100 acres, at Rs. **100**, second at Rs. 100, third at Rs. 90 per acre ‡	29,000	
		42,000

8th year (1882).

Nurseries and labour transplanting* . .	500	
New permanent houses for Manager and Assistant, and repairs to buildings † .	8,500	
Cultivating first, second, **and** third 100 acres, at Rs. 100 per **acre** ‡ . .	30,000	
		39,000

* See Note ‡, p. 165.
† See Note §, p. 165.
‡ See Note ‖, p. 165.

9th *year* (1883), *and all years after*.

Nurseries, at Rs. 500*
    Repairs to buildings, at Rs. 500 † } 1,000
Cultivating the 300 acres, at Rs. 100 per acre ‡ 30,000
                                          ————
                                          31,000

Nothing is allowed for interest after the third year, for soon after that, viz., fifth year, the garden begins to give profits on the yearly operations.

All the above figures are carried out in the table in the next chapter, page 172, and how large the profits on Tea may be will there be seen.

In none of the estimates of cost, up to this, is the expense of manufacturing the Tea included. It would have been very inconvenient to do so. The cost is so much per maund of Tea, and I prefer estimating the Tea at its market rate *minus* the cost of manufacture shown at pages 70 and 162.

        * See note †, p. 165.
        † See note §, p. 165.
        ‡ See note ||, p. 165.

CHAPTER XXX.

HOW MUCH PROFIT TEA CAN GIVE.

WE have already estimated the cost of making and cultivating a **plantation** of 300 acres. We must now ascertain how much **Tea** that area will give yearly.

It is a very wide question what produce an acre of Tea will give.

The following is an extract from the "Report of the Commissioners appointed to enquire into the state and prospects of Tea cultivation in Assam and Cachar," addressed to the **Government of Bengal,** and dated March, 1868 :—

" Average produce per acre."

"The returns of actual produce of gardens in **1867** which we have obtained are so few in number that it is **impossible to take** any general average from them. The produce in **these varies from** three-and-a-half maunds to one-and-a-half maunds per **acre, omitting the more** recently formed gardens.

"From information **received** during our tour we **have** reason to **believe that some gardens** produce more than the highest rate per acre **here mentioned; but, in the** absence of returns of exact acreage and out-turn, **we cannot notice** these instances.

"Mr. **Haworth, in** his pamphlet already quoted, speaks of the produce of Cachar gardens as follows :—

"'I believe **that** three maunds per acre is fully one-third more than the present average yield of gardens in **Cachar,** after deducting **the** area of plant under yielding age.

"'There is no reason, **that I am aware of,** why the yield of Tea **should not** soon be raised **to four maunds, and more** gradually six **maunds per** acre, equal to twenty-four maunds **of leaf** per acre (less **than one ton per** acre for a green crop, which is **still a** very small one). **Even now** there are gardens in Cachar which give an average of from five to six maunds per acre this season. Some of these gardens have really no apparent advantage over their less fortunate **neighbours, beyond** that of a somewhat better system of **cultivation and pruning;** and these improvements even are to such a small degree ahead of the general practice, that I feel justified in saying I cannot place a limit on what the increased yield should be under a more rational system of cultivation, and the application **of manures** on a liberal scale, leaving out of consideration altogether **what might reasonably be expected** from a good system of drainage in addition.'

"Mr. James Stuart, Manager of the Bengal Tea Company's gardens in **Cachar, has also given two** maunds an acre as the general average of Cachar gardens **for the** past season, including young gardens of two, three, and four years old.

"We do not think it necessary to quote in detail the opinions of all the gentlemen examined by us on the **subject** of average produce per acre. A garden that can give four maunds per acre is undoubtedly a good one, and we have no doubt there are such, or **even better; but** we do not think they are so common as to warrant our taking more than three maunds as a safe average."

Mr. A. C. Campbell, **Extra Assistant Commissioner at** Burpettah, in his "**Notes on Tea Cultivation in Assam,"** published in the Journal of the Agricultural and Horticultural Society of India, part 3, vol. xii., page 309, says :—"**Good Tea land can be made to yield as high as seven maunds per poora."** I forget exactly how **much a poora** is, but I believe **it** is nearly an acre.

In the Report to Government by the Commissioners, quoted above, at page 9, Mr. T. Burland, after estimating the cost of cultivation per acre per mensem at Rs. 9-10-2, adds :—" With the above expenditure per acre **it is probable** that much more than five maunds of Tea will be obtained from an acre of fair plant." *

All these estimates, however, **are based on the cultivation**

---

* See my estimate for cultivation at page 84. I there estimate Rs. 100 per acre per annum from the sixth year, so that Mr. Burland six years ago had **come to the same opinion about high** cultivation that I hold.

of Tea as carried on hitherto with few exceptions, that is to say, on gardens covered with weeds for many months in the year, and to which no manure has ever been given. With such cultivation, particularly on gardens planted on slopes, I think myself that the yield will not exceed four maunds *at the outside*.

High cultivation and liberal manuring will, I believe, at least double the above, if the plants are of a high class. However, here I give a table on the subject which I have carefully framed.

Estimate of probable yield per acre on flat land, good soil, in a good Tea climate, and with hybrid plants, if really high cultivation and liberal manuring is carried out.

Year	Supposed Year	Estimated yield per acre in maunds*
1st	1875	—
2nd	1876	—
3rd	1877	½
4th	1878	2
5th	1879†	4
6th	1880	5
7th	1881	6
8th	1882	7
9th	1883	7½
10th	1884‡	8

* Calculating Tea by maunds is convenient, inasmuch as pounds necessitate such lengthy figures for all calculations. The maund here employed is, however, quite an arbitrary measure. It is *not* the Indian maund, it equals and is represented exactly by 80 lbs. Any number of maunds multiplied by 80 will naturally give the lbs. of Tea.

† Up to this point, viz., the fifth year inclusive, the figures given have been much more than realised, and that on a garden with 15 per cent. vacancies. It has been, though, highly cultivated and liberally manured from the first.

‡ From the fifth to the tenth year is assumption, except that I know one garden which, to my certain knowledge, has given *more* then ten maunds an **acre, and** this in spite of about 15 per cent. vacancies. The garden is an old one, planted about 18 years ago. It is also a very small one. The soil is *very* poor, **but** the **plants** are of the highest class. It was much neglected till about eight years ago. From that time it has been highly cultivated in every way except in the point of irrigation, for it has not that advantage. It has been *most* liberally manured.

I do not think plants reach to perfect maturity under eight or ten years.

That eight maunds per acre as estimated in the table just given *can* be realised, under the conditions stated, I have no doubt whatever, but I am equally certain that the size of some gardens in India must be much reduced if even five or six maunds are looked for.* Not only must they be reduced in size, but they must be highly cultivated, must be manured, and no vacancies allowed. However, I have dwelt on all these points before, and need not repeat here, for unless the reader is convinced before this that a large area and low cultivation won't pay, it were waste to write more.

I now give a table showing the result for twelve years of a plantation such as I have advised.

* Note to Third Edition.—With high cultivation on a favourable site and in a really good Tea climate, I now believe 10 maunds per acre will eventually be realised.

TABLE SHOWING THE ESTIMATED RESULTS FOR 12 YEARS OF A 300-ACRE PLANTATION, IN A GOOD TEA CLIMATE, HIGHLY CULTIVATED AND LIBERALLY MANURED.

	Year and Rate of Yielding in Maunds		Yield in Maunds of 300 acres and its Value					Yearly Results				Final Results			Remarks.
1	2	3	4	5	6	7	8	9	10	11	12	13	14	15	16	
Year	Yield per acre as per page 170	Supposed year	Rate yield of 100 acres, planted in 1875	Rate yield of 100 acres, planted in 1876	Rate yield of 100 acres, planted in 1877	Total yearly yield in maunds	Value per maund	Receipt from Sale of Tea	Total expenditure detailed at pages 164, 165, 166	Yearly Profit	Yearly Loss	Total receipts to end of each year	Total expenditure to end of each year	Balance to credit end of each year	Balance to debit end of each year	
	Mds.		Mds.	Mds.	Mds.	Mds.		Rs.	Rs.	Rs.	Rs.	Rs.	Rs.	Rs.	Rs.	
1	..	1875	..	..	..	..	Rs. 50 per maund, after cost of manufacture, packing, and transport are deducted, see pages 76 & 162	..	22,600	..	22,600	..	22,600	..	22,600	It will be seen from this table as follows:—
2	½	1876	..	..	..	50		..	23,000	..	23,000	..	45,600	..	45,600	1. About Rs. 90,000 of capital is necessary to make a plantation as quick as this. If made more gradually, very much less would suffice.
3	½	1877	½	..	..	250		2,500	37,657*	..	35,157	2,500	83,257	..	80,757	
4	2	1878	2	½	..	650		12,500	23,400	..	10,900	15,000	1,06,657	..	97,657	
5	4	1879	4	2	½	1,100		32,500	25,700	6,800	..	47,500	1,32,357	..	84,857	2. There is no yearly profit until the fifth year.
6	5	1880	5	4	2	1,500		55,000	28,000	27,000	..	1,02,500	1,60,357	..	57,857	3. By the eighth year all the outlay is recovered.
7	6	1881	6	5	4	1,800		75,000	42,000	33,000	..	1,77,500	2,02,357	..	24,857	This table has been prepared with great care, and the authority for the figures assumed has been arrived at in previous parts. (See headings of Cols. for the pages and note at foot.) I believe this table represents truly what Tea, with all the necessary advantages detailed in the next page, can do.
8	7	1882	7	6	5	2,050		90,000	39,000	51,000	..	2,67,500	2,41,357	26,143	..	
9	7½	1883	7½	7	6	2,250		1,02,500	31,000	71,500	..	3,70,000	2,72,357	97,643	..	
10	8	1884	8	7½	7	2,350		1,12,500	31,000	81,500	..	4,82,500	3,03,357	1,79,143	..	
11	8	1885	8	8	7½	2,350		1,17,500	31,000	86,500	..	6,00,000	3,34,357	2,65,643	..	
12	8	1886	8	8	8	2,400		1,20,000	31,000	89,000	..	7,20,000	3,65,357	3,54,643	..	

* With interest, see pages 164 and 165.

At the following pages will be found the calculations for the figures assumed:—Col. 2, page 170; Col. 8, pages 70 and 162; Col. 10, pages 164, 165, 166.

The necessities for success in **Tea** are:—

1. A good climate.
2. A good site.
3. Perfect knowledge in Tea cultivation and Tea manufacture on the proprietor's part or that of his manager.
4. Seed from a high class of plants.
5. Local or cheap imported labour.
6. Facilities for manuring.
7. Cheap transport.

Do not dispense, though, with even *one* of the seven points named, for the truth is simply, that Tea will pay *very* well with all the above advantages, but will utterly fail without them.

Such is my advice to intending beginners. To those who have gardens, I say, reduce your areas till of the size you can really cultivate them highly, and procure manure at any cost.

I shall not have written in vain, and Tea enterprise in India will flourish, if the motto of planters in future be—

"A full area, highly cultivated."

CHAPTER XXXI.

PAST, PRESENT, AND FUTURE OF INDIAN TEA.

A FEW words on the past, the present, and the future of Indian Tea will now conclude this Essay, and will, I hope, be acceptable to the reader.

The subject is one of growing importance, but being a new one, there are points connected with it on which the public are very ignorant, and should be enlightened.

To begin with, the following facts are not disputed by those who know anything of the subject :—

1. Indian Teas have far more body, that is strength, than Chinese Teas.

2. Indian Teas consequently command a higher price at the London sales than Chinese Teas.

3. In spite of its higher price, it is far more economical than the Chinese produce, as, generally speaking, one-third of the quantity suffices.

4. There are lands enough in India to grow all the Tea required for England's use, and, indeed, for all her colonies.

If these *are* facts, and I confidentially affirm they are so, how is it that the following holds in England ?

1. Indian Tea is not known to the public.

2. Except in one or two shops in London and Glasgow, unknown to the mass of the people, not an ounce of pure Indian Tea can be bought in all England.

3. That India is even a Tea-producing country is scarcely known in England.*

* Note to Third Edition.—The above three statements, quite true when written, are not so now. The heavy fall in the value of both Indian and

I think I can explain some of these anomalies.

Tea is an acquired taste : by which I mean, not only that the adult who had never tasted Tea would not like it when first offered to him, but also that, with those who consume it regularly, any Tea that differs in flavour from what is habitually drunk is not relished.

It matters not whether it is intrinsically better or worse, enough that the flavour is different, for that reason it is not liked.

Indian Tea differs widely from Chinese Tea, and for that reason is rarely appreciated by those accustomed to the latter.

For a long time it appeared as if this difficulty would be a bar to the general introduction of Indian Teas in England, and so indeed it would have proved, had the short-sighted policy adopted at the commencement by one or two Indian Companies that their Teas should be sold retail **and pure,** that is, unmixed with Chinese, been followed out. It did not avail to tell John Bull it was better Tea, that it was far stronger, that it was in no way adulterated; for he simply shook his head, the flavour was different to what use had made him familiar with, **and he would none of it.**

But little by little, in spite of the above, **it made its way.** Grocers soon found that the worst, *id est*, the weakest class of Chinese Teas received *body* and were made saleable by an addition of Indian Tea. It was not long after this that the trade discovered that pretty well *all* Chinese Teas were improved, if proportions of Indian Teas were mixed with them. In short, the fact was recognised by Tea vendors that Chinese Teas were weak, **and** much improved if mixed **with Indian.**

The public were thus *educated* to relish the superior Chinese Teas in 1877, while pressing hard on the Indian producer, has certainly had the one good effect for him of making Indian Teas more widely known. They *are* generally known now, in many cases sold pure as Indian Tea, and used by all retail dealers to give the body or strength lacking in **most** Chinese kinds.

flavour of Indian Tea, and did so, when the quantity mixed with the Chinese was not so great as to make the new flavour too *prononcé*. Little by little the custom of so mixing became very general, so much so that it may almost be said to-day that if Indian Teas cannot be purchased pure, no more can Chinese. A mixture of Chinese and Indian Tea, the latter small as compared with the former, is what is now generally used in Great Britain.

This is the case to-day. What will it be in the future?

As the English palate is educated to like the flavour of Indian Tea, more and more of it will be demanded in the mixture made up for the public, and though the day is distant, nay, may never arrive, on account of its greater cost, when it will be generally drunk pure, I do not myself doubt that the demand for it will go on steadily increasing for years to come, as it has for years past.*

It is an important query if, with a largely increased demand, the supply will be equal to it. Very far from all India has a good Tea climate, which is a peculiar one, and only exists in perfection in Assam, Cachar, Chittagong, and lands in Bengal close to the foot of the Himalayas.

But in these districts alone there are lands sufficient to supply nearly the whole world with Tea, so that it is not the lands which are wanting, though the Government prices for the lands are prohibitory and will check cultivation. But in Assam, Cachar, and the Terai below the Himalayas labour is very scarce, while in Chittagong the area fit for Tea is not large, so that I do not anticipate any very sudden increase of

* Note to Third Edition.—Yes; the demand has largely increased, but, alas! production has increased in a greater ratio. In short, the supply exceeds the demand, and hence the low prices now ruling. As regards the use of Indian Teas, so much have the English public been now made familiar with their flavour, they, as a rule, reject any Teas which have it not more or less. In fact, the English public, as I predicted years ago, have now begun to like the new flavour, and even pure Indian Teas are now relished by many.

the cultivation, though year by year it *is* on the increase and will so continue.

On the other hand, I do not—for the reasons stated, viz., that Tea is an acquired taste and thus a new kind is not at first palatable—anticipate any very sudden increase in the demand. If, however, I am wrong, and from a largely increased demand the prices of Indian Teas rise, I do not doubt that the cultivation will be greatly extended, and that after an interval of four years (it takes that time for the Tea plant to produce) the supply will be equal to the then wants of the English market.

The future of Indian Tea is, I think, a bright one, and I know nothing in which capital can be more profitably invested if the business is conducted with knowledge and experience, but to embark in it without these two requisites is ruin.

A few figures may be given here. The imports into Great Britain of Indian Teas have been yearly increasing, till in 1873 they amounted to 18,367,000 lbs., and, judging from the estimate out here of the produce this year, viz., 1874, the imports into Great Britain in 1874 will not be far short of 20,000,000 lbs.*

But as the annual consumption of Tea in the United Kingdom is not less than 130,000,000 lbs., India is still very far from supplying enough to give a mixture of three-fourths Chinese and one-fourth India Tea.†

* Note to Third Edition.—The imports have been as follows during the last three years:—

1875	25,615,000.
1876	29,384,000.
1877	31,882,000.

† Note to Third Edition.—The annual consumption of all Teas in Great Britain in 1877 was—

Chinese	158,000,000
India	28,000,000
Total	186,000,000

The finest Chinese Tea sells in London in bond at 2s. 4d. to 2s. 6d., while the finest Indian in bond fetches 3s. to 3s. 6d.*

What, then, will be the future of Indian Tea? It is an important query. The industry is one which, if successful, might attain to wide limits, and help not a little to relieve the Indian State Exchequer, while it would afford occupation to many a class of Englishmen who at present look about in vain for employment.

Tea speculation has passed through the first two preliminary phases to which most new ventures are liable. First, we had the wild rush, the mad fever, when every man thought that to own a few Tea bushes was to realise wealth. In those days existing plantations were bought at eight and ten times their value; nominal areas of 500 acres were paid for which, on subsequent measurement, proved to be under 100; new gardens were commenced on impossible sites, and by men as managers who not only did not know a Tea plant from a cabbage, but who were equally ignorant of the commonest rules of agriculture. Boards highly paid, with secretaries still more liberally remunerated, were formed both in Calcutta and London to carry on the enterprise; and, in short, money was lavished in every conceivable way, while mismanagement ran rampant in each department. It is not strange that the whole thing collapsed: the wonder is it did not do so earlier.

The second stage was then entered upon. Numbers had been bitten, and the idea, once formed, grew apace, that Tea could not pay at all. Everyone wanted to sell, and down went all Tea shares to a figure which only increased the general panic. Many companies, and not a few individuals, unable to carry on, had to wind up and sell their

* Note to Third Edition.—In 1876 the *average* prices of the two kinds in bond were:—Chinese, 1s. 2d.; Indian, 1s. 10d. per lb.

estates for whatever they would fetch. Gardens that had cost lakhs were sold for as many hundreds, and the very word "Tea" stank in the nostrils of the commercial public. A few of the best companies held on, as also such individuals embarked in the speculation as could weather the storm; but some of the companies were bowed down with heavy debts, and it has been with many, from that cause, a losing race ever since.

This great smash occurred in 1867. I purpose, therefore, to examine into the future prospects of the industry, now that time has been given to test its vitality. Naturally the mistakes made at the first have not been repeated since, so the speculation has had more or less of a fair chance to show what it can do.

In the first place, the share list of Tea companies in the public prints does not at all represent the true position of Tea property to-day. It only gives the dividends declared and the value of the shares in those few limited liability companies which were able to weather the storm, but who, in common with all the others, were bowed down with debt, and are suffering up to the present time, both from that and the numberless mistakes made at the commencement of the enterprise. There are a few notable exceptions, even among the Tea companies. Some of these have done very well, pay large dividends, and are quoted at a high premium, which shows that Tea can and will pay even with the disadvantages attached to limited liability companies. I mean that in these latter work is always expensively done, and that much of the profits are swallowed up by secretaries, directors, &c., besides which, generally from interested motives, the Teas are sent home for sale which private planters know from experience is *not* the best plan.

But to return to the share list. The very many gardens held by firms or private individuals are absent, and inasmuch as many of these were begun more lately, and consequently, the blunders made in other gardens were avoided, it is evident that *their* position, if it could be ascertained, would give the true picture needed.

There is one class of plantations which it would be by no means fair to include. I mean those gardens bought for a mere song during the panic. On many of these necessarily enormous profits have been made, but it proves nothing, inasmuch as the profits, to be legitimate profits for criticism, should on the debit side include the whole cost incurred in making the plantation. To form a fair appreciation of the profits Tea planting can give, we must select gardens constructed after knowledge on the subject was attained, where **good** management, combined with economy in all details, has been carried out, and where the necessary natural conditions for success exist—and such are rare.

But first let me explain what I mean by the "necessary natural conditions for success." Manageable areas; flat or nearly flat land for the garden; a good class of indigenous and hybrid plants; local labour, or anyhow a good proportion of this; facilities for manuring; a good soil; a good Tea climate; and cheap means of transport constitute these, and where they exist I hold Tea *must*, and *does*, pay well. I don't believe in plantations of 600 or 800 acres; some of these pay, but they would pay much better if reduced in size. A garden of 300 acres, yielding even at the rate of four maunds an acre, will pay much better than another of 500 acres, yielding but two and a-half or three maunds.

The reason is obvious, the larger produce **is** against a smaller expenditure. Were I to commence a Tea plantation **to-day**, it should not exceed 300 or 400 acres in size. This passion for large areas is the rock on which, more than any other, Tea Companies have wrecked themselves; experience has already shown this, and will show it more, as time goes on.

Flat land for Tea gardens is a great desideratum. Steep lands are difficult to cultivate; the soil is continually washing away from the roots of the plants; it is impossible to manure them successfully, and the consequence of all this is that the Tea bushes do not thrive.

The Chinese plant gives a small and inferior produce, the indigenous and hybrid kind a larger and very superior one; thus I think the latter one of the "necessary conditions for success." On the other points, with the exception of manuring, nothing need be said, inasmuch as their necessity is evident; but on the point of manure I must say a few words. The Tea plant is being continually denuded of its leaves; nothing is returned to the soil; and consequently in process of time that soil is exhausted. It was held once that manure destroyed the flavour of Tea. This idea, at variance with all agricultural experience, is now completely exploded, like many others received from the Chinamen who first came from the Flowery Land to teach the art of Tea cultivation and Tea manufacture to the Indian public. Many of them had never perhaps seen a Tea bush, anyhow in many respects theirs was faulty teaching, and all experienced planters are convinced, and it is truth, that more knowledge on Tea exists in India than China at the present time.

But to return to the subject of manure. It is, and is now generally allowed to be, a necessity to the lengthened and successful maintenance of a plantation. Means for its production are now largely adopted in Assam and Cachar, and the results will be a yield per acre the most sanguine have never dreamt of. Chittagong, on this head, has great advantages; manure in any quantity can there be procured for a trifle, and the results have shown its great value.

We have scarcely yet entered on the third stage to which any new speculation, after the two first (the wild venture, and the unreasoning panic have passed), tends; but as knowledge of the financial results of Tea plantations in the hands of private firms and private individuals increases, that third stage will dawn, if it has not done so already. It consists in a sober appreciation of the subject opposed to both the extremely exulting and depressing views passed through, and when it arrives, the great and successful future of Indian Tea will be only a question of time.

ADDITIONS TO THE FOURTH EDITION.

CHAPTER XXXII.

COUNTRIES OUTSIDE CHINA AND INDIA THAT PRODUCE TEA.

So much has the **industry marched since the Third Edition was published in** 1878 **that I think** it well to add **the following pages to my book.**

I will first consider the countries *outside* India and China which produce Tea, or wish to do so.

CEYLON.

This is likely to prove a formidable competitor. **As far as I can gather, Tea** plants (of both the Assam and China kinds) were introduced into Ceylon in 1841, but **it is only during the last few years Tea** planting has been **taken up in earnest.** A Mr. Shand, who seems to have studied **Tea** in Ceylon, estimates 500 lbs. per acre as the produce when in full bearing. This is $6\frac{1}{4}$ **maunds,** and though less than the best Indian gardens give, it **is** considerably above the average **all** over India. Ceylon Tea finds a ready market in London. The parcels vary much, as they do from India, but in the **past year** (1882) many very desirable **lots were** sent home. I believe, take it all in all, **Ceylon Tea is no** better, and no worse, than Indian Tea.

With Tea prices as they are to-day, I would not myself *commence* Tea cultivation in India, Ceylon, or *anywhere*. I feel sure, therefore, if Ceylon planters rush into Tea, as they **did in India in times** past, they will regret it. But I hear that made Tea gardens can be bought there cheap, and under these circumstances Tea will probably pay the purchasers well.

JOHORE.

H.H. the Maharajah there has started a small Tea garden, but as there are in it only two acres of Tea, the whole thing is quite an experiment yet. The climate is said to be favourable, and land easily acquired. Cheap labour is the difficulty. May it long continue so! There is too much Tea already; the low prices ruling result simply from supply exceeding demand. Thus I hope Johore will *not* produce Tea. The following is from the *Tea Gazette* :—

TEA IN JOHORE.

We have lately published several articles on the subject of Tea in Johore and the prospects of Tea plantations in the Malay Peninsula. The soil and climate are all that can be desired for the successful cultivation of the Tea plant ; there is abundance of land lying idle which can be obtained on advantageous terms ; but all hopes of establishing the Tea industry on a prosperous footing are frustrated by the want of cheap Indian labour. A correspondent writes on this subject to the *Ceylon Observer* as follows :—

" I was pretty well disgusted with Johore at first. I got such fever as nearly finished me up twice. A new comer from Ceylon says he had Wellaway fever and all other fevers in Ceylon, but he never felt anything to come near the severity of Johore fever. Liberian coffee does first-class in the low country. Cocoa is being tried with apparent success. Tea is also promising. You may have seen about some samples sold in London, at a high figure. All this is nice enough, but what's the good of it when we have not a plentiful supply of labour over which we can have complete control ? So you see, the burden of my letter is an indefinite supply of labour."

Strenuous efforts are, however, being made to arrange with the Government for the importation of labourers from this country, which, if successful, will inevitably result in the cultivation on a large scale of the Tea plant in Johore. In another column will be found a description of the Maharajah of Johore's experimental Tea plantation at Tanjong Putri, Johore.

Japan

Sends **its Teas** principally to America. The Tea is of a greenish nature, **and experiments to** manufacture black Tea have not, it seems, been successful. The following should give a hope to Indian Tea planters :—

Japan Tea.

To the Editor of the *Japan Herald*.

Dear Sir,—I read your article on Tea contained in last Saturday's paper, **anent** the deterioration in quality of one of the country's **principal articles** of export, and can fully confirm the chief points contained therein.

But in addition, from my personal experience, there appears to exist a steadily increasing disregard of care in the preparation of the leaf up country, and the evil, though existing for the last three or four **years, is** much more manifest this **season,** and is worthy of being brought under the especial notice of parties **interested in the welfare** of this country's produce.

I submit for your inspection a sample of coarse leaf sifted out of a parcel of good quality, and the proportion of similar stuff in the chop amounts to fully 3 per cent., very much affecting the good appearance of the fired leaf. This defect no doubt arises from the attempted production of too great an amount of cured leaf for each hand employed per diem in the process, to be attributed no doubt to the enhanced cost **of** labour in the interior. But the defect is of vital importance for the future of Japan Teas in America. The buyer for distribution amongst consumers in that country is greatly influenced by the "appearance" of the leaf, despite its relative intrinsic quality in infusion, in comparison with a Tea of worse appearance, hence the high facing and colouring at present so much in vogue. If the Japanese producers continue the present style of manufacturing the leaf up country, so surely will Japan Teas decline in favour in America, as the foreign shipper here cannot make up the leaf prepared up country to the standard required by the American buyers, and with the prospect of a possibility of Oolongs and even blacks becoming ere long dangerous rivals with consumers in the United States, it behoves the Japanese Tea growers to turn their attention towards an improvement in production in their own country before they attempt to rival foreign competitors at this side.—Yours faithfully, YAMATO.

Yokohama, *Aug.* 19, 1881.

[We have inspected the sample of coarse leaf referred to in the above letter, and though we cannot pretend to any critical knowledge of Tea, we can confirm the statements of our correspondent, and hold the specimen at our office, where it can be seen by anyone desirous of doing so.—*Editor, Japan Herald.*]

I know not where this next extract came from, but it appears they understand adulteration in Japan:—

Mr. Yanagiya might, however, have gone a step farther, and have given particulars of the various analyses, and have mentioned that the "leaf" of the various samples showed a large proportion of leaves quite different to those of the Tea shrub, and for the presence of which not even the astute foreigner—that bugbear of Japanese commerce—can be held accountable.

We have heard this season loud complaints of the presence of leaves entirely distinct from those of the Tea plant amongst purchases. These consisted principally of wisteria, willow and a species of ash, but the native growers were impartial, and several other species of shrubs also contributed their quota to the frauds practised by the Japanese.

The probable reason of the falling off in the quantity of one of the leading articles of export from Japan is not difficult to guess at, nor can the Japanese say that they have not received full and timely warning of the danger threatening the popularity of Japan Tea. A reckless over-production, excessive and close picking of the shrubs, and great carelessness in pruning and manuring the tree—caused, no doubt, in no small degree by the high rate of wages in the interior—is militating against the realisation of a good crop, and the peasant is too intent upon immediate profits to forego the picking of the third crop of a season under existing circumstances. The result of all this has been that—at the close of last season—a quantity of worthless leaf was poured upon the market, finally sold at almost nominal figures, and shipped across to the United States, where it remains an incubus on the figures of stock, and a source of future abhorrence to any unfortunate purchaser towards anything bearing the name of Japan Tea.

The following is from the report of the Japanese Consul at San Francisco. I should have thought the Americans were too sensible **"to prefer coloured Teas:"**

It has however come to my knowledge that in the Eastern States the Tea was analyzed, and adulteration was **discovered**; such as the admixture of other leaves and poisonous ingredients which are used for colouring the Tea before it is exported, and that the markets in the Eastern States being overstocked, no Tea, unless of the best quality, can find purchasers. This is a very deplorable state of affairs. The colouring is made by the foreign merchants residing in Japan, for Americans prefer coloured Tea, and a few Japanese merchants may have imitated them, and exported on their own account.

The exports of Japan Tea to America have declined from seventeen to fourteen million in one year! Not strange if all the above is true.

The following from the *Tea Gazette* bears out what I say above as to Japan black Tea:—

JAPAN BLACK TEA.

Mr. Consul Euslie writes from Kanagawa (Japan) as follows concerning black Tea:—This has, on the whole, proved a failure, although the production continues on a limited scale. The climate and soil of this country appear unfitted to the growth of plants producing a leaf of the quality necessary to make good black. Teas resembling good leaf congous can be made with good and even handsome leaf, several samples being in appearance very similiar to Indian Teas of pekoe class, but lacking strength, and not being nearly equal to good Chinese Foochow Teas in that respect. A small amount of these Teas has been shipped to Germany on native account, a German financier providing the necessary funds; but thus far the outcome of these shipments has not transpired. The results generally of 1881 have not proved as satisfactory as those of the preceding year; the whole crop, and more particularly the first picking, shows signs of hasty and careless preparation. The amount of Tea exported from Japan was decidedly in excess of the requirements of the United States and Canada, and a considerable portion of the shipments for the year had to be sacrificed at prices which did not cover laying down cost.

All this is hopeful for our Indian Teas, as we *can* manufacture the greenish Tea they like—that is, we can do it if **they** won't take our black, but they have begun to do so.

The above mode of manufacture in Japan is new to us in India.

The process of steaming the Tea **is** as follows :—**As** soon as picked it is at once steamed, all damp or wet leaves being thrown on one side, excepting those that may be a little wet with **dew**. In order to obtain the proper application of heat, a few leaves are put into a shallow basket, spread out evenly, and the lid put on; the basket is then placed over a charcoal fire box or stove, a perfume is at once **perceived**. When the greeny smell has subsided, the leaves are removed, spread on a piece of new matting, and fanned briskly so as to draw out the heat. After the lapse of some little time the Tea is placed in a tray, and then undergoes a firing process, the length of which **is regulated either by the minute** hand of a watch or the beats of a **pulse, and depends a good deal on the** manipulator's own ideas.

JAVA.*

Much of this Tea goes to Holland and Northern Germany. I know Tea cultivation in Java is carried out very carefully and very successfully, but this one fact is all I know as to Java or its Teas.

AMERICA.

That the proper climate for Tea can be found there (a huge Continent to choose from!) goes without saying. But equally sure is it that Tea will not pay except labour is cheap.

By the extract below, it appears Georgia has been selected for experimental Tea cultivation, and I doubt not it is a good selection :—

* Much about Java and its Teas can be found in a book entitled "Java, or How to Manage a Colony," by J. W. B. Money. Crown 8vo, 2 vols. Hurst and Blackett.

Tea Planting in America.

Successful experiments have been made in this branch of cultivation in the United States, as is shown by a report just published by Mr. Jackson, a Scotch gentleman now settled in America, who was at one time manager of the estates of the Scottish Assam Company. The Commissioner of Agriculture has, at Mr. Jackson's advice, selected a tract of land in Georgia for an experimental farm, on which the raising of Tea on an extended scale will be carefully and thoroughly tried. Samples of the Teas already produced by Mr. Jackson have been sent to Messrs. Thompson, tea merchants, Mincing Lane, London, to be examined. The reply was that—" They represented Teas of a high type. The flavour, though not strong, is remarkably fragrant. In appearance they resemble Indian Tea, but the flavour is more like that of the finest Chinese black Tea, or of the hill Teas of India."

No reason why the Teas should not be good, but the labour difficulty will, I think, prevent Tea paying there, as elsewhere in America, for Mr. Jackson himself, who continues the above, asks further on, " Can we afford to pay our labourers four times as much as they pay in India and still make Tea a success ? " He, strange to say, tries to prove " yes." I say no, a thousand times no, in spite of all Mr. Jackson says. I like, however, to give both sides of a question, and so will let Mr. Jackson speak for himself:—

The stock cry continually raised against Tea culture in this country is, how can you raise Tea in a country where wages are so high ? You can cultivate Tea at a profit only in a country where labour is at the lowest possible minimum, and so on. And so it is taken for granted that the Tea culture is to be allowed to retain its antiquated forms and systems for all time, and that the skill and intelligence of a civilized nation can do nothing to raise it to a level with corresponding branches of agriculture, such, for instance, as rice growing. What would the people of South Carolina say if told that the only way to cultivate rice at a profit was to sow all their seed in nursery beds and, when sprouted, to transplant their entire crop, seed by seed, by hand, as is done in India? What would a Minnesota farmer say if told that the only implement with which he could profitably rear a crop of corn was the hoe, wielded by an attenuated skeleton of a man? If the hundreds of wealthy Tea planters in Assam were told that they must return to the original system of manufacturing their Teas by hand, they would throw up their farms in despair. Seventy million pounds of Tea are now annually manufactured by machinery in India and Java, and I have satisfied myself that green Teas, suitable for the American market, can be manufactured at one-third the cost of the black Teas prepared by machinery for the English market. There is but one division of Tea culture into which the labour question would enter at all, and that is the picking of the leaves. Everything else can be carried on with the mechanical precision of the cultivator, reaper, and floutring mill. Is not the real truth of the matter to be found in the fact that the American people know nothing—absolutely nothing—of the modern system of Tea culture and manufacture, and are therefore in no position to form a sound judgment of the possibilities of their country and countrymen in regard to Tea? I say again, as I have often said before, that the question of labour will prove no barrier to successful Tea culture in America. Let any who are interested enough in this subject to feel sceptical about it favour me with a call at No. 229 East Fourth Street and I will take pleasure in showing them what achievements modern skill and mechanical genius have already attained and what may very easily be accomplished in America. I believe that then there is a bright future in store for successful Tea culture.

In another place Mr. Jackson says he has always cultivated with ploughs, and done it successfully. Naturally this would make his cultivation much cheaper, and it is high time, as I say elsewhere, that we in India should try and do the same thing.

We, all the world knows, how ingenious, how inventive the Americans are, and thus it is *possible* they may by the use of machinery for all branches of manufacture, by improved steam-ploughs and other agricultural instruments which shall dispense with hand labour for cultivation, so cheapen the cost of Tea that its production will pay in spite of the high rate of wages ruling. Only in this way, however, *can* the industry succeed in America, and if it be done (I hope it may, for we in India shall then benefit by the ideas carried out), the United States will add one more laurel to the many they have achieved already in other branches of commerce.

NATAL.

Tea here too! Where, alas! is it not? The following is in a report from Natal:—

We have glanced at the past and seen the present condition of the Tea enterprise. The most important matter is still before us—the future of Tea in Natal. It must be remembered that an industry may be profitable to encourage for local consumption, and yet fail when it comes to be exported. This production (Tea) must be looked at as one which, if it progresses, must shortly be exported. Three hundred acres of Tea in full bearing will supply to the full the present need of the Colony and its surroundings, *i.e.*, taking the import returns as our guide; and even with increasing demand, that demand can soon be met. Therefore the importance attaching to the question, "Can we in Natal grow Tea to pay, so as to compete with other countries in the markets of the world?" The Tea-growing districts of India, till lately confined to Assam, Cachar, and neighbourhood, have now been extended to the Neilgherries and Ceylon, and these places, till lately confining themselves to coffee, are leaving that most precarious crop and growing Tea and cinchona. Both these districts at present export Tea to England. It is said that Tea is to be introduced into Queensland and the northern territory of Australia; and that the Southern States of the Union and California contemplate Tea growing. Are we justified, then, in believing that Tea may be profitably exported from Natal? Before considering this, we have to bear in mind that Tea is placed in the London market in large quantities at a very low price; China Teas as low as 5½*d*. per lb. in bond, and Indian Teas as low as 8*d*. per lb. in bond; but again the price extends to 3*s*. and even 4*s*. per lb. in bond. All these things have to be weighed and well considered by anyone before embarking in this enterprise to any great extent. In all matters of agriculture the labour question is the foremost, after it is known that the plant will flourish. To attempt to base the success of this particular industry upon any other than that of coolie labour would be foolish, as we all know that Kafirs are not to be relied upon, therefore the cost of labour has to be considered. We well know that all the Tea estates of India have to be supplied with imported coolies —the natives of the districts concerned will not work unless casually— but the cost of coolies in Natal must be more than the cost of coolies in Assam—therefore in that item the advantage must be in favour of the Indian planter. Countries such as Queensland and the United States of America must either import labour, or pay a much higher rate than we do ; hence so far as these countries are concerned, Natal will hold its own.

I have not done yet. Here is another place where it seems they mean to try Tea. I do hope that climate, soil, labour, something will be found unsuitable.

Fiji Tea.

Mr. J. E. Mason, of the Alpha Tea and Coffee Estate, Taviuni, Fiji, has forwarded to Mr. J. O. Moody, the expert, of Melbourne, samples of the first Fijian Tea produced in his part of the world; at the same time writing that early next year he hoped to pluck off 30 acres planted with Tea, and that the samples sent were hastily made in a barrel with a frying-pan of charcoal. Mr. J. O. Moody reports :—" Fiji Pekoe leaf: Handsome, small, even, golden tipped, evenly and well fermented. Fiji Pekoe liquor Very strong, full, rich, and pungent pekoe flavour, thick, with deep red infusion. An invaluable Tea for mixing, and worth about 2s. 6d. per lb. in bond. Fiji Pekoe Souchong leaf : Well made, wiry, twisted, rich, black tippy leaf, evenly and well fermented Fiji Pekoe Souchong flavour, with good, bright, red infusion. A fine Tea to drink alone, and worth about 1s. 9d. per lb. in bond. These Teas have the character of good Ceylon growths, and are in every respect suitable Teas for general consumption, and such samples are sure to meet with ready sale in Australasia or Great Britain."

Here again, I am told, the labour question is the doubtful point. Tea cannot be made to pay without cheap labour, and the sooner all these new Tea countries learn the lesson the better for **the pockets of the projectors.** I may add, the better for the Indian planter's pocket too, for *any* **increase in** the supply **is hurtful.**

In closing this chapter, I would give one **word of advice to** intending Tea planters in India, **or indeed anywhere.** There is too much Tea already, **why plant more?** If you must **" go into Tea "** you **may do so** and **probably** make money, **but it will** not be by *planting* it. **If you look** about you **can** buy a plantation **ready made for far less than you** could make such, and in doing **so there is no** reason why it sh**ould** not pay, and pay well. If **you make a garden** you **will** have five **or** six years to wait **for any return;** you attempt **what requires know**ledge **and experience to** succeed in, and begging your success, who can **say** what the **market** will be then?

I have far from exhausted the **subject of these** new Tea fields, **but my space is** limited, **and** several other points demand attenti**on.**

CHAPTER XXXIII.

STATISTICS REGARDING INDIAN TEA.

As early as **1780** a few Chinese plants were to be seen in Calcutta cultivated by a Colonel Kyd.

The possibility of cultivating Tea in India was first mooted in 1835-36, and the Indian Government started an experimental garden at Lukimpore (Assam) at that time.

Indigenous Tea was first discovered in Assam by a Mr. Bruce in 1830.

In 1845 and following **years** the Government imported **large quantities of China seed and established** nurseries on the Himalayas.

Tea planting was commenced in India by the Assam Company **about 1840, and the cultivation** was undertaken in other districts **in the following** years:—Kumaon and Gurwhal, 1850; Cachar, 1855; **Dehra-Dhoon, 1855**; Sylhet, 1857; Kangra, 1858; Darjeeling, 1860; Terai, **1860**; Chittagong, 1860; Neilgherries, 1862; Chota Nagpore, 1872; Dooars, 1875.

Thus it may be said Tea planting in India dates from 1840 by **one Company, but** 1850 by individuals.

The following figures show the imports of Indian **Teas** into Great **Britain since 1870** in millions of pounds:—

Year	Millions of Pounds	Year	Millions of Pounds	Year	Millions of Pounds	Year	Millions of Pounds
70	13	74	17¼	78	36	82	54¾
71	15¼	75	25½	79	38½	..	..
72	17	76	29¼	80	44	..	..
73	18¼	77	31¾	81	45¾	..	..

I may here remark that while the imports of Indian Teas have, since 1877, increased by 23 million pounds, the imports of China Teas have increased by 4 million pounds only in the same time.

The deliveries and stocks were as follows for 1881 and 1882 in millions of pounds:—

	1881.	1882.
Deliveries	48¾	50½
Stocks on 31st December	18½	21¾

During *the last 3 months of* 1882 the deliveries averaged 5 million pounds per month. In January, 1883, they were 5½ millions, and in February (I write in March) 5 millions.

Deliveries at this rate mean 60 millions a year.

I estimate Indian produce for 1883 at about 62 millions.

Deduct the probable quantity to be sent to countries outside the United Kingdom, and local consumption in India ... 5½ ,,

Leaving available for the home market ... 56½ millions.

Thus, if **deliveries continue at the present rate**, demand must soon equal, if not exceed, supply, and the consequence naturally must be enhanced prices, which, however, will surely to some extent check the deliveries.

There is, however, a hopeful feature regarding Indian Teas. The taste for them is increasing greatly. A very small per centage of the public drink **them pure** (a large per centage in Ireland), but the public generally are now accustomed to the strength attained only by mixing, say one third of Indian to two thirds China, and *will* nothing weaker. Thus retail dealers must continue to use them, and thus though, as remarked, increased prices *will* check deliveries, they will not do so with Indian Teas to the same extent they would with China.

Another **hopeful feature is** (for details see further on) a growing demand for Indian Tea is now established in Australia, and has quite lately commenced in America. **Thus, I think,** the increased produce from India (which in no case can be large for some years *) will probably be met **by this** outside demand, leaving no greater quantity than now available **for** the home **market. True Ceylon** (a new field) will **increase** the supply, **but it will not be by much** for some **time. Take** it all in all, I look hopefully **at the** prospects of Indian Tea in the future. I never anticipate a range of prices as good even as ruled in 1881, but a good deal better than we had in 1882, and thus enough to make **the** industry a paying one.

I have lately received a valuable paper on Indian Tea statistics from Messrs. Gow and Wilson, Indian Tea brokers. I cannot transcribe the diagram they allude to, but otherwise **I** give the complete paper as sent me:—

19, Little Tower Street, Mincing Lane,

London, 15th February, 1883.

"INDIAN TEA STATISTICS."

Dear Sir,—Now that the annual figures are made up, we beg to submit a statement showing the continued progress made by Indian Tea in public estimation, together with comparative figures relating to the consumption of China and Indian Teas,—And remain, dear Sir, yours faithfully,

GOW AND WILSON, Indian Tea Brokers.

The very considerable increase in the home consumption **of Indian** Tea during the last quarter of 1882, and January this **year, once** more attracts attention to the growing importance

---

* It will not be large because **much** in the way of extensions has not been executed lately. A higher range of prices will doubtless cause more land to be cultivated, but no produce from **such** will be available for four or five years.

of India as a field of production, and the increasing appreciation of the British public for Indian Teas, whether used alone or mixed with China sorts. Notwithstanding the check to consumption in the early part of 1882, when Indian medium and common Teas were just 50 per cent. dearer than they now are, the average monthly deliveries of the first three months were 3,670,000 lbs., or 230,000 lbs. a month more than the average of the first quarter of 1880, with prices much the same at both periods. Quotations last year receded step by step, and, as prices dropped, so we found the consumption grew, till for the last quarter of 1882, with its very low range of prices, the average monthly deliveries reached the unprecedented figures of over 5¼ million pounds.

The average monthly deliveries in each quarter of the last five years have been as follows:—

(In thousands of lbs. 000's omitted.)

	Jan.-Mar.	April-June.	July-Sept.	Oct.-Dec.
1878	3,216	3,129	2,869	3,041
1879	3,444	2,688	2,461	3,155
1880	3,441	3,418	3,522	4,228
1881	4,197	4,172	3,824	4,094
1882	3,670	4,125	4,116	5,254

During the year 1878, out of every 100 lbs. of all descriptions of Tea consumed in this country, 23, or one in about four-and-a-third, was Indian Tea. Last year the proportion was 31 per cent., or nearly one in three.

These figures show, in the clearest manner, how steadily Indian Tea is becoming popular.

The unevenness of the quarterly deliveries of China Tea in the year 1878 and 1879 is due to the apprehensions felt in those years that the duty would be increased. In consequence, clearances were hastily made before the Budget announcement, and the deliveries immediately after sank to very low figures, increasing again as stocks of retailers were depleted. In March, 1880, again there was a pressure to clear Teas, which brought up the total deliveries of the first quarter to a high level. A considerable check was given to deliveries of Indian Teas during the latter part of 1881 and the early part of 1882 through the rise of prices during that period.

The most noticeable feature of the last three calendar years is the stationariness of deliveries of China Teas at the reduction from the level of both 1878 and 1879. Approximately the deliveries of China and Indian Teas in the five years ending 31st December in each case may be given, in millions of pounds, as follows:—

	1878.	1879.	1880.	1881.	1882.
China ...	121	125	115	111	113
Indian ...	37	35	44	49	51

The deliveries of China Tea have *receded* from 125 million pounds in 1879 to 113 million pounds in 1882, while the home consumption of Indian Tea has *increased* from 35 million pounds to 51 million pounds in the corresponding years.

Notwithstanding the supply of Indian Tea for the season 1882-3 is estimated at the unprecedented figure of 55 million pounds against the actual imports in the previous two season years of about 50 million and 46 million pounds respectively, it appears not unlikely the consumption of 1882-3 will once again, as in 1880-81, overtake the supply and reduce the stocks by July next to the equivalent of less than three months' deliveries.

We find that there has been received to the 31st December last, 33,218,000 lbs., leaving to arrive 21,782,000 lbs. for the six months ending 30th June next, to make up the estimated supply of 55 million pounds which, according to Indian advices, will be available for shipment to this country. The imports of the current six months, therefore, will be but slightly in excess of those of the corresponding half-year, when 20,948,000 lbs. were received; for although the shipments of 1882-3 are expected to show an excess of more than five million pounds over 1881-2, exporters this season have hurried forward their Teas early and in the six months ended December 31st the arrivals in the

United Kingdom were 32,218,000 lbs. against only 28,947,000 lbs. in the corresponding half of 1881.

The significant feature of the **movement,** however, **is the** very agreeable surprise, month by month, caused by the publication of the delivery figures. **These** compare for the last few months as follows:—

Deliveries of the last Four Months compared with corresponding Months.

	October. lbs.	November. lbs.	December. lbs.	January. lbs.
1882-3 ...	5,132,000	5,174,000	4,457,000	5,502,000
1881-2 ...	4,353,000	4,205,000	3,724,000	4,104,000
Increase ...	779,000	969,000	733,000	1,398,000

A continuance of similar large increases is most probable, especially as we compare with the relatively small deliveries of February to April inclusive of **last** year, **when** only 10,489,000 lbs. were taken from warehouse, against 12,782,000 lbs. in the same months of 1881—a decrease of 2,293,000 **in three** months. Part of the decrease may be attributed to the then higher range of medium and common Indian Teas.

The net result of the above statistics is that—with no materially **larger** arrivals visible, even with the liberal allowance of 5,000,000 **lbs. increased shipments for** the crop year—the deliveries give every promise of showing very considerable expansion, and, as we have said, threaten for the **complete** year to more than absorb the extra supply.

To enable anyone to check and form an independent opinion on the forecast we venture to give, we present below the imports and deliveries, half-year **by** half-**year,** for the four **seasons** 1879-80 to 1882-8**3** inclusive, **with** the totals of **each** crop year:—

Imports of Indian Tea.

	1879-80. lbs.	1880-81. lbs.	1881-82. lbs.	1882-83. lbs.
1st July to 31st Dec.	23,537,000	29,142,000	28,947,000	33,218,000
1st Jan. to 30th June	15,868,000	16,819,000	20,948,000	*21,782,000
Season year	39,405,000	45,961,000	49,895,000	*55,000,000

Deliveries of Indian Tea.

	1879-80. lbs.	1880-1. lbs.	1881-2. lbs.	1882-3. lbs.
1st July to 31st Dec.	16,847,000	24,352,000	23,755,000	27,109,000
1st Jan. to 30th June	19,465,000	25,106,000	23,386,000	†28,802,000
Season year	36,312,000	49,458,000	47,141,000	†55,911,000

These figures show an estimated supply to the end of June next of 21,782,000 lbs., and an estimated consumption of 28,802,000. The former is based on the statements that the available supply for the United Kingdom will be 55 million pounds, and the latter on the actual delivery to January inclusive, and estimated average deliveries of 4,500,000 lbs. a month for the remainder of the half-year. Having these figures before us, we can proceed to calculate the effect on stocks.

	lbs.
At 31st December last we had in warehouse a stock of ...	21,716,000
Add six months' imports to June 30th ...	21,782,000
Total supply ...	43,498,000
Deduct estimated deliveries six months ...	28,802,000
Leaving probable stock at 30th June ...	14,696,000
Which will compare with (at 30th June, 1882) ...	15,991,000

* Estimated on basis of 55,000,000 lbs. available for shipment to the United Kingdom.

† Estimated on average monthly deliveries, February to June inclusive, of 4,500,000 lbs.

In stating the deliveries at an average of 4,500,000 lbs. for the next five months, we have taken this amount merely for the purpose of arriving at a conclusion. In case the deliveries of the months of February to June inclusive average, as is generally expected, 5,000,000 lbs. a month, the stocks at 1st July next will be under 12,200,000 lbs., or 3¾ million lbs. less than at the corresponding date.

We can but consider this a very healthy outlook, especially as it is simultaneous with the estimated decrease in the supply of China Tea, and the possibility that the shipments to the United Kingdom may not reach the estimate. With respect to the latter contingency, we must recollect that new markets are being rapidly developed for Indian Tea. Australia, America, and other parts than the United Kingdom took over three million pounds from 1st May to 31st December last year, compared with less than a third of that quantity shipped thence from India in the corresponding period of 1881. A continuance of this rapid rate of outside demand would considerably curtail our supply, and develope the growing Indian industry.

Gow and Wilson,
19, Little Tower Street, London, E.C.

The diagram omitted shows as follows: it gives the results quarterly, I only give them yearly in millions of pounds.

CONSUMPTION OF CHINA AND INDIAN TEAS IN THE UNITED KINGDOM FOR THE LAST FIVE YEARS.

	1878.	1879.	1880.	1881.	1882.	
China	128½	125¼	114½	111¼	114	} All are Millions of Pounds.
Indian	36	35½	43¾	48½	51½	
Totals.	164½	160¾	158¼	159¾	165½	

Thus, while China Tea consumption has decreased in

five years by fourteen and a-half millions of pounds, Indian has increased by fifteen and a-half millions!

It must be remembered that the former table given at **page** 194 deals with imports, this with consumption, and thus the difference in the figures.

The following extract from the *Tea Gazette* (January, 1883) is interesting in a statistical point of view :—

The exports to Australia (which, as it is well known, have increased more than twenty-fold in six years) now occupy a position only second **to** that of the United Kingdom; and if the P. and O. Company would see its own interest, it would facilitate by every means in its power so important a development of a great industry.

The Straits Settlements, in spite of their proximity to China, took last year ten times the quantity they took six years ago; and Persia, strange to say, has taken 54,712lbs. against 334lbs. in 1876-77—Turkey in Asia and Egypt, together, having taken also 21,488lbs. against 886lbs. in the same period.

Mr. Liotard is of opinion that these are not a tithe of the openings that might be found; and **it** is to be hoped that at the Amsterdam Exhibition and elsewhere **the Tea Syndicate will in no way relax its** efforts.

The imports of China Tea to India **have, in the six years also above** referred to, increased about 60 per cent. Speaking on this point, **we** are of opinion that the Syndicate might well make efforts to increase the local consumption of Indian Tea to the replacement of Chinas, and **we feel sure that** such organised exertion would be followed by very satisfactory **results.**

The **re-export** of China Tea from India shows four times the quantity of six years ago—by far the greater quantity going to Persia and Turkey in Asia. Mr. Liotard thinks that the N.-W. P. and the Punjab might appropriate **a good deal of** this trade; and from the character of the Teas of these districts we are disposed to agree with him. The great increase of export from Karachi shows that this, to some extent, **is** being done.

The abolition of the duty on China Tea imported to India, under the recent free trade policy, appears to have had a prejudicial effect on the planters in Northern India—who can ill afford it. The figures given at the commencement of the pamphlet show that the number of plantations in Northern India has increased in six years **from 851 to** 1,422, and the area from 4,246 to 7,466 acres; the outturn from 1,311,113 lbs. **to** 2,271,773lbs. These figures speak of great activity in production, and show the necessity for every exertion being employed to open out **new** markets. A combined Syndicate for all the districts in Northern India, on the lines of the one now established in Calcutta, is suggested, but how far this is practicable we are not at present prepared to say.

The following, **too, from the** *Tea Gazette* this year is in some respects hopeful:—

We see from the *North China Herald* that the exports of Tea from Shanghai and the Yang-tse ports to England during the current year have fallen off some six and a-half million pounds (8½ per cent.), and that there is also a decrease of some six million pounds in the quantity sent to America this last year—making a difference of nearly thirty per cent.

On **the other hand,** there **has** been an increase **of** nearly three million pounds (45 per cent.) in the direct export to Russian ports. Two large cargoes—one of nearly three million pounds destined for England, and one of almost two million pounds bound for Russia—were lost, so that the real increase of China Tea sent to Russia is only one million pounds, which would reduce **the** increase to about **15** per cent. The decrease of Tea sent to England **becomes even greater, reducing** the receipts as compared with last year **by nearly ten million pounds.** Another aspect of the question must, **however, be** considered, **namely, that** the real displacement, *i.e.*, **in** the amount **of** Tea destined for the English market, would be only **six** and a-half million pounds, and it is not safe to reckon on a recurrence of loss of such a heavy quantity by shipwreck.

The decrease **of** China Tea sent to America is almost entirely in green Teas, **there** being only a falling off of 40,000lbs. in **black, as** compared **with one of over** six millions in green Tea. **The falling off as** regards the English market is much more evenly distributed between the two varieties, the difference being **greater in** that of black than of green Tea.

While America takes from the Shanghai ports over four times as much **green** as black Tea, England, on the **other** hand, takes eleven times as much black Tea as it does of green **Tea.**

These last facts might make it worth the while **of planters in the**

North-West Provinces and in the Punjab to combine to exploit the American markets with half-chests of green Tea, for the manufacture of which those districts are famous, and for which there is so little demand at present in the Central Asian market. We merely throw out the suggestion, knowing that most of the planters in these parts could ill afford to risk much in such an experiment. It is possible that the Syndicate here, which already ships largely to America, might arrange to ship green Tea for such of the planters in Northern India as cared to join the Calcutta body.

The American demand for green Tea is so large, that a quantity representing the entire outturn of Northern India would form but a small percentage of the whole, and if Indian green Tea from the Himalayas were taken up in that market, a demand for the whole quantity produced might easily arise. Whether it would ever be able to compete with China green Tea in the matter of price we do not know, and we should think it would be up-hill work, and attended with some loss—in the first instance at any rate.

The more Tea each individual drinks, the better doubtless for the producers. It is satisfactory therefore to find the consumption *per head* is increasing in the United Kingdom as follows:—

1870. lbs.	1875. lbs.	1880. lbs.
3.81	4.44	4.59

Nearly 1 lb. per head more in 1880 than 1870!

A few figures as to Indian Teas in Australia and America will finish this Chapter of Statistics.

The consumption of Indian Tea in Australia and the Colonies stands as follows:—

1880-81	...	...	Little under ¾ of a million lbs.
1881-82	...	...	Nearly 1 million ,,
1882-83	...	...	Estimated 2 million ,,

This is a satisfactory increase, but when we consider how vast is the great Australasian field, it stands to reason two millions is but a small fraction of what it eventually may be.

The outdoor rough life, led more or less in the Colonies, makes its inhabitants the largest Tea drinkers in the world. For instance, each white denizen in New Zealand drinks nearly three times as much Tea as each person in Great Britain!

The following was the consumption in lbs. per head in 1878:—

United Kingdom.	Victoria.	N. S. Wales.	Queensland.	New Zealand.
4.66	6.92	7.53	9.16	11.05

I now give, in millions of lbs., the consumption in 1880 in the same Colonies:—

Victoria.	N. S. Wales.	Queensland.	New Zealand.
$5\frac{1}{2}$	5	2	3

But what vast tracts exist outside these. The total consumption of all the Colonies must be very large. We make the best Tea in the world in India, why should we not have a large share of the market?

The population of Australia is nearly $2\frac{1}{4}$ millions, and of Tasmania and New Zealand nearly $\frac{3}{4}$ million, say three millions in all, or say three-quarters of the population of London. What a field exists there for Indian Tea!

AMERICA.

The yearly consumption (Canada is included) is over eighty million pounds, nearly all supplied by China and Japan. It is quite lately Indian Teas have been sent to America; so far, their reception has been favourable. But the Americans are accustomed to a greener Tea than we make in India, and this will prove a difficulty. Still we can make the Tea they like, *if* they will buy it. It is early to speculate much as to America, but I think we shall succeed little by little, especially as in the States they are awaking to the fact that both China and Japan Teas are adulterated.

In closing this chapter I must put on record the fact, known to all in India, that the great success achieved in Australia, and the opening thus early attained in America, is entirely due to the labours of the Calcutta Tea Syndicate, and that I firmly believe, much as they have done, they would have done still more had they been properly supported by larger supplies of Tea by the planters in India, who, as a class, are strangely blind to the advantages of co-operation. I can only hope in this respect they will do better in future.

CHAPTER XXXIV.

MARKETS OUTSIDE GREAT BRITAIN.

I HAVE forestalled a good deal on the above in the last chapter, so this will be short, but, I hope, cheering.

AUSTRALIA.

This, from the correspondent of the *Tea Gazette* in Melbourne, as to the size of chests, should be attended to:—

> If the planter wishes to get his Tea direct into consumption, the packages must be small, to suit buyers. In the Colonies a large trade is done in 38lb. half-chests. **They are within the purchasing power of a numerous class, and** are easy to **handle.**

A fierce fight has been going on in Melbourne between the advocates of China and Indian Tea. The latter say China Tea is often adulterated, but this is disputed by the former. Of course *I* cannot say which is right, but chemical analysis, to which China Teas have been subjected in Melbourne, would seem to prove that in some cases they are *not* pure. We all know China Teas in London have, in several instances, been pronounced unfit for consumption, so it is *possible*, of course, that similar Teas are sent to Australia.

The Tea trade in China has taken alarm at our attempts on the Australian market. This is what the *North China Herald* (an organ of the China Tea trade) said lately:—

> There are no squeezing mandarins in India; there is European supervision in the packing and firing of the leaf, and the plantations are connected with civilisation by the railway and the telegraph. Everything is done to give India an unfair advantage over China. Consequently, India tea of the same quality is far cheaper in London

than the ill-regulated produce of Hankow and Foochow, and it is only the conservatism of the consumer, who is not yet entirely habituated to the Indian flavour, that prevents our losses being much heavier than they are. Every year this preference for the leaf that has been longer known is wearing away, and our buyers will soon have to reckon with its disappearance. As yet, Indian Tea is hardly taken on the continent of Europe at all; but here, too, it will penetrate sooner or later, as it is doing into America and Australia, and then there will be no corner of the earth where the sway of China Tea will be undisputed. Until foreigners can supervise the packing of the leaf in China as they do in India, the produce of the latter country will continue to have an unfair advantage. The time no doubt will come when we shall be able to go up and buy the raw leaf on its native hills, pack it by our own methods, and bring it down by railway to Shanghai for shipment; but *for years yet we labour under the disadvantage of having to buy it just as the Chinamen choose to prepare it, without any real knowledge of the total crop at any time, or any immediate power to manipulate the Teas to suit the tastes of consumers.*

Mark you, this is an enemy's opinion. May his prognostications be accomplished to the letter!

The following is from the *Tea Gazette* lately received:—

THE CALCUTTA TEA SYNDICATE.

We are glad to learn that this most useful body intends to continue its operations in opening up, wherever possible, new markets, although there will be no more soliciting supplies of Tea for Australia—the feeling being that the trade in this direction may now be left to take care of itself.

The Tea Syndicate has done a great good, and those able to ship to Australia should at once arrange to take the fullest advantage of the opening made for them. We would have wished that the Syndicate had continued actively its operations there, but perhaps they are right in leaving, now, the further development of the trade they have so successfully founded to private enterprise. It will be the fault of owners themselves if they do not take advantage of the large market opened to them.

I conclude my notice of Australia as a market by the

following, also **from the** *Tea Gazette.* Matters there certainly look promising for the Indian planter:—

THE NEW AUSTRALIAN TEA ASSOCIATION.

Our friends in Australia, now that they are convinced of the purity and good quality of our Indian Teas, have determined, **we are** glad to see, to follow in the wake of the Calcutta Tea Syndicate, and push by *united* effort Indian Teas throughout the Australian Colonies. Knowing full well that no half-hearted measures would be likely **to** succeed, and **that** the **efforts of a few** individuals **would not** meet the requirements of the market, our friends in Victoria and New South Wales have *combined*, and formed an association **under the title of the** "Calcutta Tea **Association,"** for the **sale** of pure **and** unadulterated Indian Teas **to wholesale** merchants, storekeepers, **and** customers in general. Large **and** handsome premises have been taken **in** King Street, **Melbourne,** and Charlotte Place, Sydney, in which **the** operations of the Association are to be carried on **on** a large **scale.**

AMERICA.

The following is from the *Daily News* — a Calcutta paper:—

We were glad to note that our American cousins were being induced to give some orders. If only Indian Tea was once taken up, **and** became popular, its future would be secured. The teeming masses of people **in the** States would consume more Tea we should imagine than all the English public, provided Indian Tea took the place of China. Australia so far has done well, but the market there would be **easily** glutted, whereas, if its use became general, it would be almost impossible to glut the American market. The millions of settlers in **America** and in Canada all use Tea at their meals very much as an Englishman takes his beer, so that the inland consumption must be very **large. In Australia,** every shepherd carries his pannikin of Tea, and the amount he swallows in twelve months must be pretty considerable. In the backwoods of America and Canada, each wood**cutter** consumes nearly half a pound of Tea weekly, so that, with its millions of people, America could easily dispose of millions of pounds **of Tea,** which would not only clear off all the surplus Tea in the

London market, but **would** probably cause **a deficit**. **We** wonder if in our time this golden **era will take** place.

This from the *Tea Gazette* :—

TEA IN AMERICA.

A petition has been **presented** to the United **States** Congress asking for the prohibition **of the** importation of adulterated Teas from China and Japan, which **are at** present extensively **sold**. This, it is thought, will lead **to** increased attention being paid **to** Indian Teas, **which** are well known to be pure and unadulterated.

Again from same paper :—

The circular lately addressed to the local Tea planting interest by the Committee of the Calcutta Syndicate, reporting the results of Mr. Sibthorp's efforts to create a market for Indian Teas in America, opens up **a vista of** unprecedented prosperity in the future.

That the population of America, the bulk of which consist of the **same races** among whom Indian Tea has grown in favour so rapidly in **the United Kingdom, should persist in rejecting it after a fair trial** was *à priori* highly improbable. **It was, therefore,** reasonably **to be** presumed that whatever **difficulty might beset the** opening up of this new market would **consist chiefly in the obstacles** to securing such a **trial.**

Mr. Sibthorp's report not only bears out this view of the case, **but** justifies a confident expectation that the obstacles **in** question, so far as they have any real existence, will speedily disappear. In Chicago, so far from having had to encounter any of those strong trade prejudices which were met with at first in Australia, Mr. Sibthorp found the leading importers, Messrs. J. Doane and Co., ready to render every assistance and confident of being able to dispose of five thousand half chests the first season, without forcing the market. Similar success seems to **have** attended his efforts in New York, **and a telegram has** been received **from** him ordering **a** thousand half chests for shipment to that port.

The importance of **this new market is** immensely enhanced by the **circumstance** that the American consumption **of Tea** is destined to **increase,** owing to mere **growth** of population, **at a** rate not to be looked for in any other country; at such a rate, in fact, that if India could only secure the annual addition to the demand from this cause, she would probably have to double her production in less than a generation to enable her to meet it.

So far from seeing any reason why she should not secure this amount of custom in the New World, we see none why the proportion of India to other Teas consumed in America should not ultimately be as large as in England, where there was **once a** strong prejudice against Indian Tea.

What possible foreign markets have we besides Australia and **America**? Russia and **many European countries are** on the cards, and if the **Calcutta Syndicate** will continue its work great results may ensue. Those who know the Continent often say, and it is true, that no good Tea can be had in France, Germany, or Italy (it is *not* so in Russia), **and** retail dealers have offered again and again (made the offers to me) to take large quantities of the Indian Tea of which I have shown them samples. As **this is so,** why not supply them? But it cannot be done well to any extent by individual planters. The Calcutta Syndicate could easily **do it,** and I quite believe they would find the work in Europe easier than in America.

The Amsterdam Exhibition, so soon to take place, affords a great opening, and from all **I hear it will be taken** advantage of. Inhabitants from all countries will be there, and the fame **of our T**eas should thus spread throughout Europe. The *Tea Gazette* says :—

THE AMSTERDAM EXHIBITION.

It is intended to have Indian Tea well **represented at the forthcoming** Exhibition at Amsterdam; **and we trust that** the most will be made **of the** opportunity. There **is no reason** why we should not succeed in Holland as **well as we** have succeeded in *America* and *Australia*. The rapid strides going on in production must be met by exceptionally active exertions to open out new markets, and to see that those recently opened out are not allowed to drop for want of fostering.

The **effect** of this opportunity will be by no means limited to Holland, **as** in all probability thousands will flock to the Exhibition from adjacent countries, and many from all parts of the world.

We hope that every advantage will be taken of future International Exhibitions in any part of the world by an adequate quasi-permanent organization in Calcutta, and **we sincerely** trust that the existing Calcutta Tea Syndicate will not **cease its most** useful operations until all the **world bows to the great god Indian Tea.** The operations in countries other than Great Britain during the last few **years show** what important developments in the Tea trade of this **country** are now taking place, and every exertion is necessary to maintain these successful results—for which the industry is so much indebted to the **Syndicate.**

THIBET.

This is a large, mountainous, and table land country on the northern side of the Himalayas. It is at a very high elevation, intensely cold, and very thinly populated. The Thibetans drink much Tea per head, but they use Brick Tea; this is made of the coarsest leaves compressed with some glutinous substance.

There **is no** difficulty **in its manufacture. At** present it is supplied by China, which is close by, but not nearer than India. Many think much of our coarse Tea (particularly from the Himalayan gardens) might find a market in Thibet, **and I** incline to the belief they are right. The quantity **would not be very large,** "but every little helps."

Formerly much Tea was **sold to** the native tribes over the **northern border** by the gardens in Kumaon, Gurwal, and Kangra. Why I know not, but I hear the trade has fallen off to some extent; the Teas are taken to the Central Asian markets.

I have done with foreign markets, **but** there is yet **another** and a very large one regarding which nothing has yet been done: I allude to the market among the natives of India, in other words

The Local Market.

The following is from the *Calcutta Englishman* on the subject :—

The letter of our correspondent " A. E. T." calls attention for the hundredth time to the failure of the planting interest to make the most of the local demand for Indian Teas. It is only necessary to compare the prices realised at the public auctions with those at which even the most liberal of our retail firms offer to supply their customers with such Teas to see that but a very small fraction of the difference between the prime cost of the Tea and what the consumer has to pay for it goes into the pocket of the planter. It is probably no exaggeration to say that while the consumer pays, on the average, from twelve annas to a rupee per pound more than the actual cost of the Tea laid down in Calcutta, the planter may think himself fortunate if he can appropriate from half an anna to an anna of this sum. By whatever course of argument the fact may be justified, it is certainly not justifiable by the equity of the case as it appears to ordinary minds. For it is the planter who has borne the heat and burden of the day, and the proportion which the capital invested by him bears to the ultimate return is immensely greater in his case than in that of the retail dealer.

On whom does the blame for the continuance of this state of things, if blame there be in the matter, rest? Hardly on the public. They would only be too glad to allow the Tea planter, say, four times his present profit instead of allowing twelve times that profit to a middleman or a series of middlemen. The public, however, can give their custom only to those who bid for it, and who consult their convenience in the arrangements they make to secure it.

It is evidently the planter, and the planter alone, who can move in the matter. But whether out of regard for the interests of the retail dealer, or from a belief that the game is not worth the candle, he does not move. If there were a retail Tea trade worthy of the name, in the proper sense of the term, in Calcutta, it would probably not be to the interest of planters to enter into competition with it. But though we have many retail establishments who deal in Tea, its sale is, in the great majority of cases, only one item of a very multifarious business, the profit on which, as a whole, is probably not excessive under all the circumstances of the case.

As to the game not being worth the candle, that is possibly the case if only the present demand is considered. But we are persuaded that it is otherwise if regard is had to the expansion of which that demand is capable.

If Indian Tea were procurable in the bazaars in parcels of moderate size at a reasonable **advance on auction prices,** we believe that a large native demand for it would rapidly grow up. As it is, an extensive business goes on in China Tea of the most wretched quality, some of it sold in packets of a few ounces, and **some of it loose in** still smaller quantities. Even in Calcutta this Tea is sold at prices which would pay the Indian Tea planter a handsome profit, while in the interior it is sold at rates which would have been high fifty years ago.

Surely a Syndicate which extends its efforts for the popularisation of Indian Tea to such distant and widely separated markets as Australia and America might profitably make some systematic effort to promote its use among the vast population at its doors.

The time may be far distant when the great bulk of this population will adopt Tea as **an ordinary beverage;** but the way in which the habit of using it has spread during the last ten or fifteen years, among all classes of the vast **population of** Calcutta, affords an indication of possibilities very well **worth testing.**

When last in India I **wrote on this subject** largely, but all to no avail. The following was one of my letters which appeared in the *Tea Gazette* :—

THE MARKET AT OUR DOORS.—CONSUMPTION OF CHINA TEA IN INDIA.

The *Statesman,* **in a** recent article, observes as follows, while discussing the maritime trade of British India :—

"**Perhaps the most** anomalous import we have is Tea. It is hardly conceivable that while Indian Tea continues to advance in public estimation at home, we should not only use China Tea in India, but that in increasing quantities."*

In 1876-77 the imports of China Teas were a little *under* two millions, but in 1880-81 as much *over* three millions ! The *Statesman* **states, and** truly, that the reason of this is simply " that Indian Tea is **sold in** too large packets to be easily obtainable by the general public,

* **With** few exceptions **it is** bought by the Natives alone and for the reason given above.—E. M.

for it seems, as regards Indian Tea, the smallest quantity that can be bought is one **pound, whereas an ounce of China Tea can be purchased.**"

Further on, the *Statesman* kindly alludes to my advocacy in the *Tea Gazette* of a company to sell Tea in small packages to the natives, stating also that such a trade is "capable of almost unlimited expansion at a fair profit," which is exactly **what I have, for some** time, been trying to hammer into the heads of those interested in the **Tea industry** of India.

Now, Sir, is it not absurd that while the *bête noir* of our industry **is** "supply in **excess of** demand," and while, with this dread, we are trying (it seems with success) to **open up new markets at the Antipodes and in America, we are neglecting a market at our very doors, the limits of which, I hold, no man can foresee, for is it not a market where the possible buyers number 200 millions?**

Is it not also more than absurd, nay a very **shame to those interested** in our industry, that while we **have a** better article **than China Tea, we allow, by our supineness and lack of enterprise, more than three million pounds of** an inferior article to be sold in the birth place of the better? **And why?** simply because we *will* not supply it in the form the teeming **crowd of natives willing, nay anxious, to buy can** avail themselves of it!

Since I advocated in your **paper the formation of a company to sell Tea to natives** in small packets, **and showed, I thought** conclusively: 1—That the capital **required was not large** (say one and a-half lakhs). 2—That the **shareholders might** expect very fair dividends. 3—That there was no assignable limit to **the** trade which might be developed. 4—That if such a company was started and worked well, **all fear for the future of** Indian Tea would be at an **end.** 5—That **every Tea owner,** who became a shareholder, would advance **his own interests by many times** more than the dividends he would receive—since **then I** have obtained from England estimates of **all** the machinery required to bulk **and** pack the Teas, **advice from the** best firms **as to** *the mode* **so successful** in England, and **I am more than** ever convinced **that the company would be a money-making one, and that, in** two words, **we shall sadly** neglect **our own interests if we do not accomplish it.**

Again, since my **former articles I have spoken** to dozens of Tea **planters and Tea owners** on the subject, and all of them think highly **of the scheme, while many only wait for** the company to be launched to take shares. I could name more than one influential native also who is willing to join, and this is a good sign, for, in my opinion, a moiety of the directors should be natives. I will myself become a large shareholder, though I cannot offer my services on the board, for it must be in Calcutta, and I do not reside there.

I am convinced, if the company is launched, the shares will be taken up in a week.

But if no one in Calcutta is public-spirited enough to launch such a company, why should not an association of a few individuals try to carry out the scheme. I quite believe Tea proprietors would help them, at starting, by supplying, on reasonable credit, the coarse Teas suitable. Were this done, the thin edge of the wedge would be driven in, and, if the association succeeded, they might later transfer the business at a fair profit to a company.

I had written so far when I saw your remarks on the same subject in your last issue. I cannot agree with you in thinking an association would be *better* than a company, but I say, failing the last let us have the first—in fact, let us make a beginning.

I give here below, to save the trouble of reference, the last part of my former article:—

"I will now, in conclusion, shortly estimate for how much two and four ounce packets could be sold to the consumer.

"Supposing suitable Teas could be bought at six annas per lb. (and all Tea planters know that a very large supply of broken Teas with some red leaf would be available at that price), one ounce would equal 4½ pie or 9 pie for 2 ounces. We may then calculate thus for each 2 ounce packet:

	R.	A.	P.
Tea	0	0	9
Tin foil, company's mark, labour of making up packet, wear and tear, bulking machinery	0	0	3
Profit to company	0	0	3
Price at which company could sell 2 ounce packets ...	0	1	3
Profit to dealer or middleman	0	0	3
Profit to retailer	0	0	3
Cost to consumer for 2 ounce packet	0	1	9

"As making up a 4 ounce packet would be cheaper in proportion, and the profit to company, middleman, and retailer need not be double the 2 ounce rate, we may fairly say that 4 ounce packets could be sold at 3 annas.

"I have sent to England for an estimate of the necessary machinery, so that if my project meets with favour, there will later be no delay on that score."

Surely the above figures, and I believe they are sound, have *the look* of success about them.

I hear it has been suggested that paper packets would deteriorate by keeping, but protected by a good wrapper of tin-foil inside, I feel sure this would not be the case. EDWARD MONEY.

Nothing has been done to this day; and thus, to our shame be it said, we are allowing a market capable of indefinite expansion to remain dormant.

CHAPTER XXXV.

MAKING INDIAN TEA KNOWN IN THE UNITED KINGDOM.

SEVERAL plans have at times been proposed in India with a view to make the merits of pure Indian Teas known in England. When I was last out there I saw the following letter in the *Calcutta Statesman*, and it appeared to me the plan suggested was in every way an excellent one:—

HOW TO PUSH THE SALE OF TEA.

To the Editor " Statesman."

Sir,—Referring to your leader of to-day on the subject of selling Tea at home, I agree with you that Tea-growers should combine for retailing, as they have, through the Syndicate, combined for opening up new markets, but there must be the same spirit of enterprise in the one case as in the other. Now, the mere opening up of shops for the sale of Indian Teas, involving, as it would, rents, expensive establishments, and bad debts, would not afford the necessary scope, nor would it meet the case.

The system of auction in Mincing Lane must with all its drawbacks continue, but it is surely possible to extract some good from it. Let agencies for such a combination as you propose be established in all the large towns in Great Britain, and weekly auctions of packets of Tea from 2 ounces to 5 lbs. or so be held in different parts of each town, so that every day except Sunday there would be an auction going on somewhere. Let the sales be *bonâ fide* to the highest bidder and for cash on the nail, and I will promise that before a year is over, as high prices will be paid at these auctions as are at present realised by Cooper and Cooper, whilst the demand would soon greatly exceed the supply.

If something of the same kind were done in the bazaars of India, the taste which so decidedly exists among natives would develop rapidly. MATT. DREWS.

Calcutta, *January 4th*, 1882.

I wrote the following remarks on the above to the same paper:—

INDIAN TEA SALES AT HOME.

To the Editor "Statesman."

Sir,—Your article of Wednesday on the above, and a letter from Mr. Drews in Thursday's paper, have interested me much. As you truly say, it is more than absurd that the public at home should pay 150 per cent. for our Teas above the prices at which **they are** sold in Mincing Lane, and that this tremendous profit, minus 6*d*. duty, **should** all go into the hands of the retail dealer. Absurd as it is, it **is still a great** fact, and the absurdity can only be increased in one way, **and** that is, if we remain quiet, accept the position, and do nothing.

That we ought to move, and move quickly, is very certain. How **best to act requires serious** consideration, and ample discussion.

You advocate a company or association to sell our Teas retail in all the large towns in Great Britain, and advocate a subscription of Rs. 10 per month by each garden in India, until the business could support itself. Nothing *can* be done unless **we all subscribe a** small sum to set it going, and the amount you mention (Rs. 120 for one year; the necessity would most assuredly last no longer) should frighten no one, while, if done generally by the Indian gardens, it would be ample. I would suggest, therefore, that we should begin the matter as set out below.

The following none of the very many interested in Tea can deny:—

1. The large profits made **on Indian Teas at home are** not realised by the producers, but by **the retail dealers.**

2. We can easily undersell the said retail dealers, to the tune of 50 per cent. **or more, and still work at a** large profit.

3. If the retail dealers were so undersold, an enormous custom would ensue **to us,** or rather the agents we employed.

4. If Indian Teas were procurable at a fair price all over Great Britain, because Indian Tea is superior to China, because those who have drunk Indian never revert to China, because thousands would then taste our Teas for the first time, and continue their use—I say, because of **all this,** little by little, **the consumption** would increase in a ratio we do not dream of now.

5. The consumption so **increased, we should** necessarily, because demand exceeded supply, **get** good prices at **the** public marts in **Calcutta** and London, and **in** consequence thereof the value of all Tea property in India would be greatly enhanced.

I believe all the above would *certainly* follow on a general well-combined movement on our part; but let us take the worst view. No one can deny that they *might* do so. Would Rs. 120 be a large stake from each garden for even the chance? Let us *begin* thus: Open a list in your office for the names of those gardens willing to join. One year's subscription, at Rs. 10 per month, should be the limit from each garden. When enough names are collected to warrant further movement, call a meeting in Calcutta, and let the next steps be decided on, and in the interval—agitate; I will help to the best of my power, and collect opinions from all sides.

Open the list with the names of the three gardens I represent (as per enclosure), equivalent at once to a subscription of Rs. 360.

Now, as to the question—*how* to do it? I give you my views, but let them be criticised and discussed. We want to do it, and to do it the best way.

What I have been suggesting for months in the *Tea Gazette*, as the best thing to do in India—*viz.*, to sell Tea by auction in convenient forms as to quantity for native consumption—is really what I advise for England. I am quite at one with Mr. Drews on this point. (I wish you would reprint his valuable letter above, and then my allusions to it would be understood.) Retail shops and all they would entail, *viz.*, intricate supervision, rents, establishments, and what not, necessitate details quite outside our legitimate sphere as producers. No organisation we could devise would carry on successfully two or three hundred shops at home. We (that is, the company or the association) *could* not efficiently superintend such a complicated business, and we should be cheated right and left. But let others, I say, do the work for us at their own risk, as follows :—

Sell Teas in whole, half, and quarter chests, in tins of 10, 5, and 1 lbs., in packets of 8, 4, and 2 ounces once a week (the market day) in country towns; daily, in different localities in London, Birmingham, Edinburgh, Glasgow, Dublin, and such like cities—all by auction to the highest bidder for *cash*, in lots which would suit both retail dealers and retail purchasers. Never mind if there be a loss at the commencement; the quantities sold, till we felt our way, need not be large.

What would be the result? Retail dealers would shortly sell as much Indian as China Tea, *if they could get it*. Our Teas would go into thousands of houses where it has never been tasted yet. The demand would increase on all sides; prices in Mincing Lane, and consequently in Calcutta, would rise, and no fear of a glutted market could then exist. In two words, Indian Teas would, I believe, six months after such operations were commenced, become the rage in England, and we, **the owners of** Tea property, would add 50 per cent. to the value of our estates.

Is not even the *chance* **of all** this worth an **outlay of Rs.** 120 for each garden? I am proud to head the list with my **Rs. 360**, and I do beg of all interested in Tea to follow my lead.

In the plan I have sketched, like Mr. Drews, **all the operations** would be simple. **The** necessary supervision would **be small**; **the** details easily arranged. **The Teas would of course be** bought in **the** open market in London **and distributed for** public auction to **the** different localities. **There might be** some loss at first (it is for this the **capital is wanted), but if always sold to** the highest bidder, there **would be none—nay, a** handsome profit after a time; and though I do *not* think with Mr. Drews, nor should **I** wish, that the prices would eventually equal Cooper and Cooper's, I do think that the said firm would soon find it useless to advertise their *cheapest* Indian Tea at 3 shillings a pound—Tea for which they certainly paid no more than 13 pence!

I may add that I quite agree with the last paragraph **of Mr.** Drews' letter; but a sale for India and a sale for England **are two** different things, and I will not treat of both **together.**

EDWARD MONEY.

Western Dooars, *January* 7, 1882.

Alas! in this case, like **the one** of supply of Tea to natives, nothing practical came of **it**. A *very few* gardens agreed to **subscribe, and the** matter dropped.

Of all the plans that have been mooted, this of Mr. Drews I believe to be the best. I wish a small company in England would try to initiate it. No greater boon, in my opinion, could be conferred on the Indian Tea industry; and were such a Company, with good names, launched in England, a large proportion of the shares would probably **be taken in India.** A very moderate capital would suffice.

CHAPTER XXXVI.

TEA MACHINERY.

So much has it been extended and improved since the Third Edition was published, I have much to say on this subject.

I will divide it into two headings, "Tea Cultivation" and "Tea Manufacture." Of course the machines for the last far outnumber the first, which are very few, but much of great importance to the industry will find its place under the first heading—

Machinery and Implements for Tea Cultivation.

Formerly, with prices **as they** ruled, Tea paid under **most** circumstances. It is *not* so now. Unless Tea, and good Tea, can be made cheap it is hopeless to look for profit **from a** Tea garden. To cultivate cheaply, and efficiently, **is therefore** all important (far more important than has hitherto been recognized), and assuredly the more machinery can be made **to take the** place of hand labour, the sooner shall we attain **that end.** On this point I need only observe that in most of the Tea districts in India labour has to be imported at a great cost, varying from Rs. 50 to Rs. 100 per **coolie**, and anything which would lessen this want would **materially** help to success.

The following, signed "**Nil Desperandum**," appeared in the *Tea Gazette* in August, 1881. I quite agree **with the writer and** have myself often expressed the **same** opinions:—

PLOUGHING AND HOEING MACHINERY.

Dear Sir,—On looking over your columns I have been surprised to see the small attention paid to agricultural machinery : in fact, I can't find the subject mentioned, although one would imagine it was as important if not more so than manufacturing machinery. Various agricultural instruments, such as ploughs, &c., have, I know, been tried in old times, and not with the best results to the bushes ; but there is no reason why, because the ordinary machines have failed, that planters should be sunk in the belief that that costly article the coolie must endure as long as Tea does.*

I will now consider the cultivation implements I know of.

Planting Pots.—These are made of clay, cow dung, and cut straw. They are placed in the nurseries and the Tea seed planted in them. When the seedlings are big enough to put out, pot and all is buried where the Tea bush is to be. The pot being broken a little when placed in the ground, the rain soon destroys it. The seedling *does not know* it has been transplanted, and the check of six weeks or more, experienced by all transplants, is entirely avoided. I know not who invented the pots, but the idea is an excellent one.

Jebens Transplanter.—This is an implement for lifting seedlings without injuring the rootlets or disturbing the soil around them. It is noticed at page 79 favourably : since that time (1878) it has been used more or less in all Tea districts. I have seen many opinions both for and against it. I believe the truth is it works very well in light soil, and with smallish seedlings, but does not answer in hard soil or with plants above 2½ feet high. Where the soil and size of seedlings are suitable, it certainly saves much of the check experienced otherwise by transplants.

I know of no other peculiar implements for Tea cultivation.

* " Nil Desperandum " evidently foresees what must be sooner or later. All interested in Tea, owners, planters, and inventors, should aid to achieve the result.

The greatest expense connected with cultivation is, naturally, **opening the soil** or digging; the spade is never used in India and would not **answer. Coolies** dig with a kodali, a thing something **like a** spade, with the handle set at right angles to the blade. Could we dispense with this, and cultivate between the lines of Tea with ploughs of any suitable pattern, whether worked by steam or animal power, **an enormous saving** would be **effected.** I am sure the *whole* space between two lines of Tea can never be so done, round each and every bush the soil *must* be opened by hand; **but the centre** space, say about 2½ to 3 feet, could, I am convinced, be so worked, and I think it is only a question of time when it will be so treated.

The planting community are gradually appreciating the fact that something *may* be done in this way. The following appeared in the *Tea Gazette,* **end** of 1881, *re* ploughing by steam :—

Ploughing v. Hoeing.

Dear Sir,—I am glad to **see by the letter of a** "Man in the Kundah" that some managers **have taken up the idea** of ploughing instead of hoeing. It is an idea which I have been dinning into the ears **of** Tea planters ever since I saw a Tea garden. **Mr.** Lyell deserves credit, and so will everyone who assists to introduce ploughing instead of hoeing. The saving of labour would be immense. The gentlemen who are interested in the subject will be glad to learn that I wrote home last month to several leading agricultural machinery people asking **the fullest** particulars as to *steam ploughing machinery*, with a view to seeing how far suitable it would be for Tea cultivation. As soon as all my information arrives, and I have thought the matter out, I will give the planting community my opinion. I have, as far as I am personally concerned, already formed it, and am confident that at no very distant date the steam plough will supersede the *dhangar* or other hand labour. But **of course I** must **make out a** strong case for **it, or** my opinions would be supposed to arise from a professional predilection for machinery. F.

Siligoorie, 27*th November,* **1882.**

TEA MACHINERY.

Again, "Nil Desperandum," quoted above, continues:—

I enclose a report on Darby's Digger from the *Times* and *Pioneer*, which shows that it is an instrument possessing the principle we require in deep hoeing, viz., turning the earth completely over, and bringing the subsoil to the surface, although of course far too unwieldy, costly, and weighty to be used in Tea. It is, however, the first step in the right direction, as it closely copies spade action; and we may hope that before long a machine with that principle, and capable of being **worked in a Tea khet,** will be brought **out**. For light hoeing, last **cold weather** I procured from Messrs. Vipan and Headly, Church **Gate, Leicester,** England, two expanding horse **hoes,** which I worked **all the hot weather,** and which did their work admirably and at a much cheaper rate than can be done by hand **labour. Two of these hoes hoe a 12-acre khet** in six days up the lines **of** Tea and across them, but to make a thorough job it is better to go **over** the work again. The total **cost of this**:—

Planted 4′ × 4′

For one hoe	Pay of boy and man 12 days ...	=	3 6 0	
	Food of bullocks @ 4 as. per diem, Barley @ 24 per Rupee ...	=	2 0 0	
Cost of light hoeing 12-acre khet ...	... ...	=	5 6 0	
			2	
Against			10 12 0	
Nirrikh for 136 bildars, light hoeing, **240 spaces,** 4′ × 4′, per diem @ 0-2-9 each	... ...	=	23 6 0	

Or a saving of more than 100 per cent.

I gave one **12-acre** khet four of these light hoeings during the hot weather, which so thoroughly destroyed the grass seeds that, although heavy rain has fallen here for the last month and a-half, the grass in this khet **is thin and not** more than 6″ high, a fact which, to those who know how the jungle springs up in cultivated ground in the Doon when the rains set in, will be a sufficient proof of the success of these instruments. The frame of the hoe is only 7″ high, and when the blades are buried in the ground is only 4″, and as the handle projects from the centre of the back of the hoe and not from the sides, there is **no danger** of the bushes **being injured. The hoe** will expand from 14″ to 20″ at back, and from 3″ to 7″ in front; and as the standards **of** the blades are curved outwards, the hoe in its greatest expansion **cultivates a** breadth of 27″ of ground. I found that one bullock was too weak to drag a hoe, although a good pony was quite equal to the work, so put in a pair of bullocks. The bullocks and hoe take up between them three rows of Tea at once, the bullocks on each outside row and the hoe in the centre one. A boy walking up the centre row leads the bullocks, which are harnessed to the hoe in the same manner as bullocks are harnessed to the country ploughs, but with longer julas of course. These hoes are, I find, useless during wet weather, as they clog dreadfully, but during hot dry weather they are invaluable. What we now want is a machine that, either by bullock, horse, or steam power, will do our deep hoeing as well as the light hoe does the light hoeing. This is a matter which I consider of vital interest to owners and shareholders, as, unless in these days of very low prices we can reduce the cost of production considerably, we cannot hope that Tea will pay a fair interest on the money expended, and great length of time lost in getting up a garden.

NIL DESPERANDUM.

In the above, two **bullocks to** drag the plough or digger **are evidently** contemplated. My experience is, that two **draught cattle** cannot be used, simply because there is not room for them between **the lines** of Tea.* If animal power is used, it must be **a single** bullock alone. How to harness a single bullock to the plough **is the question.** A collar with a hinge below, which allows it to open at **top,** may be put on from below, and then the sides fastened together at the top. But I advise another plan, which I have seen most successfully **practised** in Austria. The traces, joining together, **and** thus becoming one behind the bullock, are fastened **to the** horns, and tightly connected with a leather pad across the animal's forehead. The bullock thus pulls by his head, and I am sure he can pull in no more efficient **or easier way to** himself. Bullocks in pairs, or singly, are **thus harnessed for plough** work in Austria, and I have seen single animals dragging ploughs of much greater weight and **power than we** should require in our Tea gardens.

* "Nil Desperandum" takes up three spaces—one bullock in each outside space and the hoe in the centre. I don't like the plan. It *could not* be done where the tea plants are high.

Given a proper plough, and I feel sure a large strong bullock thus harnessed would be successful.

A really good Tea garden plough has yet to be invented. All that **is** necessary is to give some agricultural machinists here **at** home the conditions necessary for **success, and I predict what we want would be soon** forthcoming. I will myself try **to do so, let others do the same;** one of us is sure to succeed.

I give all these extracts to show that many think as **I do.**

Cultivation with ploughs **of any kind can never be** feasible except on flat land. The hill gardens in India must **in no case hope to** introduce it; but I sincerely trust the **planters in India** who own level gardens will not rest till **they have solved** the problem, and that **Messrs. Kinmond,** Jackson, and other **inventors of Tea** machinery will give their valuable **aid. The** following two letters from the *Tea Gazette* show the difficulties to be encountered in steam cultivation:—

STEAM CULTIVATION FOR TEA.

Sir,—As promised in your last issue, **I now write to say that I have** received from England the catalogues and price lists of Messrs. Howard, **of** Bedford, Messrs. Barford and Perkins, and other makers of steam ploughing machinery. Messrs. Howard seem to think that the greatest difficulty would be in lifting the return rope over the bushes. This would be certainly a difficulty, but the idea of steam cultivation for Tea is so valuable that it is well worth while thinking this out. I will in your first issue for January give a *resumé* of all the information gleaned from **the** illustrated catalogues and the letters from the engineers at home on the subject of steam ploughing, and will then be glad to co-operate with any gentlemen interested **in** Tea by giving my professional opinion and assistance without fee in endeavouring to solve this matter. I trust, should I ever have **to** write another series of articles on Tea machinery for the *Tea Gazette*, the steam plough may figure as one of the machines which **I will** have to describe as in use on Tea gardens.

Meanwhile the principal difficulty in the way seems to be the **shifting of the** long wire pulling rope over the row of bushes. Let those interested in the subject try to devise a speedy and economical method of doing this.—Yours, &c.,   C. B. FERGUS, C.E.

Siligori, 17th December, 1882.

As to Steam-Ploughing on Tea Gardens.

Sir,—As **promised,** I give you a letter regarding the question as to whether steam-ploughing could be wholly or partially introduced **as** a substitute for manual labour in Tea gardens. I have been in **com**munication with several of the leading makers of steam-ploughing machinery in England, but notably with Messrs. Howard, of Bedford, and Messrs. Barford and Perkins, of Peterborough. These gentlemen forwarded me their illustrated catalogues in duplicate, one set of which I sent to you.

The first question that ensues in regard to the subject is, " Would it pay, even if found feasible ?"

In Assam, Cachar, Sylhet and other places, where labour is scarce, it is probable that the introduction of steam cultivation would be a **great boon to the Tea planter.** **The first cost** of a steam-ploughing apparatus with ropes, plough, and everything complete as in use **in** England on what is called the " single system," **that is,** working **with** only one engine, is about £950. This is heavy, but as a much lighter cultivator would be used for Tea, I think the cost might be reduced to £800—say Rs. 10,000 on the garden. Under moderately favourable circumstances the machinery, making all allowances for native attendants, and the usual difficulties we have to encounter in India through their laziness and stupidity, should cultivate 800 to 1,000 acres per month of twenty working days. The remaining ten days might be occupied in the rains by taking the engine and gear from place to place where it might be required ; for, as the expense of a steam-ploughing engine and apparatus would be too much for any concern, except a very large one, to bear, I suggest that two, three, or four gardens unite and purchase one. There need be no clashing or quarrelling about terms at the end of the season : each should pay his share of the cost of fuel, up-keep, wages, **&c.,** according to the number of days it was on each garden. It would thus be to the interest of each manager to forward it **on to** the man whose turn was next, without delay. Remember, please, that in saying that it would cultivate so many acres in such a time, I mean that it would cultivate two ways—that is **up and** down and **across.** There would remain a little hand-hoeing, &c., round the inner part of the roots of the bushes, but not much, as the cultivator I would design would go partly underneath the laterals and still not hurt the **roots, the** outer lines being much shorter than the inner ones.

Now it is a simple matter to calculate, according to **the rates of the** district in which the reader may be, **the** comparative cost **of cultivating** 1,000 acres of Tea by hand and **by** the steam-plough. The **plough would be worked** for Tea by an 8-H. P. portable engine of any **maker's manufacture.** Wages for one engineman, one cooly to **cut wood, possibly one pair bullocks and cart-driver** to bring barrels of **water, two coolies to shift the anchors, and two more** to assist them **(possibly) in shifting** the **rope, added to the cost of fuel,** and 15 per cent. **per annum added for** repairs **and deterioration,** seems to be the cost **of working.** This would be lessened by **the rope and** anchor-men **and the wood-cutter on the days when** the plough was not at work. Add, however, the cost of elephants or bullocks to take the engine, &c., from garden to garden, and I think it will **be** found that the saving in expense would be very great on the side of the steam-plough as regards cooly labour.

Now, as to the feasibility of the scheme. It is difficult, **without the aid** of plates, to describe how steam-ploughing is done. The engine remains stationary at one **corner of the field. Near it is a** large double windlass, which, **when the cultivator is at work, winds** up the dragging rope with one **barrel of** the windlass, whilst from the other the rope is uncoiling, which will drag the plough down the next furrow. When the plough comes **to** the end of the furrow, two men, one at each end of the rope, shift the anchors, on which are the pulleys round which the rope runs: one furrow breadth forward the plough is double, one set of coulters and shears being at work, while the other set is tilted up in the air by the weight of a man **who sits on** and guides the plough. When the plough is **to return** it **is not** turned round, but the man simply tilts up into the air the set of ploughs that have done their work, and brings down the others. Of course ploughs like this **would** not do for Tea: a special cultivator would be needed. At the end of the furrow the motion of the windlass is reversed, and the drag rope becomes in its **turn** the following rope. In England there **is** an ingenious mechanical **contrivance** for shifting the anchors, which **does** away with two men, as it works automatically. Now the greatest difficulty in the whole matter will be best explained to the reader in Messrs. Howard's own language in their letter to me. They say:—

"The obstacle to the use of steam-ploughs through rows of bushes or trees is the practical difficulty of bringing the slack or following rope into position for following the implement back on its return journey. The rope cannot be lifted over the intervening row of bushes, and to employ draught animals to take the rope up the next alley between the bushes would add to the expense of the work, and would impede it." They continue: "If it is important that the land be broken up to a depth of 9 inches, and the obstacles to effecting this by animal power are practically insuperable, the steam plough worked on the single system, with animals to convey the slack from end to end of the land, would probably be the most effectual and economical method of working."

Now if this difficulty could be overcome (and I confess it is a rather formidable one), I quite believe that on fairly straight land, even if somewhat sloping, with straight rows of bushes, and the land clear of stumps, steam cultivation would be easy. On hill gardens, or gardens where the Tea is irregularly planted, on ground much traversed by nullahs or having stumps left in, the steam cultivator could not work. There may be some method of lifting the rope over the bushes. Coolies might be stationed at intervals along the row, and with the aid of a very light block and tackle might hoist long bights of the rope high enough to clear the bushes. The block and tackle would be fastened to the top of a light pole. One man would hold the pole while the other hove up, and (the pole being midway between the two rows) might incline it over till above the next row and then lower away. A strong 10ft. bamboo, a pair of light wooden blocks, and an inch and a half Manilla rope, would be all that would be requisite. Other projects for effecting this may strike some of your readers, and what I want is, that those who may think the idea of steam-ploughing of any value should co-operate together to work it out in a practical form: I will give every assistance in my power.

We can scarcely hope, in the present depressed state of the Tea market, that proprietors will club together to subscribe to bring out a set of steam cultivating apparatus in order to institute experiments on the subject. Should 1883 bring better times, something of the sort might be done, and it is as well to have the matter well thought out and discussed beforehand, so that should a series of experiments take **place**, people would be **prepared for** any contingencies which might arise, and **perhaps** be **better prepared to** overcome these difficulties through the matter having been previously well discussed.

It is now the **season** for opening out Tea gardens, and one piece of advice I would give to planters—that is this. It is quite possible that steam ploughing for Tea cultivation is a **thing** of the future, **or may** be nearer than you imagine: therefore be careful to have your lines of Tea very straight, both along and **across, so that there** would be no obstacle to the plough or cultivator working. If **you** object to the expense of taking out stumps, they may remain in, as they could be taken out afterwards.

I trust your readers, Mr. Editor, will not view this subject **with indifference,** but will co-operate in endeavouring to solve the problem. —I am yours faithfully, "TEA MACHINERY."

Though the signatures **differ,** I conceive Mr. C. B. Fergus, C.E., wrote the second as well as the first. He **has** evidently **pondered the matter well.** Let others do so too, and I foretell that the day is not far distant when *flat* Tea gardens will, in a great measure, be cultivated by steam or animal power. When this is so, even 8 annas (say 10*d*.) per lb. for our **Tea** all round should pay **us well.**

Tea Manufacturing Machinery.

The processes in Tea manufacture, as generally practised in India to-day, are—

1. Plucking.
2. Withering.
3. Sorting green leaf in a measure, and separation of Pekoe Tips.
4. Rolling.
5. **Fermenting.**
6. **Drying or firing.**
7. Sorting.
8. Final heating before packing.

No. 3 is not always **done, the** others invariably.

I will consider the machines invented for each process, in the order of the said processes.

Plucking.—No machine has ever been invented for this, and I do not think any is possible.

Withering.—In any but continued wet weather no artificial means are necessary. The leaf, spread thinly and exposed to the action of the air below and around (former attained by any kind of mesh), withers perfectly.* In continued wet weather artificial means are sometimes required. The various Dryers in use (see further on) are sometimes supposed to furnish the means, but their use necessitates much labour, nor is the result satisfactory. A good withering machine (it must be on a large scale) might, I think, be easily invented; there is none at present. Why do none of the inventors of other Tea machinery try to succeed in this?

Sorting Green Leaf.—This is sometimes attempted in a rough way by the use of sieves of different meshes. To separate the fine from the coarse leaf, and in some cases to eliminate the Pekoe tips, is the object. A machine by John Greig and Co., of Edinburgh, professes to do the latter. I have never seen it, but I doubt any machine abstracting the Pekoe tips alone. A machine which would, however, separate the fine from the coarse leaf previous to rolling is, I think, quite feasible, and it would conduce much to good Tea. This, again, is an opening for inventors.

Rolling.—This is perhaps the most important of all processes in Tea manufacture. The object of it is to break the cells in the Tea and liberate the sap (fermentation could not take place otherwise), and further to give a tight

---

* In wet weather especially the warm air generated in the factory by the fires in it helps the process.

roll or twist to the leaf. Formerly this was always done by hand (it is so done in China, I believe, to this day), but the process was lengthy, expensive and dirty. I might perhaps add inefficient, for doubtless machine-rolled Tea is better done (better in appearance, better in liquor) than hand-rolled.

I will now consider—

Tea Rolling Machines.

The inventors are Jackson, Kinmond, Haworth, Lyle, Greig and Thompson. There may be others, but I have not heard of them.

Jackson has invented five machines. The details of each, how much each can do, the testimonials regarding them, &c., would fill many pages. All can be seen in the illustrated catalogue he supplies, so I will only offer a few general remarks. All planters know Jackson's rollers, and they are held in high estimation. His last invention (if I mistake not) is the Rotary Tea Roller, which is on quite a different principle to the others. It consists of an elongated revolving barrel or cylinder, with a polygonal *internal* surface, and a roller with a fluted *external* surface, mounted within the said barrel its whole length. These revolve in opposite directions (the roller the quicker) and the leaf is rolled in the annulus between. It is not yet known what the success of this last invention will be. Not so with his Cross-action and Excelsior Rollers. These are first-rate machines, and all who have tried speak well of them.

Kinmond invented the first Tea roller (see page 117), many years ago. Many improvements resulted, eventually, in his " Improved Double Action Tea Roller," which is a very good machine and has given satisfaction to the many who have used it. From all I have heard and seen, however, I doubt if, **take** it all in all, it is equal to Jackson's **Cross Action** Excelsior. Kinmond, **some two** years ago, **invented** a "Centrifugal Roller." It was made in two sizes. The smaller seems to have done well, not so the larger; one of the latter on the Phoolbarry garden (in which I am **interested) has** proved **a failure.** But Mr. Kinmond has quite lately materially altered the said Centrifugal machines, and is confident that they *will* do well. **He is** now leaving for India **with** one, and anticipates good results.

Tea machinery is still so much in its infancy that **the best machines are likely to be improved upon, and perhaps superseded by others, but as things are now, I think, though some** do not agree **with** me, that Jackson has carried off the **palm** in rollers.

The following two letters on rollers appeared in the *Tea Gazette,* **and** are well **worth attention :—**

KINMOND'S IMPROVED PATENT DOUBLE ACTION TEA ROLLING MACHINE.

Sir,—You have so repeatedly asked planters to supply you with information regarding "Tea machinery" that it is **a matter** of surprise **to** me you have not been flooded with letters on the subject. I know very little about Tea machinery, as I am not an engineer, but I gladly contribute my quota of knowledge on the subject. I have been rolling leaf for some time past in one of Kinmond's old machines, styled his "Improved Patent Double Action Tea Rolling Machine." A machine for *fine* leaf I do not believe there is in existence. I have seen several machines at work on different factories, and I should say **for** *fine* **leaf this machine** of Kinmond's **cannot** be beat.* A few **improvements could no doubt be** made, **and** I feel sure Mr. Kinmond himself is aware of this, **and is** quite competent **to** make them. I have seen Mr. Kinmond's "Compound Action Centrifugal" at work. I do not consider it a success. It certainly cannot hold a candle to his "Patent Double Action." **I would** strongly recommend Mr. Kinmond to improve the latter, and forego the former, unless he can make some

---

* This, after the previous sentence, is obscure.—E. M.

very material alterations to it. The roll from the "**Centrifugal**" comes out hot and flat, whereas that from his "Patent Double Action" **is** turned out not only perfectly cool, but has a perfect twist.* For *coarse* leaf, Jackson's "Excelsior" is a splendid machine. I should **say a** factory could not want two better machines than one of Kinmond's "Patent Double Action" and one of Jackson's "Excelsior" Rollers—the former for *fine*, the latter for *coarse* leaf. Will some of my brother planters kindly give their experience, and thus further enlighten an anxious ENQUIRER.

Tea Rolling Machinery.

Dear Sir,—I **will be glad if** some of your numerous readers **will** kindly furnish **results** of trials, or of experience, of Kinmond's **Compound Action Centrifugal Tea Rolling Machine.** I have tried it repeatedly, and find it not only heats the green leaf a great deal too much, but in addition cuts, I may say into mincemeat, about 5% of the leaf in the process of rolling. I am not an engineer, and therefore cannot state for certain where the fault lies, but I fancy the ribs of the two revolving plates **are somewhat at fault.** If they were broader and bolder, the machine might, perhaps, be **a** better success. **The green** leaf does not come out sufficiently rolled. The major **portion** of the roll is too flat. Perhaps Mr. Kinmond will kindly help by giving a hint or two to a perplexed Tea-house "**Assistant.**"

Haworth's Roller.—This **machine was invented long ago. The** leaf is placed **in bags and so** rolled. **In** some respects **the** machine **resembles a** mangle. It has not been largely **used, and thus is not** much known. I have no personal experience of its worth, but have heard much of it from an old friend of mine, Mr. Carter, of the Chandpore Tea Estate, Chittagong. He has, I believe, had one from the first on his plantation, and thinks very well of it. Mr. Carter is a **first-rate** judge **on** all **Tea matters. He** conducted some experiments to test the value of Tea **rolled by** Jackson's and Haworth's Rollers, and did it with great **care,** that the quality of leaf, the withering, the drying, all **but** the two modes of

* I agree with "Enquirer" in this.—E. M.

rolling should be *exactly* the same. The samples were then **sent** to Calcutta and valued. Results as below :—

Messrs. Carritt and Co.'s report on the samples is dated Calcutta, 29th October, 1881, *viz.* :—

Chandpore leaf rolled by Haworth's machine :—Large irregular open unassorted leaf, brisk, fair flavour, little strong—Re. 0-9-9.

Chandpore leaf rolled by Jackson's machine :—Leaf preferable, closer rolled, liquor inferior, not very strong—Re. 0-9-0.

Sungoo leaf rolled by Haworth's machine :—Rather large **irregular** loosely **twisted** unassorted leaf, flavoury, little brisk—Re. 0-9-3.

Sungoo leaf rolled by Jackson's machine :—Leaf little preferable, liquor inferior, wanting briskness—Re. 0-8-9.

By above it appears Haworth's gave better liquor, and Jackson's the best Tea in appearance. From all I have heard I think it likely Haworth's roller has not received the attention it deserves.

Lyle's Roller.—I have never seen this. From the drawing **before me** it has no resemblance to other rollers. The **inventor** claims for **it simplicity,** cheapness, strength, durability, good rolling, and large outturn **with** a minimum **of labour.** One testimonial I have seen **speaks** very highly **of its** capabilities.

Greig's Roller.—This I have not seen or heard of. I **can** only give **the** description sent me by the inventor :—

The Greig Link and Lever Tea Rolling Machine, worked by one man, and suitable for rolling the finest nibs without breaking them, or to crush the coarsest leaf into broken black at will. It can roll a large or small quantity equally well. Price £70, delivered in Edinburgh. Small size suitable **for cattle** gear, £45. Cattle gear, £20, delivered in Edinburgh.

The Calcutta Agent **of the Luckea** Moung Lung Tea Estate, Sonada, Darjeeling, in sending remittance for a large size machine which has been working there all the past season, says: "I am informed the machine does its work in a most satisfactory manner, rolling better than by hand : I am pleased to have to state this."

Thompson's Challenge Roller.—This (quite lately invented) though given last is likely, by all I hear, to stand **well** among rollers. I have no drawing **or** description of it, but *why* I think well of it is that a Tea engineer, Mr. Ansell, of Kurseong, who thoroughly understands Tea machinery, thinks so highly of the machine that he has recommended its purchase by the Phoolbarry Tea Company. I have every faith in Mr. Ansell's judgment, and feel confident therefore the machine **must** be a good one. One feature and **advantage claimed for it is,** " free contact of the leaf throughout the roll with the outer air."

I may conclude my remarks on rollers with a quaint **letter** (from *Tea* ***Gazette***) **by a native.** If he can judge of Tea machinery **as well as he** can write English his opinion is worth preserving :—

TEA ROLLING MACHINERY.

Dear Sir,—On the subject of Tea-leaf rolling machinery, the **(to** all appearance) strangely opposite results I have obtained from machines of the same make have led me **to the** following conclusions, viz. :—

1. All " genuses " of **machines are equally good.**

2. There **are hardly two** " **species** " **of the same genus which give** similar results.

3. **Changing the** " fixings " **of a** machine makes all the difference **in the world.**

Ergo a good mechanic will have a good machine **whether he** patronize Jackson, Kinmond, Haworth, or any other inventor.

I think with your correspondent " A Voice from Assam" that the machine that gives the roll quickly, and in a continuous supply, is the best.

I would defy any man to prove that any *inventor* has it " all his own way," for I certainly have not found it so in my experience.

Yours truly,
KOL MISTRY.

Before going to press I received drawing and description of "Thompson's Challenge Roller." It is impossible to judge of its merits by the drawing, but some very strong testimonials are appended—one much in its favour from Mr. Ansell, the Tea engineer above mentioned. By the testimonials (more than one from men I know) the following advantages appear to have been obtained :—

"Balling" of the leaf is avoided.
The tips are kept quite bright.
Heating prevented.
Simplicity of "feed" and "discharge."
One attendant, a minimum of motive power, and low priced.
A good twist attained.
Simplicity in the machine, and ease of transport and erection.

If all the above are facts, I quite think the "Challenge" will prove a great success.

The following, written by me to the *Tea Gazette*, may be worth the attention of Tea-rolling machine inventors :—

Suggestions for Improving the Drums and the Faces of the Rollers in Tea Rolling Machinery.

Sir,—The following idea, suggested to me by a planter up here, may be practicable or not, but in any case it is worth letting the patentees of Tea-rolling machines know it.

In days gone by when iron worked in contact with iron on the faces of rollers the colour of the outturn (that is the infused Tea leaves) was quite destroyed. That is now remedied, but there is still an evil of less importance. The wood on the said faces of the rollers absorbs the sap of the leaf, and unless they are washed very clean, the said old sap is apt to contaminate, more or less, the new leaf. Could not this be rectified by making the faces of the rollers of porcelain or iron (like camp crockery) and the drums of opaque coarse **glass**? Both these, if they would **stand**, could easily **be** washed quite clean.

I give the idea, given to me, for what it **is** worth, and would invite the opinion of other planters on it.   EDWARD MONEY.

Darjeeling, *November 10th,* 1880.

Fermenting is the next process in the list. After the leaf is rolled it is put together; some make it up in truncated balls, some put it in baskets, but in either case it is allowed to stand until a given amount of fermentation has set in. This is done in the warm atmosphere of the factory. Naturally no machine is required for this process; but shelves, at varying height from the factory floor, are useful to regulate the fermentation, inasmuch as the higher the shelf the warmer the air, and warmth hastens the process. This plan of shelves was devised by Mr. J. Fleming, at the Phoolbarry Garden, and it seemed to me to answer well.

Drying or *Firing* comes next. Up to this point the leaf is of a brownish green colour, and soft. After the drying it is black and crisp, in fact, made Tea. By the drying process all the moisture in the mass is driven off. For many years charcoal only was used to fire Tea, and it was an established belief that *the fumes* given out by the said charcoal had some chemical effect on the Tea—in fact, that good Tea could not be made without it. When, twelve years ago, I published the First Edition of this Essay, I had begun to doubt the soundness of the above belief, and four years later I had thoroughly satisfied myself of its fallacy. It was not, however, till 1877-78 that I devised *a means* of firing Teas without charcoal. The invention was well received, and thought well of. At all events, it *proved* what I had long urged—viz., that any fuel, if contact with the smoke was avoided, would dry Tea. My invention was a very crude one, and **quickly superseded by far more** perfect designs; **still** I have the satisfaction **of** knowing that on this head I have done much to perfect Tea manufacture, and that the conviction I had attained **to** in 1874 is now general and practised throughout **India.** (Pages 119-121, 295, to end of Addenda, bear out the **above** remarks.)

I will now **consider the various**

Tea-Drying Machines.

Robertson's Typhoon.—This is a late invention: it was noticed in the *Tea Gazette* in 1881. It had, however, made a great noise at end of 1880, and so well was it spoken **of,** many, in the early part of 1881, purchased it. The following was the report as to its merits (*Tea Gazette,* September, 1881):—

ROBERTSON'S TYPHOON.

Mr. J. M. Robertson, manager of the Arcuttipore Tea Company's Gardens, has invented **a new Tea-drying** apparatus which he has named the "Typhoon." A number of the planters of his district met at his garden, by invitation, to test the merits of his machine. We quote the verdict recorded by them in their own words, and also append the brokers' report on the Teas which were manufactured in their presence during the trial.

The "Typhoon" **is** a simple and inexpensive construction of brick **and** iron, which **can be** erected without skilled labour. The heating material used is coke, and the quantity of coke required for a maund of Tea is stated to be one quarter of a maund.

The out-turn from the "Typhoon" we found to be at the rate of one half maund of thoroughly dried Tea per hour, and the manner in which **the work** was done **was to our entire** satisfaction, some of us thinking that the apparatus was capable of doing **more.**

The inventor leads us to understand that **the** entire cost of **construction** and material will not be over Rs. 300, and we do not see **that this sum** need be exceeded.

We are unanimously of opinion that unless the dryers at present in use are very materially reduced in price, they will be beaten off the field by the " Typhoon."

Messrs. William Moran & Co.'s report on the Teas is as follows :—

Typhoon Teas.	London value.	Cal. Equi. Ex. 1-8½.
Pekoe, very well made leaf, with **ends**, good brisk flavour	1 10	14
Orange Pekoe, very well twisted leaf, good amount of tip, very good brisk flavour ...	2 0	15¼
Br. Pekoe, leafy **black Br.** Pekoe, some ends strong	2 1	1
Pekoe Souchong, **well twisted leaf, some ends** good flavour	1 3	9
Souchong, small **good even grey leaf,** brisk	1 1	7¾

The above are very desirable Teas as regards leaf and liquor.

The following are some of the chief features and advantages of this machine :

1. The low cost.
2. Durability, there being nothing except the **trays that can** suffer from wear and tear.
3. The small quantity of fuel required—about ¼ maund of coke for kutcha firing 1 maund of Tea.
4. Ease in stoking, **the furnace** not requiring attention oftener than once every one and a-half to two **hours.**
5. Absolute **and immediate control over the** temperature, which can be raised or lowered instantaneously.
6. No " **getting up heat** " required. In fifteen minutes after beginning to **light the fire** the apparatus is ready for work.
7. Requires no troublesome cleaning out.
8. Quantity. The apparatus is capable of drying at least 40 lbs. an hour, **and** has frequently dried over 50 lbs.
9. Quality of Tea is equal to that obtained **by any process** hitherto introduced.

Of course **all the above** was very favourable, and its low price gained it many purchasers. **I think,** as a *first* success, it beat any machine **yet** invented. But, alas! its fall was sudden **as** its rise, **for,** judging from several letters in the

R

Tea Gazette, the purchasers were not satisfied with its capabilities, and I doubt consequently if it is now manufactured; still I may be wrong.

Allen's Tea Drying Apparatus.—I have never seen this, and have not heard much about it. Advantages claimed for it are—1. Quick drying. 2. Coke can be used as a drying agent, 10 seers to one maund of Tea. 3. Only manual labour required. 4. Not necessary to turn the Tea. 5. Perfect control over temperature. I have three testimonials to its merits before me, one from an engineer, and all three speak highly of it.

The following letter from the inventor to the *Tea Gazette* gives further information:—

ALLEN'S PATENT DRYING MACHINE.

Dear Sir,—Some time back your valuable paper contained a description and rough drawing of my Patent Drying Machine. I now beg to say that the machine is in the market.

I will simply state here that it can dry one maund of Tea per hour, or about equivalent to four maunds of leaf.

It cannot burn the Tea as in other machines, yet it thoroughly dries it at one fill of the machine.

It takes half a maund of Tea at each fill, and every leaf of this is done in exactly the same time; no turning over, changing of trays, or further looking after the Tea, after the roll has been placed in the machine on the trays.

Temperature can be lowered from 300° to 100° in two or three seconds, and run up again in five to seven minutes.

It will burn any fuel. Fireplace $2\frac{1}{2}' \times 3'$, when kept regularly three quarters full of firewood or coal about 6 to 8 inches thick, while machine is drying, will suffice (half a maund of fuel to a maund of Tea should be ample). The appearance and fine flavour of Tea dried in this machine by fan beats charcoal; no gloss is lost on the Tea from shaking up and turning over, and the Tea is black, with glossy appearance and good flavour.

The following are valuation and reports on this machine's dried Tea, by Messrs. William Moran and Co., to whom some of bulk or rough Tea was sent.—Yours, &c., J. C. ALLEN.

I omitted to extract the broker's reports, but they were favourable. I think it likely this Dryer is well suited to small gardens, which cannot afford steam motive power.

Davidson's Sirocco.—Many of these, over 200, have been set up in all the Tea districts; it has done good work in its time: had it not done so it would not so long (some years) have commanded attention. When it came out it was, I think, the best machine going. I doubt much that being the case now. It requires no motive power, and is thus, in that respect, cheap to work. The following letter to the *Tea Gazette* in many respects embodies my views of the machine:—

THE SIROCCO.

Dear Sir,—As both sides of a question, *viz.* for and against, should be stated before the public for their judgment, I think I may say that, as far as we have seen in *print*, the " Sirocco " is a " first rate Tea-drying machine." I beg to state that *all* does not appear in print, though what does appear there may be quite true, and quite right too for the seller to get as many sales of it as he can, for who would be such an ass as to cry down his own invention or anything else he wished to profit by. The " Sirocco," as I have seen (and I have seen over ten, and amongst them the latest improved ones), does not thoroughly fire off the Tea without burning it: the Tea must be taken out of the machine when three parts fired, and allowed to cool, when its own heat, and the fact of it being gathered in one place, give sufficient heat to finish the kutcha firing, but pucka batti is required after that. Again, the advertisement would lead one to suppose that the drying is effected by means of the draught of hot air entirely: now if this were the case, when the fires are first lighted in the machine, the hot air would at once be of sufficient heat to dry Tea; but this is not the case, for the whole iron work, in fact, the whole apparatus, iron work, &c., has to be heated up by fire, and when a litle off red hot, the Tea is put in and fired. I do not mean to say that hot air does not ascend through the Tea, but I contend that the heat of the iron has more to do with the drying; there is no detriment to the Tea, I feel convinced, whether it is dried by hot iron or hot air, but there is a very considerable detriment to the machine. Let purchasers ask any engineer, or even blacksmith, **how** quickly iron burns away, and he can tell them.

Up **to date no** doubt the "Sirocco" has seen its run: over 200 **are** advertised **as in** use, but **it is now** beaten by two machines which **have come out** lately, and which beat the "Sirocco" entirely as to quantity dried and simplicity of working, and for durability should last any time by careful looking after. One is Robertson's, which is firebrick, and the other Allen's; both these machines for durability cannot be surpassed: the difference in results between the two is, that one dries every tray of Tea in the same time without turning over, and the other requires to have the Tea turned over and the **trays changed,** &c., as in the "Sirocco."

The "Sirocco," no doubt, was a good Tea-drying machine in its **time, and** the inventor deserves the greatest credit for it, but it has been improved upon, **as is** always inevitably **the case in** machinery.

I trust no offence will **be** taken by the "**Sirocco**" **inventor, as such is not intended.** Any answer of his will be gladly **read.**

Cachar. Yours faithfully, PUCKA TEA.

There may have been an answer, but I did not see it.

Gibbs and Barry's Tea Dryer.—This machine has been lately invented. I saw it when not as complete as it is now. I have tried to get details, but failed. It must have merit, however, for though a late machine, some thirty-six **are now** in operation; I heard one good judge speak **very well of it.** More are, I hear, being despatched to India. **No trays are used** with this Dryer.

Shand's Dryer.— This hails from Ceylon. Steam for drying **Tea is not quite a new idea. I saw** an apparatus to **use steam in Cachar years** ago. The great advantage claimed for this Dryer is that Tea cannot be burnt. It is quite **a** new invention. This, from the *Tea Gazette*, describes it :—

A NEW TEA DRYER.

A gentleman in Colombo, Ceylon, a Mr. C. Shand, as we mentioned in our last, has invented a new patent Tea Dryer. The following is a description of his invention :—

The barbacue-shaped steam-heated **Tea Dryer is the cheapest**, most economical and safest drying machine.

As this machine **can be** made any length **and** width, the quantity of leaf which can **be** manufactured is only limited by the extent of drying surface. One, 5 feet wide, and 15 feet long, will admit of about forty pounds of Tea being spread as thinly as on Sirocco trays, and, if heated to 150° Fahrenheit, would dry a maund per **hour.** The steam for heating thin galvanized **iron** drying surface is generated in the space (3 inches) between it **and the** thin boiler plate bottom.

The machine, which **is made** steam-tight, **is** partially **filled with water,** and placed **on a** fire **stove. It is** evident that a comparatively **small quantity of fuel will generate sufficient** steam to heat **a large surface, especially if the smoke flue is placed** under the whole length **of the** machine.

As it is impossible to fire-burn the Tea, dried by the steam-heated Dryer, the enormous advantage of being independent of the care and judgment of coolies, and of the necessity of uninterrupted European supervision, is too evident to require comment.

Then comes the figure of the Dryer with the following note :—

"Barbacue-shaped Tea Dryer.—The far end should be slightly higher than that **over** the fire, to allow the space over it to be full of water.

An apparatus for escape of steam and supplying water is inserted in the end plate covering the boiler."

The *Ceylon Observer*, referring to **the** above, asks **the** following questions :—

Is it really impossible by means of steam to over-heat, though we **may** not, indeed cannot, **"fire-burn"** Tea ? And when a boiler is **employed to generate** steam, **do we** become quite independent of the care and judgment **of** coolies, and avoid the necessity of uninterrupted European supervision ? Will not a thermometer be necessary to indicate the proper degree of heat, will it not require close watching, and will there not be danger **of the** boiler exploding if neglected ? The danger may be reduced to a minimum, but we **should be** glad of proof that it cannot exist.

Mr. Shand in reply **writes**—With reference **to your** remarks and queries regarding my Tea-drying machine, will you allow me to mention that, as it is not intended **to** sustain any pressure of steam, the drying surface cannot easily be heated **over** 150 degrees.

As a matter of course, the **Tea takes** a longer time to dry than when **made by** Siroccos, in which the temperature is maintained at **275 degrees, but** the extent of drying surface available makes this a matter of secondary importance.

I did not mean that no care or attention is required to keep up fire and supply boiling water periodically from a cistern placed over the flue; but you **can** understand **that** the same **care,** judgment and observation is **not** required to dry Tea at a comparatively low temperature **as at a very** high one: for instance, **it does not** injure **coffee** to allow **it to remain** on the barbacue after it is **thoroughly dry; but** put it **in** a roaster, and what care and judgment **is not required to** perfect **the** roasting!

No doubt, by the use of Siroccos and other modern appliances, **the risk** of fire-burning **is** now greatly diminished, but these still require **great care in** shifting **the** trays **and** watching the thermometer. This constant watching is obviated by the use of my machine, and all the superintendent has to do is to feel when the Tea becomes crisp and dry. He **has the** security that, if this is neglected **to be** done at the **moment it is** sufficiently dry, no injury takes place by **its** remaining on **the heated surface.**

The **machine is especially adapted for redrying Tea** before packing, this being an operation carried on **at a low** temperature, and requiring a good deal of care.

There are, it is well known, two difficulties connected with the proper manufacture of Tea, requiring at present the constant supervision of the superintendent: these are fermentation and firing. **If** the necessity of closely watching the latter can be dispensed with, it gives the superintendents more time to direct the fermentation, on **which the** colour of the infused leaf, and consequently the value, so **greatly depends.**

I have now considered all the Dryers I know of except Kinmond's and Jackson's. I have purposely left these to the last. While in the case of Rollers I thought Jackson had done best, in Dryers I most decidedly award the first **place** to Kinmond.

Jackson's Dryer.—A long and exhaustive report upon it from Mr. Carter, **of the Chandpore** Garden, Chittagong, appears in the *Tea Gazette*, November 7, 1881. It is too long to insert here. No one can read it and doubt that the trials were most carefully conducted, and without bias of any kind. The results are not in favour of the machine. Moreover, were Jackson's Dryers a real success I should have been aware of the fact long ago. I incline to the belief Mr. Jackson thinks he can do better, for he has lately brought out a Self-acting Tea Dryer regarding which the following appeared in the *Tea Gazette* :—

Jackson's New Self-acting Tea Dryer.

Messrs. W. and J. Jackson have invented a new apparatus that will deal with the Tea itself throughout the drying process, and thus, they submit, secure a perfection in the dessication of the leaf not hitherto obtained. The objects arrived at by the new invention are as follows :—

1.—After the leaf is fed into the machine it requires no more attention until it is discharged dry.

2.—Every individual leaf is simultaneously exposed in precisely a similar manner to the action of the heated air, thus producing an unvaried and perfectly even dried leaf.

3.—The Tea is steadily but very slowly kept in motion, thereby dispensing with the tedious and tiring watchfulness of attendants, hitherto required in Tea drying on the tray system.

4.—There are no trays about the machine to handle, and it is, therefore, thoroughly durable and cannot get out of order.

In operating with the machine, a boy or attendant has simply to spread the leaf on a slowly moving feeding web or band, which carries it forward and places it in the machine, where it is steadily but inactively kept in motion, and in due course is discharged dry and crisp from a shoot at the delivery end ; so long, therefore, as the attendant continues to supply the machine with leaf, it will steadily dry and discharge it, and should he have occasion to leave the machine at any time, no injury can take place to the leaf in the apparatus, as it must pass on and be discharged.

The leaf is continuously, but very slowly, turned over, disentangled and individually presented to the action of the heated air by a peculiar combination of concentric cylinders, thus ensuring not only the most uniform fermentation, but the drying of each leaf being simultaneously effected alike **must** produce an unvaried briskness and quality of liquor not obtainable from any of the methods of drying at present known.

The machine will dry about forty maunds of green leaf per day, **and** will be approximately 9′ long, **3½**′ wide, and 8′ high.

The apparatus will take **very** little driving, which can either be effected by steam or hand power. It is very simple, easily erected, and self-contained.

I know nothing about this new Dryer beyond what **is printed above, and** I rather doubt if any have yet been set **up.** *If* the advantages detailed are truly all realised, they **are** doubtless of much value.

Kinmond's Dryer.—I shall devote **extra** space to this, for I *believe* in it. I have seen it working for a long time on the **Phoolbarry** Garden, and **I** continue since **I** left India to receive good **reports of it**. This is what the inventor **himself says of it recently :—**

This Tea-drying machine continues to give great satisfaction. The improvements made last year considerably increased **the** out-turn of Tea, and reduced the amount of fuel required. Further improvements **have** this year been introduced in fastening the iron plates at the corners of the trays with copper rivets, and otherwise strengthening the trays, remedying many small defects suggested by planters who are using the Dryers, and in improving the arrangement of the fire-bricks over the furnace. The latter, as well as some of the smaller alterations, were suggested by Mr. Ansell (inventor of the sifting machine which bears his name), an engineer who has had great experience in and around Darjeeling in erecting and working all the three sizes of these Dryers.

This is the only Tea-drying machine which can keep pace with the largest rolling machines. It **is** made in three sizes. The capacity of the **smallest or** No. 1 Dryer **is one** maund of pucka Tea per hour. The capacity of No. 2 Dryer is two maunds per hour, and that of No. 3 Dryer is three maunds per hour. The consumption of fuel is less than one maund of wood fuel to one maund of pucka Tea dried.

One of the great advantages of this Tea Dryer is the facility it gives for *final firing* before packing. The enhanced price of Tea which has been dried and final fired in this Dryer is well shewn in the high average of 1s. 6d. per lb., which the Scottish Assam Company's Teas have fetched this season. See letters annexed from their superintendent in Assam, Mr. Cruickshanks, and their secretary in Edinburgh, Mr. Moffat.

When *final* firing Tea with the Dryer, it is found convenient to place a fine gauze cover over the top trays in each compartment, to prevent any of the Tea dust being carried away with the hot air which passes through the Tea.

In order to get the maximum quantity of work from the Dryer, the trays must be spread with rolled leaf twice as thick as that used when Tea is dried over charcoal, where there is no forced current of air, and after the Tea has been *half-dried*, then the Tea on *two* trays should be spread on *one* tray, and the drying finished. In the Dryers now in course of construction, the trays have been made one-half deeper, so that the half-dried Tea on *three* trays should be finished in *one* tray. The out-turn of the machine is greatly diminished when the foregoing method is not observed; and owing to its non-observance, many of the Dryers in use have never been worked to their greatest capacity.

The Dryer should be lined outside with one thickness of bricks—they are the cheapest and best non-conductors of heat—inferior or badly-burned bricks may be used. Both ends of the Dryer should be lined, and both sides and elbows as high as the trays. The top may either have a lining of bricks, or four inches thick of sand or clay. When the Dryer is lined round with bricks, it not only greatly reduces the consumption of fuel, but by preventing the radiation of heat, it enables the men to increase the out-turn of pucka Tea.

The Dryer is extremely simple and compact—the No. 2 size occupies a space of about 7 feet long and 3 feet wide. The fan of this Dryer requires about half a horse-power to drive it.

The fan should be driven at a speed of 500 revolutions per minute. The pulley on the fan spindle is $7\frac{1}{2}$ inches diameter and 4 inches wide.

Owing to the satisfaction given by these Dryers this season, an exceptionally large number of orders are on hand, and although a number of each size is generally kept in stock, the patentee will be obliged to those requiring Dryers for next season to kindly send in their orders early.

No. 1 Dryer, capable of drying one maund of pucka Tea per hour, £150; **No.** 2 Dryer, capable of drying two maunds of pucka Tea per hour, £220; No. 3 Dryer, capable of drying three maunds of pucka Tea per hour, £300. These prices are f.o.b. in London.

London Agents—Messrs. Geo. Williamson and Co., 7, East India Avenue; Calcutta Agents — Messrs. Williamson, Magor and **Co.,** 4, Mangoe Lane.

The best of the three sizes is No. 3. **I have** quite lately **sent out** two of them, one for the Phoolbarry, one for the Leesh Company's Gardens, both in the Western Dooars. I **think** the prices are much too high, and might with advan**tage (to both** inventor and planters) be reduced; but as to the excellence of the machine there **can,** I think, be no doubt. My opinion is shared by many. I have before me many testimonials as to its excellence. Space forbids me inserting them here, but Mr. Kinmond or his agents will send them on application.

In March, 1881, **so** satisfied was I even then with the Dryer **(both** the manager, **Mr.** Pillans, at Phoolbarry, and I am still more so *now*), **I wrote** the following to the *Tea Gazette*, and I give it here as details are embodied :—

KINMOND'S TEA DRYER.

To all interested in Tea in India, and their name is legion, Tea manufacturing machinery and its capabilities must be a subject **of great** interest.

Though Tea prices may, and I think to a certain extent will, revive, **the old** scale which existed previous to the late serious fall will never probably **return.** How serious **the** fall has been will be appreciated when I **state that** gardens which previously realised 14 **annas to 1** rupee for **their** produce think **now** they do well if they obtain an average of 10 annas. Thus, an average of 12 annas (even if **the** partial rise I hope for **takes** place) will probably be more than **most** Indian plantations will get in the future. In **two** words, the Tea **industry** of India is passing through **a** period of depression and a crisis which argues " the survival of the fittest." Not only must plantations, destined to last, produce largely, they must also make good Teas at **a**

small cost. This latter, I hold, both as regards quality and economy, *can* only be attained by the use of machinery; and thus, what is the best kind of rolling machine, the best description of dryer, equaliser, and sifting apparatus, is **an all**-important point.

Tea machinery is still quite in its infancy. Various as are the machines in use, and superior as some are to **others, perhaps none of** them are yet quite perfect. Still, planters **cannot afford to wait for** ultimate perfection, for though **any machines bought to-day** will probably be more or less out of **date in a few** years' **time, he who** waits *must* go to the wall in **the meanwhile.** Realising **this fact, as** those who **know** the subject do they (and they are many) ask **eagerly:—**

"**Which of the several machines for the** different **processes in Tea manufacture shall we buy?**"

I have not now, perhaps, the knowledge **to discuss fairly the** several merits of **the various machines** for each different process, but as Tea Dryers hold an **important place in the** list, and I have, perhaps, an exceptional experience **of one** kind, I purpose **to give** your readers the benefit thereof.

Years ago, **when I first** mooted **the idea that Tea could be** fired **without charcoal, it was scouted.** It was said, "**The fumes** of charcoal **had** some chemical and necessary effect." "**The Chinese would not have** used it **from time** immemorial had **a substitute, and a** cheaper one, been practicable." Such were the objections. **It is now no** longer a question. A great part, perhaps **the greater part, of the** Indian produce **is to-day worked with other fuel, and it is only a** question of time when *all* **of it will be so. It is** generally admitted that Tea prepared in Dryers is more valuable than that fired over charcoal; **and** begging the question that the fumes of charcoal are *not* necessary (the old idea is very nearly exploded), it is reasonable that it should be so; for, if there is one thing certain in Tea manufacture, it is that speed is necessary. Charcoal drying took on an average 45 **minutes; Tea is fired in** the best Dryers in eight minutes. In respect of speed, Kinmond's **Dryer (which** is the one I advocate) is certainly unequalled.

When, as in large factories, 30 or 40 **maunds of** Tea have to be made daily, it is evident that, *cæteris paribus,* **the** machine which will do most in a given time and given space must **be** the best. In these respects also Kinmond's **Dryer** stands well, **for the** small size (No. 1) will **do one** maund, and **the larger** size (No. 2) **will turn out** two maunds per hour. In other words, in a working day of 12 hours (and I allow no more, for I do not believe in night work) 12 and 24 maunds daily are the capacities of the two sizes. Considering that the said two **sizes, with necessary** stokehole, tables, &c., occupy respectively not **more** than 200 and 260 square feet of space in a factory, the satisfactory results, in both **the above respects, are unquestionable.**

Tea made at night, both because **the colour of it in its** different stages cannot be well seen (let the light be what **it** will), and also because superintendence cannot then be so close, **is never so** good as day-made Tea. This is *why* I do not believe in night work; and it is also a very important extra reason why machinery (which by its speed enables all the necessary Tea to be made by daylight) will prove **such a great and lasting advantage.**

When Kinmond's Dryer was first constructed, it was proposed to **work it** at 300 degrees. Later experience has proved 260 degrees is **better** and sufficient; but of course more time is thus taken, and with **the** old sizes one and two maunds per hour could not be turned out at **the lower temperature. The machines are now** made one-fifth larger **to obviate this.**

The fan is worked at 600 revolutions per minute, and this is found to be the **best speed.**

Several alterations, and important **ones,** have been **made since the first** machines were constructed, but I will mention them shortly, for **they** will only be understood by those who know the Dryer—1. The trays now take out alternately both sides. 2. The fine Tea or dhole trays take out independently. 3. Outside bearings are supplied to the fan shaft or spindle; thus the lubricating oil cannot now run down **into the fan casing.** 4. The chimney is moved forward, and thus heats a larger amount **of air** and reduces fuel. After the necessary temperature has once been obtained, one maund of wood will fire one maund of Tea. This **is an** outside estimate.

The great feature **in** Kinmond's Dryer **is the** fact that a *separate* blast of hot air is forced through **the** Tea on **each tray.** In all other Dryers **I** have heard of, the *same* hot air passes through each tray successively, and moisture is consequently more **or** less carried upwards through each. It is principally in this respect, and in the large quantity of work it executes, that I consider the excellence of Kinmond's Dryer to consist.

It remains only to give shortly the results of a long series of experiments with Kinmond's Dryer. The valuations were made by more than one Calcutta broker:—

Class.	Charcoal dried.	Machine dried.
Pekoe	Rs. 0 11 0	Rs. 0 14 0
Broken Pekoe	Rs. 0 10 0	Rs. 1 1 6
Pekoe	£ 0 1 6	£ 0 1 10
Broken Pekoe	£ 0 1 5	£ 0 2 7

These were **made from** the same leaf, at the **same** time, with every care. In one of my gardens, after Kinmond's Dryer was obtained, the Teas averaged upwards of **2 annas per lb.** more all round.

The Dryer can also be **used for** withering leaf, but in my opinion no Tea Dryer is fit for that work, inasmuch **as** to do a large quantity takes far too much time.

Artificial withering **is** only necessary **when** the weather is wet and cold, and the machine **to** do it should **do a** large quantity *at a time*. No Tea Dryer *can* do this. A machine fitted for that work has yet to be invented, unless Baker's Wet Leaf Dryer, of which I have heard good accounts, but have not seen, would answer.

EDWARD MONEY.

Since the **above** was written, further improvements **and** alterations (suggested by Mr. Ansell, **the T**ea engineer, and Mr. Pillans, manager at Phoolbarry) **have been carried out.** The machine is now very perfect, **and I consider it the best Dryer at present in the market.**

Mr. Kinmond has invented quite lately a coke-burning Dryer. **He** is now taking this with him to India to try it, and has sent me the following prospectus of it :—

The Coke Burning Tea Dryer has been made to meet **the want of Tea districts** where wood fuel is scarce, and coke can be **obtained at a** reasonable price. The upper part of the Coke Burning Tea Dryer is exactly the same as the No. 2 Wood Burning Dryer, which is adapted to burn any kind of fuel, but its capacity is a little more, being from 2¼ to 2½ maunds pucka Tea per hour. One **maund of** pucka Tea can be dried with the consumption of about ⅛ maund of coke. Besides its large capacity for doing work, and its small consumption of coke, the Coke Burning Dryer has other advantages. It is nearly one-half less in weight than the Wood Burning Dryer, which means one-half saving in freight. It requires no foundation or brickwork of any kind; and taking into consideration the quantity of work it does, it is the cheapest Dryer in the market—costing only £180, f.o.b. in England.

I know nothing of this Coke Dryer. Its price compares favourably with his other Dryers.

In April, 1881, the following leader, written by me, appeared in the Calcutta *Statesman*. Though other Tea matters are included (all of interest), I give it here as further testimony to the merits of Kinmond's Dryer:—

The days are passed when Tea planters hoped to make a fortune in a few years. There are mainly two reasons for this. Firstly, the prices of Tea have fallen greatly, in many cases 30 and 40 per cent. This is due to the fact that supply, in the case of Indian Tea, has overtaken demand. Still, there is some comfort to all interested in the industry to be derived from the low prices which have ruled during the last two years. So cheap have Indian Teas been that the attention of the trade has thereby been directed to them, and consequently the deliveries of the last few months have exceeded any known previously.* It is calculated by those best able to judge, that if the present rate of deliveries in London continues, the stock in June next will not exceed twelve million pounds, and the truth is, strange as it may appear, that below this point it is not well that the stock in hand should fall, because, if it does, dealers will not be able to meet their requirements, and will then perforce buy more China. Low as prices are, we therefore, nevertheless, consider the statistical position of Tea to-day as good. There is another point which should give comfort and hope to the Indian planter, in spite of the fact that we are heavily handicapped in our race with China, inasmuch as owing to more expensive labour our cost of production *must* exceed theirs. This source of hope is the great point now generally admitted, that Indian Tea is better and goes further than China Tea. The experience of each of us can quote instances of individuals dropping China Tea, and taking to India; who knows of anyone doing the reverse? We admit the taste for Indian Tea is more or less an acquired one. Still, the public at home have already been educated to the taste by the yearly increasing proportion of Indian mixed with China Tea. Speaking generally

* They are still higher now. The last three months they have averaged five millions.—E. M.

(though the exceptions are many and increase yearly), it is true that Indian Tea is not obtainable pure, but no more is China. The bulk of the Tea now sold to the public in the United Kingdom is a mixture, three parts China and one Indian, and all points to the fact that in a few more years the general mixture will be half-and-half.

We are thus surely paving the way, in other words, teaching the English public to like Indian Tea, and the broad fact that, once used, it is never abandoned for its rival is surely a very hopeful feature. The truth is that were it possible to *make* the population of England, Australia, and America drink Indian Tea for one week only, the demand after that week would be enormous, and we should hear no more of "supply exceeding demand;" nay, more, many thousands of acres would at once be added to the present cultivation in India.

But we have somewhat wandered from the question we set out with, viz., *why* Tea does not pay now as it once did. The first reason we have given; the second is that there is now no market for Tea seed. This last reason is little dwelt on, but it is a very important factor. The days were when Rs. 300 per maund, and even more, were paid for Tea seed, and though this did not last long, the price for many years up to 1878 was about Rs. 100. Now it is simply unsaleable. The receipts for Tea seed, during all these years, formed a large part of mature garden earnings, and, to quote one instance, thereto in a great measure were due the big dividends paid by the Assam Company.

But though Tea prices may, and we think will, improve, it is not likely we shall ever again see the rates obtainable formerly. This being so, it is probable that only those plantations in the future will pay that produce Tea cheaply. How is this to be done? Those gardens that are heavily weighted by unsuitable climates, by a bad class of plant, by slopes which are too steep, by inordinately expensive labour, or other causes, will have a hard time of it, but plantations with natural advantages need in no way despair. Though, as we said above, we cannot, in the matter of cheap labour, vie with China, we have a great advantage over the Flowery Land as regards economy of production in another respect. We allude to the use of machinery, which does much now, and will do more and more as each year passes, to reduce the cost of production. Machinery in the manufacture of Tea is, we believe, almost unknown in China. There each and every operation is performed by hand; here in India many now do, and eventually all will, wither, roll, fire, and sort by the help of machines. It says **not** a little for the enterprise and the inventive genius of the Anglo-Saxon race that, while **in** China the manufacture of Tea dates **back** many centuries, and **yet** all the Tea is still made by hand, we in **India, who** have only planted **Tea** some forty years, have invented machines and **use** them **to-day for each** and **every** operation in manufacture. It is but as **yesterday that we** imported Chinamen to teach us the *modus operandi*. **We** now **know far** more than they do on the subject, and verily the pupil **has** beaten **his master.**

Though machinery reduces the cost of production, and in more **than one** case improves **the** quality **of** Tea, and planters know it, the **difficulty** before them to-day is to know which is the best machine for **each operation.** Unanimity on this point is not to be expected yet. **One swears** by Jackson, another by Kinmond, others by Ansell, Barry, **Lyle,** the inventor of the Sirocco, and **so** on. The machines and **names** of inventors are many, and each has its disciples. Perhaps the **most favourite** rolling machines **are** Jackson's **and** Kinmond's, but we see the **latter** has just produced what he calls a "Centrifugal Rolling Machine" which he thinks will supersede all others. We have not seen it, though it **is at work on** several gardens, and so can give no opinion about it; **but another of** Kinmond's machines, his Dryer, we know well. It was long **a moot point** if Tea **could be** efficiently fired by any other agent than **charcoal.** Many affirmed **that** the fumes **of** charcoal **were** necessary; and **when,** years **ago,** Colonel Money, **so well known** by his writings in Tea **matters,** affirmed **from** experiments **that** charcoal was not necessary, but that any fuel **would** do the **work, few** believed him, for people said it was impossible **to** credit that **the Chinese** would have gone on using charcoal (so much more expensive than **other fuel)** for centuries, were it not a necessity. What Colonel Money **then** predicted has already **come to pass.** Much of the Tea now **produced in** India never **sees charcoal at all, and it is** very certain that **in two or** three **years all Indian Tea will be fired** by machinery. We say this is certain **simply because, apart from the** saving effected **by using** other fuel, the **value of Teas** fired by machinery is increased. **It is natural it** should be **so because,** by the **use** of **the** best machines **invented for** that purpose, **the heat** can be regulated to a nicety, an impossibility by the old mode of charcoal firing.

Kinmond's Dryer is, in our opinion, the best Tea Dryer machine yet invented. Space forbids our describing it minutely (besides, only those, and they are few, who understand Tea machinery would appreciate our description), but its general features we will shortly touch on. **In the** comparatively **small** space it occupies in a factory, and in the large quantity of work it does in a given time, we think it unrivalled. This last feature does away with the necessity of night-work, which, apart from other drawbacks, is prejudicial to the excellence of Tea, because, among **other reasons, its colour** cannot then be appreciated in its several **stages.** Tea made **at** night is never **very good.** With sufficient motive power, sufficient rolling machinery, **and Kinmond's Dryers,** the factory (let **the leaf gathered be** what **it may) can** be **shut up at** dark. Kinmond's **Dryer may yet be** improved upon by himself or by others, but **as it now stands it** possesses a feature peculiar **to itself, and all important. The hot air,** driven by a fan (the speed of which, **under control, regulates the** temperature), does not pass successively through **the** different trays, for the hot air, drying the Tea in each tray, has **a** separate inlet **and outlet.** By this **means** is avoided the objection of carrying the moisture absorbed **by** the hot air from one tray to the **other.** Another peculiarity in the machine is, that the same air is used again and again, being re-dried and re-heated each **time.** By this **two** advantages are obtained: (1) fuel **is** saved, **it is easier** to heat **air** which still retains caloric than **fresh air;** (2) the aroma of Tea is very volatile, and when hot air, which dries it, **passes** away, some of the essence and strength of the Tea **goes with it.** But here the same air being used **again and again, the volatile essence** (how much who can say?) **is returned to the Tea. It is reasonable to** suppose that this will increase the **value of the Tea;** indeed, we know it did so materially **in one garden last season.**

We do not doubt that the unanimity wanting at present amongst planters as regards machinery will more or less come with time, but only long experience can settle the merits of rival machinery. One thing, however, **is very** certain—if **the** exports of Indian Tea ever vie in quantity **with China,** it will be **due** to the use of machinery in manufacture.

I may state that Kinmond and some other inventors of Dryers claim for them that in wet weather green leaf may **be** withered by their **means.** But, **as I** stated some pages **back, I do** not think any Dryers suitable for withering. *That* **machine has** yet to be invented.

s

To conclude my remarks on dryers, I give (again from the *Tea Gazette*) **an estimate** of the cost of drying by the old primitive mode with charcoal, and with machines. There **was no signature** to the letter. I cannot say if the figures **assumed are quite** correct, but in any case the machines **have much the best** of it :—

TEA DRYING MACHINERY v. CHARCOAL.

Dear Sir,—Tea drying by machinery *versus* Tea drying by charcoal fires over choolahs is, I believe, still discussed as to the relative merits **of each. I will try** and give you a fair estimate of cost, and speak **from experience as** far as I know relative to the merits, ills, &c., &c., **of both** modes of firing.

1st. Charcoal firing and its merits.—Except for those who persist **that the** fumes of charcoal are necessary to make good Tea, I can see **no merit** whatever in charcoal drying, either in cost, quality, rapidity, **saving of** labour, or anything else, over machine-dried Tea.

Cost per maund Tea *of Tea* dried over choolahs by charcoal.

	R.	A.	P.
Charcoal at 8 annas per **maund, 1¼** maunds ... =	0	12	0
1 Battiwallah at annas 4-6, kutcha firing ... =	0	4	6
Do. pucka firing, say ... ... =	0	0	6
Cost of firing by charcoal ... ... **Rs.**	1	1	0

N.B.—Notice the labour staff required for three months in the **year** to make charcoal; the immense space (and heat) taken up by choolahs; cost of timber used for charcoal; the number of trays, gauze, iron, &c., &c., required; the masonry and carpenter's work always more or less out of repair; loss of small tea falling through trays, &c., &c.

Now let us take

Cost of machine-dried Tea per maund.

	R.	A.	P.
1st. Those machines which dry by coke, say cost of coke ... ... =	0	8	0
3 men at annas 4-6 per 5 maunds Tea = about	0	2	8
Cost of drying per maund Tea for a machine, drying by coke 5 maunds in 10 hours	0	10	8

I now give an estimate of cost of 1 maund Tea dried by a machine of similar capabilities, but drying with any sort of fuel—coal, wood, grass, bamboo, &c., **say 2** maunds of firewood at 6 pie per maund = 1 **anna** per 1 maund Tea.

N.B.—Price of firewood at 3 pie per maund should be nearer the mark.

3 men's pay, annas 4-6 for 5 maunds in 10 hours = annas 2-8 per maund. The analysis of the above comes to this—

	R.	A.	P.
Charcoal drying ... ... =	1	1	0
Coke ,, ... =	0	10	8*
Wood fire ,, ... =	0	3	8

We read of machines drying with any fuel, and doing double the Tea of what I have estimated above, and how people can still stick to charcoal beats me.—(No signature.)

Sorting or Sifting is the next process—that is to **say**, dividing the Tea (by passing **it through sieves) into different** kinds, as Pekoe, Broken Pekoe, Pekoe Souchong, and Broken Tea. All do not divide it thus, for some make **other kinds** also. In the body of this Essay (page 122) **I say**, "I do not believe in any present or future **machine for sifting** Tea." I did not then; that **was in the early days of Tea**; but I was wrong. A sifting machine, on the large scale on which Tea is now made, is essential for every garden.

Jackson's **Sifter.**—I have seen this, and heard it well spoken of, but I have no experience of it.

Greig's Sifter.—This I have not seen, but from the drawing I have I should doubt if it would sift enough per day for a large garden.

Pridham's Sifter.—This is quite a new thing. I know nothing of it.

The fact is, the manager at Phoolbarry and I have been

---

* I should be glad to be set right if I have not rightly calculated the price of coke.—(*Writer of the letter.*)

so thoroughly satisfied with the Sifter we use there (Ansell's) I could conceive nothing better, and I have not therefore looked into the matter of Sifters.

In January, 1881, I sent an article to the *Tea Gazette* describing *Ansell's Sifter*, and as I thought then I think now. I believe it is by far the best Tea Sifter yet invented. Many are the testimonials, too, in its favour. The price, £80, is too high; but the manufacturers (Ransomes, Head and Jeffries, of Ipswich) advise me they propose reducing it to £70. Even that, I think, is too much; but there can be no question the use of it effects a great saving in a factory.

This is my article:—

ANSELL'S SIFTING, SORTING, AND FANNING MACHINE.

January 27, 1881.

In the days gone by, Tea cultivation was, to those commencing a Tea career, *the* thing to study. Those days are passed. None are embarking in new gardens, and but few are extending existing cultivation. Prices have fallen so wofully that all that Tea planters think of to-day is how to make what they have *pay*. *I* believe in Tea still. I think the present low range of prices cannot last, and I think so simply because I know Tea will not be cultivated year after year at a loss. But the present crisis is very serious; it means, in five words, "the survival of the fittest," and even the fittest will not succeed, unless every advantage is taken of all existing Tea knowledge.

Tea manufacture is now the most important branch in the industry. We have advanced greatly in the last few years; but Tea manufacture, as regards economy in doing it, is yet comparatively in its infancy. Still we have done a great deal since the indigenous plant was discovered in the jungles of Assam, now nearly fifty years ago; we have advanced more in Tea manufacture than the Chinese, who have been making Tea many centuries. That is to say, I affirm that the Indian Tea planter of ordinary intelligence knows more of both Tea cultivation and Tea manufacture to-day than any of his Chinese contemporaries. The Chinaman grows Tea, and makes Tea, as he taught *us* to do it twenty to thirty years ago. The pupil in this case has certainly beaten his master. We have made some improvements in Tea planting and Tea cultivation, but where we have left our teachers far behind is in manufacture. "Johnny" makes his Tea as his father made it before him, taught by his grandfather who made it the same way; and, for aught we know, no improvements, in that way, have taken place in the course of many centuries. All is hand labour; machinery to them is unknown. The most primitive ideas in Tea manufacture are still adhered to. In support of the latter, I will quote one instance: Tea, from time immemorial, has always been dried by charcoal in China; no other way is known there now. **How is it here in India? A large proportion of the produce** is fired with other fuel, **aided** by machinery; **and it** is only a question of time (and **a very short time) when the whole of it will be thus prepared.** I could quote other instances: let this suffice, for **no** comparison can be **drawn** between Tea manufacture as followed out in China and India in this year 1881. The former **is** as crude as it was two or five hundred **years ago**: the latter (though still far **from** perfection) **in** its many details, in its numerous machines cleverly contrived to save labour **and** better the Teas, is a striking illustration of the activity, **the energy, the** inventive genius of the Anglo-Saxon race!

An Indian Tea factory, well set up with machinery—that is **to say** with a green-leaf drying apparatus, rolling **machines, Tea dryers,** equalisers, and sifting and sorting machines, **all driven by** an engine of 15-horse power—offers a wonderful contrast **to a** Chinese Tea factory, where all is **handwork.** But more strange still is the comparison alongside of the fact, that in the former **case the** industry dates back only some thirty **years; in the latter** many centuries.

Tea machinery **is destined to work** great results in India. When brought to perfection (it **is far on** the road now), it will so cheapen the cost of manufacture that, though labour is dearer with us than in China, we shall, thanks thereto, be able to lay down our Teas at cheaper rates than the produce of the Flowery Land. **If** Indian Tea ever vies in quantity with China in the Tea-consuming countries of the world, it will be due entirely to the economy effected by our machinery. I do not myself anticipate that Indian Teas will ever beat China out of the field, but, inasmuch as our Teas are better, because the taste for Indian Tea is growing apace, I do believe the day will come (it will scarcely be in our time) that the Tea exports from India will equal those from China; and, as I said before, to machinery, far more than to anything else, will that end be due.

There is therefore no question of more importance to the Indian planter to-day than Tea machinery. It is a difficult question too, because so many machines, for each of the different necessary processes, are vieing in competition for public favour. "Which is the best machine to buy?" is the question one hears asked daily. I propose, with your leave, to write a series of articles on Tea machinery, pointing out, as far as in me lies, the advantages and defects of those which commend themselves most to me, for I wish to give planters, through your paper, the advantage of my experience; and as my expressing an opinion in no way precludes others from doing the same, and I know your columns are open to all, I would invite discussion on rival merits, and thus certainly benefit the Tea industry.

I will to-day describe what, I think, is the best Tea sifting and fanning machine extant. It is true it is the last machine used in manufacture, but that does not signify; I will take all the others in turn.

The said machine is the invention of an able man and engineer, Mr. C. W. Ansell, well known in the Darjeeling district for his knowledge of Tea machinery. He has been for many years employed as an engineer in Tea factories. I heard of his machine when I was lately in England, and went down to Ipswich to the manufactory of Messrs. Ransomes, Sims, and Head to see it. Though difficult to judge of it, as there was no Tea wherewith to test it, I was so pleased with the principle that I ordered one. The cost was £80. It has now been working on one of my gardens some thirteen months, and in every way it has proved a great success. But to describe it, as far as I can, in a few words:—

Its length is 19 feet, its breadth 5 feet. The Tea, in bulk, is delivered through a hopper from an upper floor, on what I will call the A end of the machine, to distinguish it from the other end, which I will name B. The principle of all other sifters (except Jackson's), as far as I know, is, that the succeeding trays of differing wire mesh are arranged one below the other, the slope all being the same way, that is—from A to B. This plan is objectionable in the following way: if the Tea has been well rolled and clings together, a good deal of the fine Teas that are in the mass or bulk often passes some distance down, perhaps over half the tray or wire-mesh length, before falling through. If they do so, and the object is to sift out any particular class on the next succeeding tray, there is only half the length of mesh left to traverse to effect the object, instead of the whole length of the tray. This is obviated in practice by pushing the Teas continually back up the inclined tray; but this is done at the expense of extra labour and making the Teas dusty and grey.

The above objection is obviated in Ansell's machine. It consists of four slopes, but each of these incline downwards, alternately, different ways—*viz.*, No. 1 (the upper), from A to B; No. 2, from B to A; No. 3, from A to B; No. 4, from B to A, and below the mesh of each slope is a carrying tin tray, sloping the same way, which carries all the Tea which falls through each mesh down to *the head* of the succeeding slope, while in each case the Tea which will *not* pass through the mesh is delivered separately. The above arrangement, however, does *not* hold with the upper or No. 1 slope. This consists of two wire trays or meshes, with the carrying tray below the lower one. Such of the bulk as will not pass through the upper tray is delivered on the head of No. 2 slope, at the B end of the machine. What passes through the upper tray, but will not pass through the lower, is delivered by a side shoot at the B end of the machine, and is "No. 1 Pekoe." What passes through both sieves on to the carrying tray is also delivered by an opposite side shoot from the B end of the machine, and is "Broken Pekoe." Between Nos. 1 and 2 slopes is an air chamber, which, as the bulk left on the upper sieve of No. 1 slope falls on the head of slope No. 2 (a blast being sent through it by a fan at the A end of the machine), drives out of the said falling bulk all red leaf, stalks, fannings, &c.

No. 2 slope receives the bulk at the B end of the machine, after the red leaf and fannings are taken out as stated above, and what will not pass through the mesh is delivered at the back of the A end of the machine, and is "Congou;" while what does fall through the mesh into the carrying tray below it (which is still bulk, consisting of "Pekoe," "Pekoe Souchong," and "Souchong" mixed) is delivered at the A end of the machine on to the head of No. 3 slope.

What will not pass through the mesh of No. 3 slope is delivered at the B end of the machine in front, and is "Souchong;" while what does pass through the mesh of No. 3 slope on to the carrying tray below (still bulk, consisting of "Pekoe" and "Pekoe Souchong") is delivered on to the head of No. 4 slope at the B end of the machine.

No. 4 slope has no carrying tray: it would be useless. What will **not pass** through the mesh is delivered at the A end of the machine, and is " Pekoe Souchong ;" while what does pass through the mesh falls on the floor of the factory and is the remaining " Pekoe," that is, " Pekoe No. 2."

The sorting is **so** far finished, and the results are the following Teas, placed round the machine thus :—" Pekoe No. 1," at the left side of B end ; " Broken Pekoe," at right side of B end ; " Red Leaf and Fannings," some distance in front of B end ; " Souchong," also in front of B end, but nearer to the machine ; " Congou," **at back of A end** ; " Pekoe Souchong," also at back of A end, but nearer **the** machine ; " Pekoe No. 2," on the floor below the machine.

With Teas thus minutely sorted, all possible requirements are provided for, and the planter can, by mixing or otherwise, make any number of classes he may choose.

It will be observed that " Pekoe " is taken out twice, resulting in " **Nos. 1 and 2 Pekoe.**" These differ slightly, but **are** better mixed **together.** " **Why take them** out separately," **some exclaim,** " to mix **them together again ?** " But there are three very good reasons : firstly, the " Pekoe " **is taken out at the** commencement, previous to fanning, to prevent the small or **broken** Pekoe tips being blown out in that process ; secondly, the " **1st Pekoe**" **being** taken out thus early, its appearance is not injured by passing **over** a large **amount** of seive-mesh area ; and thirdly, *all* the " Pekoe " **is thus extracted,** which it could not be, as far as I can see, by any other process.

From all the kinds detailed above, I make only four—viz, " **Pekoe,** " " Broken Pekoe, " " Pekoe Souchong, " and " Broken Tea ;" **but others can do as they will.***

The machine is of course driven by steam.† The movement of all **the trays is a backward and forward one of** 3 inches longitudinal semi-circular motion, **the latter movement** being imparted by the steel spring hangers. Only **a small amount of power** is required **to drive the machine, viz., under half horse.**

I must here conclude my description.

Now as to the amount of **work** the machine will **do.** I speak from **actual** experience when I state what follows :—

It will **sift and** fan seven maunds **of** Tea per hour. The only hand

---

* I advise only these four kinds. When the trader becomes more sensible, three or even two would be better, but as it is now four are necessary.

† With a driving belt from the engine shafting.

labour required to supplement it is a few (a very few) women to pick out any foreign substances out of the "Congou."

At our garden in Western Dooars, 1,260 maunds of Tea were made in 1880, and all sifted by this machine, the hand labour besides being only 44 women during the whole season, or about one-fifth of a woman per day.

The machine requires only two men to work it continually, and one boy to feed it from the upper floor.

I can think of no possible objection to this machine, or even of any possible improvement. I believe, in the case of a 300-acre garden with a decent amount of produce, the machine, in its saving of hand labour, pays for itself in one year, whilst the Teas are much improved in appearance by its use, and fetch higher prices.

EDWARD MONEY.

I add two more letters in favour of the machine from the same paper :—

ANSELL'S PATENT TEA SORTING AND WINNOWING MACHINE.

Sir,—In respond to your call for information regarding Tea machinery, I am happy to supply you with my experience of Ansell's Patent Tea Sorting and Winnowing Machine. I have been sifting the whole of my Teas through it this season, and am therefore in a position to state what I think of it. I consider it a most useful machine, and a great saver of labour. With four men, I do with it in one day an amount of work which without it I would have to employ from twenty to twenty-five men to accomplish.—Yours, &c.,

"SIFTER."

ANSELL'S SIFTING MACHINE.

A correspondent writes from London to the *Ceylon Observer* as follows:—Ansell's Patent Tea Sorter seems to be an article which will later be much used in Ceylon. In a memo. before me there is an extract from Messrs. George Williamson and Co., who say:—" The manager of our Majilighur Garden writes :—' I have now had sufficient experience of Ansell's Sifter to be able to report very favourably upon it. It does its work thoroughly and cleanly, and, owing to the comparatively small space it occupies, little or no loss occurs even of the finest dust. Sixteen maunds in nine hours is what I find to be about its capabilities, and four boys do all the work connected with it. It has effected a great saving in the Tea house this year, and has quite done away with hand-sieving, except equalizing the broken Pekoe and broken Tea—a very trivial operation.'"

Packing.—This is **the final** process. Unless Teas are packed directly they are made, they require to be heated once more to drive off any moisture imbibed. This can be done in a way in most of the dryers described, perhaps in Kinmond's best of all.*

This concludes my remarks on Tea machinery; but I **shall not** have a more appropriate place than this to mention **the ornamental** tin boxes devised **by Messrs.** Harvey Bros. **and Tyler, as a new mode** of packing Teas. The following **is an article of mine** on the subject to the *Tea Gazette,* written in 1880:—

I saw lately tin Tea boxes made to hold 20 lbs., which are manufactured by Messrs. **Harvey** Brothers and Tyler, 21, Mincing Lane. I was much pleased with them, **for I** foresaw that by their use great good to the Indian Tea industry **would accrue.** I went to Mincing Lane, and had a long talk with the **firm,** and came away convinced **that** the fact of the said boxes should be known far **and** wide in India.

The boxes measure 15¾ by 10 15-16ths by 10 **5-16ths.** They are handsomely illustrated with Indian Tea plantation subjects.† Each **piece runs** into a groove in the adjoining one, so that one minute will **put a** box together, and a touch of solder here and there completes it; **they are then perfectly** air-tight. The boxes are very sightly. Price **is now 2s. 5d. per box.** Boxes sent to Calcutta up to this have been charged 2s. **7d.** The price is dependent on the fluctuating price of tin, which is somewhat lower now. Of course they are sent out in pieces. Cases holding pieces for 100 boxes weigh 4 cwt. The firm tell me that Messrs. Schœne, Kilburn and Co., and Messrs. Begg, Dunlop and Co.,

* Heating before packing has to be done on a large scale. None of the Dryers notified are large enough. A special machine should be devised.

† Top is "The Tea Garden;" front, "Weighing Leaf;" back, "Packing;" ends, "Elephant with Howdah," **or,** if desired, the plantation mark.

TEA MACHINERY.

in Calcutta, have consignments of the boxes, so any of your readers can see them.

In my opinion there are several advantages to be derived from their use :—

1. They will help to open up new markets. The ungainly, unwieldly packages we have used hitherto are certainly detrimental, at least where Indian Teas are not known. **By the use of these** tin boxes the sale of our Teas would, I am sure, **be extended at home,** and they would also give great facilities for successfully introducing **Indian Tea** into Australia, Canada, the **United States,** the Cape, &c. It seems some Indian Tea has **already been sent home** in these tins, and I am told it met with **a ready sale,** quite to 8*d*. per lb. over what it would have brought in chests. This is, of course, too good to last, but less than one penny **a lb. increase would pay for their use.**

2. The sale **of Indian Tea in India would be developed by** using them.

3. The tares **of these boxes is and must be exact, viz., 3 lbs. 15½ oz.,** so only a few would **be opened at the Custom House,*** and the great loss by the deterioration of **Tea being exposed** (few know how great it is) would be avoided.

4. There is no doubt Tea will keep better in transit in these boxes than in our old packages. How often are the latter broken and the lead torn! This evil would be quite avoided.

There seems to me to be but one doubtful point. The boxes cannot be sent loose on board **ship : how then** are they to be packed? Chests holding **four tin boxes were recommended, but they do** not smile on me. True, they might be made very light : still they would

* The following are the numbers to be opened by the Custom House regulations :—

From	1 to	5			1 to be turned out.		
,,	6 ,,	40	..	..	3	,,	,,
,,	41 ,,	80	..	..	4	,,	,,
,,	81 ,,	120	..	..	5	,,	,,
,,	121 ,,	200	..	..	6	,,	,,
,,	201 ,,	300	..	..	8	,,	,,
,,	301 ,,	500	..	..	10	,,	,,
,,	501 ,,	**800**	..	..	12	,,	,,
,,	801 and upwards		..	..	16	,,	,,

This applies to packages of all sizes and kinds, **if** the tares are equal or nearly so. If the difference in the tares are not great, an average is struck. If tares are various all are turned **out** !

add to the size, weight, and cost considerably. I think crates of strong light battens **would answer perfectly, and six,** or perhaps eight boxes might then be placed in each. However, this is a matter of detail, **which experience would quickly decide. To continue the** advantages:

5. Teas packed in these boxes, **and so sold,** would not be used for bolstering up China rubbish. **They** would be drunk pure, and thus the great desideratum of teaching the **public, both** here and abroad, to use Indian Tea by **itself, would** be, in a measure, attained.

I do not **say** that any planter should pack *all* his **Teas in** this new way. The mass of Indian Tea, do what we may, will still be used to mix with China. Again, the highest class of Indian Teas are not **the** ones **to** commence with. As a rule they are too expensive for the public **to use them** alone. Ordinary Teas, or perhaps a mixture which **could be sold** cheaply, and would be a good household Tea, is what I should recommend. **It is just** this kind which is now such a drug **in the market, and necessarily the** diversion of some **of this** into other **channels would help us greatly.**

6. **A considerable saving in the loss of** Tea at the Custom House **would result by the use** of these boxes, as the following figures will show. To begin with, **the trade allowance** of 1 lb. per package which is now allowed the buyer, and which **is** of course a loss to the producer, would be avoided; for this allowance does **not apply** to any package under a gross weight of 28 lbs., and these tins with 20 lb. 2 oz. of Tea in them, will weigh gross only 24 lbs. 1½ oz.

To make the figures below clear, I must state that the rule of the Custom House is to discard fractions of a pound both in the gross and the tare. But **in the** gross the number *below* is written, in the tare the number *above*. **Thus,** if the gross weight of a package is 132¼ lbs., the gross is written 132. **If the** tare of a package is 37¾ lbs., it is written 38. **Now to** take **one extreme case, to show the loss on our** ordinary **Indian packages: a chest weighs** gross, say, **132** lbs. **15 oz.; it is still written 132 lbs. The tare of the said** package weighs, **say, 37 lbs. 1 oz.: it is written** 38. The tare deducted from **the** gross **gives the net weight of Tea.** In this case **132** minus **38 equals 94 lbs., which is all the producer** is paid for. **But the** net **weight of Tea in** the box is 132 lbs. **15** ozs., minus 37 lbs. 1 oz., equals 95 lbs. 14 ozs., and thus on such a package there is a loss of exactly 1 lb. 14 ozs. Add to this the trade allowance of one pound, and the whole loss is 2 lbs. 14 ozs., which is about **3 per cent.**

TEA MACHINERY.

It will be observed that by this custom the advantage, as regards the duty of **6d.** per lb., is on the side of the payee, but none the less is it to the loss of the producer. The case quoted above is, of course, an extreme one, but in practice I believe the loss of Tea on Indian packages, including the trade allowance, is not much under 2 lbs. In the case of our ordinary Indian packages, if we could regulate our tares exactly, so as to make the gross weight only one ounce above the whole number, and the tare one ounce **below the whole** number, the loss would necessarily be much decreased. This, however, is impossible, for, as a rule the tares are **one or two pounds less when** they arrive in England than when they left the garden, owing **to the** wood drying in transit; **and thus it is quite a chance what the real tares come out here.**

But, with the tin boxes in question, the tares, that is their weight, **being fixed and equal, and not liable to** change, we can so arrange the weights that the **loss will be very trifling, thus** :—

		lbs.	ozs.
The box weighs		3	15½
We put in Tea		20	2
Gross Weight		24	1½
In the Customs the gross is written		24 lbs.	
And the tare is written		4 ,,	
The Tea paid for will be		20 lbs.	

that is a loss **of only 2 ounces, or not much above half per cent.,** instead of three per cent., as shown in the old packages.

Shortly, to conclude this point. In the case of the old packages by no means can **we** help ourselves; but, as shown, with the tin boxes, the loss need be very little.

Roughly, **the** cost of using these tin boxes would be, all told, from 1½d. to 1⅜d. per lb., and with our lead-lined boxes it averages perhaps per penny. **The difference of a** halfpenny, or even three farthings, one pound **would not be much** for the advantages detailed.

One point I have forgotten. If 500 boxes are ordered, the plantation **mark is put on the** ends of the boxes gratis. If less than 500 are **ordered, the additional** cost for this would be about £5.

I hope the Syndicate in Calcutta will try these boxes. I shall certainly do so.

I enclose the directions for making up the tins, and hope you **will** insert them at the foot of this letter.

Reading over the above, there is one point I find not observed on **as regards the loss of** Tea at the Custom House. By the mode of weighing, as explained, the producer often loses 2 or 3 per cent., but **still**, strange to say, in practice, this loss is sometimes more than counterbalanced by the **increased** weight of the **Tea** due to the moisture imbibed while exposed (if boxes are broken in the transit) anyhow at the Custom House. But I need not point out that this gain is dearly bought by the deterioration of the Tea. **The Custom** House procedure is bad in every way. More on this subject later.

EDWARD MONEY.

The following is also from the *Tea Gazette*, and is much in favour of the boxes :—

PACKING OF TEA IN TIN BOXES.

In our issue of November 7th, 1881, we inserted a short editorial **note questioning, on the** authority of certain correspondents, the advisability of using tin Tea **boxes for the packing of** Tea, at the same time asking our readers to favour **us** with their opinions on the subject, in case we were misinformed. Our invitation has met with a response from several quarters, and the correspondence we have received leads us to alter the opinion we formerly held on the subject. **A** gentleman largely interested in Tea, but in no way connected with the manu**facturers** of the patent tin boxes, writes to us from England :—

"I made enquiries as to the condition in which Tea packed in Messrs. Harvey Brothers and Tyler's lacquered tin boxes is turned **out in London.** I found that the Tea was not at all injured by this method of packing, but that **its** condition is quite as good as that of Tea packed in chests. Messrs. W. J. and **H.** Thompson assured me that you were entirely mistaken **in** your remarks as to the contamination, but they thought that an objection to the packing in the lacquered tin boxes was the **labour** of putting **up in these** boxes. Catalogues were shown me **in** which I saw that **the Teas** in the lacquered **tin** boxes fetched higher rates than the **same** Teas packed in chests, **the** difference being in one case 3*d*. per **lb.**"

This is certainly a most favourable testimony, and coming as **it** does from a disinterested **party, who writes simply in** defence of what he considers the right, we cannot but accept of his statement in its entirety.

Another correspondent writes :—

"I now give you a few of the sales of these boxes **made at** public auction during the last month, shewing the preference **of the** trade for Tea so packed, and the higher prices realised.

	Public Sale 3rd November.	s.	d.	
Koliabar.	28 chests **Pekoe** ...	1	10½	per lb.
K. Assam.	28 **cases, each** 4 tin boxes	2	¾	,,
	Public Sale 16th November.			
M.L.B.D.S.A.	30 chests Pekoe ...	2	¼	,,
	30 cases, each 4 tin boxes	2	2¼	,,
,,	20 chests Souchong ...	1	3½	,,
	20 cases, each 4 tin boxes	1	4¾	,,
	Public Sale 23rd November.			
M.L.B.L.P.	20 chests Pekoe ...	1	6¾	,,
	19 cases, each 4 tin boxes	1	9¾	,,

"In every case the above Teas were packed out of the same heap in India, and the difference in the selling price arises chiefly from the *better condition* of the Tea on arrival, and the growing preference of the country trade for Teas so packed."

The following is **worth notice** :—

Hoop Iron.

The *Ceylon Observer* says: "The planters should note the following (writes to us **a London firm**)—From quotations lying before us the prices of 22 gauge iron hooping are as follows: ½in., 165s. per ton; ⅝in., 110s. per ton; ¾in., 70s.; ⅞in., 60s.; 1in., 50s. Thus by using one inch hooping, less than one-third the price is paid. The narrower the hooping, the more difficult is it to manufacture."

It is also not so strong.

CHAPTER XXXVII.

WEIGHING AND BULKING OF INDIAN TEAS AT CUSTOM HOUSE.

One misapprehension with some exists on this head. The *weighing* is done by the Customs to ascertain the amount for duty. The *bulking* is done at the request of the vendor, the broker who is to sell it, or the purchaser, and it has to be paid for.

Two distinct injuries are inflicted on the producer by the present Custom House system—

1. The Tea is much damaged by exposure.
2. The quantity found is *always* less than the actual.

Now as to No. 1. When we consider how damp the London atmosphere is at the best, how in foggy days it teems with moisture, is it not very certain that Teas exposed to it, often for days, deteriorate? What care we take in India heating before packing—carefully with lead and solder, excluding all air—and then the Teas on arrival here are treated as above! It is simply monstrous.

The following extract from a letter to *Home and Colonial Mail* sets out the case forcibly:—

The blame ought not entirely to be laid upon the planter, however, for certain facts have come to our knowledge during the present week as regards the manner in which Indian Teas are bulked at some of the London warehouses, which somewhat explains how depreciation in quality comes about. We bought several breaks of Tea in the sales this week, which were stated to be bulked and ready for sampling six days before the sale; and yet we know for a fact that some of those very Teas were not put back into the chest till the day after the sale, if even then. More or less moisture is always to be found in the London atmosphere, particularly in rainy weather, and there can be no question that incalculable injury would be done to a fine Tea by seven days' exposure on the floor of a warehouse. The damage and loss falls entirely on the buyer. The effects of it are not seen at once, but there can be little doubt that a gradual depreciation sets in, consequent on the absorption of moisture. No redrying process follows; the Tea is simply filled back into the chests when seven days of neglect have done what mischief is possible. Is it to be wondered at that samples drawn from such a break of Tea a few months after it has been bulked in London will have lost all their freshness and malty smell? J. C. TAYLOR AND COLMAN.

I have no reason to think the delay above is very unusual, and I must add to the above, that when the chests are closed no attempt is made even to cover the top with lead, much less to resolder it. Some paper on top is all attempted. I need say no more to prove that the quality of Indian Teas is *most* seriously damaged at the Custom House.

Now as to No. 2. The loss in quantity to producer.

The following article, which I wrote to the *Indian Tea Gazette* in 1881, shows how invariable the loss must be:—

The loss of Tea by the mode adopted at the Custom House in England is great.

When Teas are sold at Calcutta, though the English Custom House regulations do not then affect us immediately, they do so indirectly. If purchasers in Calcutta gain by our Teas, they will bid more; if they loose, they will bid less. Besides, many Teas are sold in London.

To understand what follows, it is necessary to remember that—

Garden Invoices *never* go to Custom House. Custom House arrives at weight of Tea by weighing the package for "gross," and then turning out Tea, weighing box, lead, nails, iron hooping, in fact all but Tea, for "tare;" gross weight, minus tare. is the weight of Tea they demand duty on, and the weight so found by Custom House is all the

T

producer or importer gets paid for.* It follows, therefore, that the less Tea declared by Customs means a loss to producer and a gain to buyer. To the latter in two ways, viz., less Tea to pay for than is really there, and a saving of 6d. per lb. duty! But to show, now, how the loss occurs. When weighing for gross, the fractions of a pound are discarded; when weighing for tares, the pounds above the actual weight are written. The *greatest* loss that can occur by this method, on one package, is 1 pound 14 ounces of Tea. It (this greatest loss) *must* always occur when the gross is 1 ounce short of a pound, and the tare 1 ounce more than the pound.

No. 1 Example.

Gross and tare can be put at any figures **as to** pounds. It will always come out the same. Say, therefore,

	lbs.	oz.	
Gross	132	15	} actual weights taken at
Tare (deducted)	37	1	Custom House.
Actual Tea in chest	95	14	

By rule quoted the gross and tare weights **are** set down at Custom House—

	lbs.
Gross	132
Tare (deducted)	38

Actual Tea thus paid for = 94 pounds—on which duty is also paid. **Therefore** the loss on the chest is 1 pound 14 ounces.

The *least* loss that can take place (when ounces **occur in gross** and tare) is 2 ounces. To insure this the gross must be 1 ounce more than the pound, and the tare 1 ounce below.

No. 2 Example.

Say any figures in pounds.

	lbs.	oz.	
Gross	133	1	} actual weights taken at
Tare (deducted)	36	15	**Custom** House.
Actual Tea in chest	96	2	

* If tares are nearly equal, and if Teas are well bulked in India, only some packages (about 10 per cent.) are opened, and an average tare struck. But this in no way saves the loss in *quantity* of Tea, though, of course, less Tea is thus *injured*.

But again, by rule quoted, it is written by Customs—

	lbs.
Gross	133
Tare (deducted) ...	37
Actual Tea paid for ...	96 pounds, on which duty is also paid.

Therefore the loss on chest is 2 ounces only.

Now did weights turn out the same in London that they were on the garden, we could, by doing as in last example, insure only the above trifling 2 ounce loss. But it is *not* so. The wood dries and thus makes both the gross and tare less. The loss then comes out anything between 2 ounces and 1 pound 14 ounces.

I find the following simple rule will give the exact loss on each and every weight of both gross and tare.

Rule.—Add the ounces above a pound in the gross to the ounces short of a pound in the tare. The sum of the two, in ounces, will be the loss of Tea on the package.

This is only part of the article. I break off here to add a few remarks more appropriate now than what I then wrote.

There are means by which this varying loss, of which the maximum is 1 pound 14 ounces, can be reduced to 4 ounces only on each and every chest.

I admit the procedure is scarcely practical, but as nothing can demonstrate better the absurdity of the system as pursued at the Customs, I give it here.

How can we insure the *least* loss, taking into consideration the fact that the weights of both the gross and tare, because of the wood drying and lightening in transit, can never come out the same at the Custom House in London as they were on the garden.

We can do it thus: the Tea if well packed in a chest in no way alters in weight during transit. If dry, when put up, it cannot become lighter; if the leaden covering is airtight, it can absorb no moisture, which would of course make it heavier. I therefore beg the question that it is **a fixed** quantity, for it must be so if well packed.

We have therefore only to consider the gross and the tare, and, as shown, the loss in Tea, varying from 2 ounces to 1 pound 14 ounces, depends entirely on the weights these are found to be at the Custom House. In other words, if we can insure the gross there being but little over any even number of pounds, and the tare there being but little below any other even number of pounds, we attain (approximately) the least loss we can be mulcted in.

Begging the question that we can add to, or detract from, the gross weight of each chest in the Custom House (before it is put into the scales by the officer there) by the addition or subtraction of a few nails if the weight is nearly what we want, or pieces of hoop iron if the actual varies much from the desired weight—I say, if we can do this, we can insure approximately the minimum of loss. I go to show how this is to be done.

Pack the Tea in the usual way, but whatever the quantity it is desired to put into the chest (it can be varied with each class, for it matters not what the weight is in pounds) add to it 4 ounces, **and** be very careful that the whole weight of Tea is exactly the number of pounds required, plus 4 ounces—for the whole success of the plan depends on this weight being **exact**. Nothing more is required to be done at the Factory than has been done hitherto, for it matters not one straw, as regards the success of the plan, what the gross and tare of each package is, nor what the weight of Tea is, as long as exactly 4 ounces above an even number of pounds is there; neither does it signify how much the wood lightens in transit, and thus decreases the weights which were found at Factory for gross and tare.

The next step must be taken at the Custom House in London. Let the importer or the producer's agent attend and weigh each package himself nicely, any time before the weights are to be taken **by the Customs.** Then let him *make* each package **2** ounces above the even **number** of pounds. This will be easy enough, by the addition or subtraction of a few nails or hoop iron. For instance, suppose the chest to weigh 140 pounds **6 ounces, he would** take away nails or hoop **iron** weighing 4 ounces. If it weighed 140 pounds 13 ounces, he would, by **adding 5** ounces more nails or hoop **iron,** make it 141 pounds **2** ounces. **All would then be** finished, and each and **every package so treated would give** a loss in Tea of 4 ounces only.

If my plan could be carried out (as the minimum loss otherwise is 2 ounces, and the maximum 1 pound 14 ounces the mean is one pound), we save a loss of the said pound on *each* chest, minus the loss we compound for, *viz.,* 4 ounces. That is to say, we gain 12 ounces on each package which, in a break of 2 or 3 hundred chests, means a good deal to the producer or Customs!

I will give one example **in figures.** Any other possible figures can be tried; it will always come out **the same,** *if* the weight of Tea **is exactly 4 ounces** above any given number of pounds.

No. 3. Example.

	lbs.	oz.
Results at **Garden. Tea,** any number of pounds with 4 ounces added (say)	100	4
Tare (any figure) (say)	43	6
Gross at Garden	143	10

The wood lightens in transit any amount (it is immaterial), say 15 ounces.

	lbs.	oz.
The weights at the Custom House then become { Gross	142	11
{ Tare	42	7
Weight Tea as before	100	4

At Custom House (as detailed) by adding 7 ounces of nails or hoop iron make

	lbs.	oz.
Gross ...	143	2
Tare ...	42	14
Weight tea as before ...	100	4

The tare will thereby necessarily be increased 7 **oz.** and become

These weights are written at Custom House

	lbs.
Gross ...	143
Tare ...	43

Weight of Tea found by Customs is ... **100 pounds** which is a loss of 4 ounces only as stated.

Were the plan feasible, the gain to the Indian planters **would be large.** Say this year (1883), fifty-seven million pounds are imported, and ninety pounds per chest is taken as the average, **this gives over** 600,000 chests, **and** 12 ounces **saved on** each = 450,000 pounds, **of** Tea, which at 12 annas per pound, Rs. 3,37,000.

The **gain to the Customs would be** 450,000 sixpences = £11,250.

This increase to **the Customs would be** attained by simply (though still keeping **under** the **actual** weight of **Tea in each** chest) taking the contents more correctly.

The above shows, if figures will show anything, that a great loss to both the producer and Customs takes place **by the system** in vogue. As the only object of the Customs *should* be to arrive at the true weight of Tea in the most expeditious and **simple way,** how very absurd is the system pursued! What the *tare* is can in no way signify to them; all they really want is **the** weight of **the** Tea. The absurdity of **the** system is proved **by** the fact (demonstrated) that the **results to both** producer **and** Customs *can* be altered by the **addition or** subtraction **in** the Custom-house of a few nails! How easy to weigh the **Tea itself!** What possible objection **can exist?**

WEIGHING AND BULKING OF INDIAN TEAS.

The Indian Tea Districts Association having failed to move the Customs, have quite lately addressed the following Memorial to the Secretary of State for India:—

To THE RIGHT HONOURABLE THE EARL OF KIMBERLEY, HER MAJESTY'S SECRETARY OF STATE FOR INDIA.

The Petition of the Indian Tea Districts Association sheweth—

That your Petitioners are a body representing the interests connected with the cultivation of Tea in British India, in which enterprise British capital to the extent of over fifteen millions sterling has been invested.

That the industry dates from the year 1838, when the first consignment of Indian Tea, consisting of 456 lbs., reached the London market.

That the imports of Indian Tea for the year ending 30th June, 1882, were 49,503,000 lbs., having a value of more than £3,300,000 sterling; while the estimated importation for the current season is upwards of 55,000,000 lbs., or fully one-third of the entire consumption of the United Kingdom for the year.

That the contribution to the Revenue accruing from Customs' import duty on the above quantity of Tea will exceed a million and a quarter sterling.

That the whole of this large quantity is manufactured and packed on between 2,700 and 2,800 separate estates, situated on various parts of H.M.'s Indian dominions.

That the boxes in which the Teas are packed are in great part made of such wood as can be obtained on the several estates, or purchased from the neighbouring Forest Department, and it is very important on economic grounds, as also in the manifest interests of the districts, that this should be exclusively the case.

That it has been found, under these conditions, practically impossible to meet the imperative Custom-house standard of close uniformity of tare weight when the chests reach the Bonded Warehouses here.

That your Petitioners have reason to complain of the system of weighing the Teas in the said warehouses for the purpose of levying the duty.

That the present system of weighing is to weigh each package in he gross, then to turn out the contents, weigh the empty case, and **thus arrive at** the nett weight of the contents.

That the only exception to this rule is when the package, *i.e.*, the empty cases, in a Break closely approximate in weight.

That by the said system **of** weighing, two serious injuries **are** inflicted on the grower and importer of Indian Tea, viz.:—

> In the first place, a loss of weight is sustained **by** the fractions over the even pound in both gross and tare being given against the seller, and in favour of the buyer, amounting, it may be, to 1 lb. 15 oz., or an average of about 1 lb. in every **package** weighing **over 28 lbs.** gross, in addition to the usual trade allowance of 1 lb. per package.

> **Secondly, and by far the** more **serious** grievance, very great injury is caused to the Teas by the process of turning them out of the packages, in which they arrive hermetically sealed, for the purpose of weighing the empty packages. The Teas are thus exposed to the atmosphere, the humidity of which they readily absorb, and sustain further serious injury and depreciation by breakage from rough handling **in** the process of repacking : **the lead** linings also are so torn in the process as **to** be **rendered** comparatively useless for the purpose for which they were intended, eliciting loud complaints from the trade of the rapid loss of condition **of** the Teas.

That the concession of this Petition, by rendering it unnecessary **to turn** out more than a small percentage of the chests to test the **correct** weight of contents, would admit of the Teas being bulked in India ; and while it would free the industry from **an** injurious and vexatious restriction, and admit of the Teas reaching the consumer in **a** purer and sounder condition, it would also greatly simplify and reduce the work of the Customs.

That the foregoing statistics significantly demonstrate **the** import-**ance** of the Indian Tea industry to both England and India, and constitute **a claim to the** favourable consideration of both Governments, especially that of India, on the ground of the benefit accruing to the districts in which it is conducted, and the increment of State revenue to which it has directly and indirectly **conduced.**

That having regard to the existing close and hardening **competition with** China, Japan, and other Tea producing countries, your Petitioners naturally feel aggrieved that **the** important industry they represent should be hampered in the contest by the restrictive **and** superfluous impediment forming the subject of their petition.

That your Petitioners have unsuccessfully urged on the Commissioners of Her Majesty's Customs the **adoption of this change of** system, and therefore venture to **address your Lordship**.

That your Petitioners beg to refer to the accompanying copies of correspondence between the Association and the Commissioners of Her Majesty's Customs annexed to this Petition.

That the accompanying Memorial signed by the leading mercan**tile firms and others in** Calcutta, interested in the growth and export of Indian Tea, **is** an illustration of the **feeling in** India on the subject of this Petition.

Your Petitioners therefore pray—

That your Lordship will kindly take such steps as may be necessary to secure for your Petitioners the relief sought for.

And your Petitioners will ever pray, &c.

T. D. FORSYTH,
Chairman of **the Association**.
ERNEST **TYE,**
Secretary.

The following reply was received :—

INDIA OFFICE, S.W.,
28th February, 1883.

SIR,—I am directed by the Secretary of State for India in Council to acknowledge the receipt of the Memorial addressed to the EARL OF KIMBERLEY by the Indian Tea Districts Association, respecting the method of weighing Indian Tea at the Custom House. In reply, I am to inform you that the Memorial has been forwarded to the Lords Commissioners of Her Majesty's Treasury, with the expression of LORD KIMBERLEY's hope that **whatever is** practicable may be done to remedy **the grievance complained of by** the memorialists in the interests of the Indian Tea trade.

I **am,** Sir, your obedient servant,

(Signed) J. K. CROSS.

The Secretary, Indian Tea Districts Association.

It is possible, therefore, that some improvement will now be accomplished.*

But at the CRUTCHED FRIARS Warehouse (belonging to the East and West India Docks) a great advance has already been made. The Tea there is now bulked, and re-packed by **machinery**. The Directors most kindly invited me to come and witness the **process**. I went, and was more than pleased with what I saw. The machinery, and all connected with the process, is so well described in an article in the *Home and Colonial Mail*, I cannot do better than give it here :—

TEA BULKING AT THE EAST AND WEST INDIA DOCK COMPANY'S WAREHOUSES, IN CRUTCHED FRIARS.

It is not a little strange that the importance of effecting improvements in the present system of Tea bulking, which has exercised the minds of Tea growers and importers so much of late, should have hitherto been neglected or ignored by the proprietors of the various bonded warehouses in London wherein the Tea is bulked and stored. That Tea may be, and only too commonly **is**, bulked by an antiquated and unsatisfactory process is a fact which **is** well known to all who are interested in **the** matter. How **this result is arrived at** will be **seen later on**; at present we desire to show that **at least at** one warehouse **the** question has received the attention **which it deserves**, and **to** explain, **so far** as may be possible, **the steps** which **have** been taken **in** the matter.

It is, then, that old and powerful body, the East and West India Dock Company, who have taken up the matter. At the instance of Mr. Du Plat Taylor, the able and energetic secretary of the company, supported by the equally energetic warehouse superintendent, Mr. Robert Adams, the arrangements for bulking Tea at **the** warehouse **of** the Company have been very greatly improved. More than this; there has been invented and set up a special and very ingenious **machine** for the bulking of **Tea in** a manner **which avoids** all the **failings of the old** system. What this machine **is, and what its** peculiar merits **are**, will best, and perhaps only, be clearly understood by **a**

---

* Since I wrote the above the Customs have framed new rules for Indian Teas. The absurd **tare system is done away with.**

brief description of the two systems as we lately saw them in operation at the warehouses of the company in Crutched Friars, which we may mention are nearer than any others to Mincing-lane, an advantage securing to planters and importers the certainty that their Teas will be sampled by the trade generally.

Under the old system, then, each chest of a break, after having been subjected to certain preliminary formalities, is opened, and the Tea turned out in a heap on the floor of the warehouse. When this is done the Tea is bulked by means of wooden spades, each spadeful being thrown to the top of the central heap, so that it falls over and **on all sides. Here the Tea lies until it is placed** back again **in the chests** after they are tared, there **being** a considerable interval at **some of the** London warehouses between the bulking and refilling. The refilling is thus accomplished. The Tea is first put into **bags and** weighed on a machine at the side of the bulk. The bag and chest are then taken off the weighing machine and the contents of the bag are emptied into the chest. The Tea, however, requires some pressure to force it into the chest, and this pressure is obtained by an expedient of a very primitive kind. When the chest is partly filled a man gets in and presses down the Tea by treading on it. So soon as the Tea is all **in** the chest the package is properly secured, and the operation is completed.

Now the serious faults of this plan are at once apparent. **In the** first place the Tea, being in heaps on the floor of the warehouse with a large surface exposed to the atmosphere, runs the risk of losing a great deal of its **freshness and aroma,** this risk being largely increased by the doors of the warehouse being kept open in order to discharge or to **receive** merchandise in all weathers. No atmospheric influences **are** calculated to benefit Tea. Then, again, the shovelling of the Tea by means of wooden spades, and the treading into the chests, can hardly do otherwise than injure the Tea—the filling in a minor degree and the treading to a more serious extent, the result being, of course, that the Tea is depreciated.

The East and West India Dock Company have made the best of this primitive method of Tea bulking. In the first place it is insisted on in their warehouses that previous to trampling the Tea into the chests, a cloth shall be placed over it to preserve it from the dirt of the man's **boots, and** to some extent from injury—a precaution which, strange as it may seem, is not taken in every bonded warehouse. Then, again

Mr. Adams, the warehouse superintendent—who could hardly have the interests of planters and importers more at heart were he "in Tea" himself—uses his best endeavours to refill the boxes with as little delay as possible, and thus to prevent it from being injured by undue exposure to the atmosphere. He also keeps the floors of the warehouse as clean as practicable. But feeling that the best efforts, however well devised, and however strenuously carried out, must necessarily be attended with but partial success, the East and West India Dock Company have erected—as has already **been mentioned—a Tea** bulking machine, a device which is ingenious and meritorious, and which seems to be, so far as it has been tried, a great success.

This machine, designed by Mr. Tydeman, of the company's engineering staff, and constructed under his supervision, consists, firstly, of a large hollow revolving drum weighing nearly two and a-half **tons, and of** sufficient capacity to thoroughly bulk about 50 chests of Tea. The drum is made to hold about 100 chests of Tea, which leaves ample space for the bulking of the above quantity. Inside this drum are frames fitted at intervals with iron rods, and extending at varying angles from the **axle of** the drum to its extremity. Externally the drum has two openings for the **reception** of the Tea, and two smaller ones for its discharge. In a line with the axle of the drum, some height from the floor, **is a platform to which the** chests are conveyed by a double lift which simultaneously ascends with a full chest **and** brings down an empty one. Adjuncts to the machine **are a** weighing machine, a presser, and four beaters—of the two latter the nature and object will be immediately apparent. The process of bulking **as** effected by this machine is briefly as follows: The drum being revolved till its receiving openings are level with the platform, a chest of Tea is raised, as before explained, and the contents examined on the door of the drum, which falls back into a horizontal position for that purpose, then by closing the tray or door the Tea is passed into the drum. The lift then brings up another full chest and takes down the emptied one, **which is** at once taken **to a scale** for taring purposes, and so the process is continued till the break is exhausted. This filling process can be carried on at **both sides** of a drum at once, as there are two openings and two lifts. The Tea being in, the drum is made to revolve, when the iron frames thoroughly mix the Tea in a very few revolutions —three would suffice.

The drum has now to be emptied, and this operation is effected

WEIGHING AND BULKING OF INDIAN TEAS.

in the following manner:—The revolution of the drum is stopped when the openings through which the Tea is released are brought over the weighing machines—there are two for greater expedition—on which are placed the chests ready to receive it. The delivery doors (worked by levers) being opened, the Tea is allowed to descend till the chest is about half full, when the presser and beaters are brought into play by hydraulic pressure. The presser is a piece of flat iron about an inch in thickness, removable at pleasure, and varies in size to fit either a chest or a box. The beaters are four pieces of the same metal, which support the chest so soon as it is on the weighing machine. When the chest is partly filled, the beaters are released, and, by the action of a wheel, are made to strike all four sides of the chest, and thus shake the Tea down. The presser is also brought down to press the Tea in. The action of both of these agents can be regulated to any required degree of force. Thus by degrees the chest is filled, and (the supporting beaters having been released and the presser raised) is weighed and ultimately removed. Such, in brief, is the action of the new Tea bulking machine. One or two points, however, remain to be mentioned. The power by which the machine is actuated is hydraulic. The presser will not injure the Tea. The beaters serve the triple purpose of holding the chest in position on the weighing machine, of supporting it should it be of weak construction, and of materially assisting the repacking of the Tea. The beating action does not in any way injure the chests. Our readers will also be pleased to know that certain very marked improvements even upon the above described are already in hand by this Dock Company—improvements which will greatly increase the value and usefulness of their machinery for bulking Teas.

To descant on the advantages over the old system of bulking which are possessed by the machine which has been described would be little better than a waste of time. Yet some few points may be briefly referred to. First, cleanliness is secured, for from first to last the Tea is never touched by hand or foot. Again, the Tea cannot be injured, nor can it lose its aroma, for it is never exposed to the atmosphere at all. Instead of being allowed to lie on the floor of the warehouse for any period, the entire process of bulking is completed without break or delay. The Directors of the East and West India Dock Company are not, of course, so sanguine as to imagine that the old system of bulking will be at once abandoned; indeed, they have, as has been mentioned, taken steps to improve that system; they do, however, think that it should be abandoned, and to that end have adopted the Tea Bulking Machinery as an alternative, and an immeasurably superior process. That they are justified in this view there can be no doubt in the minds of those who have witnessed both the systems in operation.

The said machinery is at the CRUTCHED FRIARS Warehouse alone, and it is, of course, very desirable the machinery should be adopted in all Tea warehouses. This end will **be** quickly brought about if those who send their Tea home, **and** the importers here, insist on their Tea being sent to this **one** warehouse that has the machinery.

What an advantage to owners and managers of Tea estates is the fact that Tea bulked by machinery at CRUTCHED FRIARS is not exposed to the changeable English **atmosphere, or** at least not for more than a few minutes, **and** consequently is not so likely **to be** classed as "flat." How many planters are there who, after taking especial care in the manufacture of their crop, find to their chagrin that on arrival in London (and after exposure probably for some days), the shipment is described as "flat," and worth **so many** pence per lb. less than if the atmospheric exposure had not occurred.

It appears **to** me that very little, added to the help this new machinery gives, would now do away with *all* the injury the producer and the Tea has hitherto borne in the Customs. So much has now been accomplished by this machinery, the Tea is well bulked, and *receives no injury whatever thereby*. But two further improvements are required:—

> 1. That the actual weight of Tea in each chest (discarding ounces) be recorded, and that thus the loss to the producer and the Customs, detailed above, be avoided.

2. That the lead at top of the Tea be carefully **replaced and resoldered, so that every chest shall leave the Custom House in as good condition as it entered it.**

Very little addition to the machinery detailed above would accomplish the first. The **chest ready to receive the** Tea, plus the lid and top lead (which **should have been** carefully removed), might be weighed **on the** platform **at** the side of the big drum (by simply making the said platform a weighing machine) and weighed again when filled, with the **lid and lead laid on it. The** difference of the two weights **would, of course, be the weight of the Tea.**

The second is a question of expense; it would **not be** great if done systematically. The chest should be carefully opened, and the top lead removed in a square piece *nearly the size of the box*. When replaced, a narrow strip of lead, soldered down on either side, would make the covering complete.

Justice will not be done to Indian **Teas till this last is** accomplished.

Who should bear the expense? The chests are received into the Customs for the benefit of the Revenue, and who can doubt, were the question tried in a Court of Law, that they are bound to return them in as good condition as they were received. They do *not*, and have never done so, and I only wonder the trade has stood it so long, and has not sued them. Were the course I advise followed out, there would remain no cause of complaint, and the trifling cost of soldering on the lid again should **doubtless,** therefore, be borne by the Customs.

But in reality the Customs would sustain no loss—in fact, the other way. I have shown clearly at page 278 *that were the weight of Tea correctly recorded, the Customs would receive in duty upwards of £11,000 each year from Indian Tea more than it does now.* To re-solder the lids on the boxes would cost nothing like that; and highly as Indian Tea is thought of now, how much higher still would it stand were it not injured to the frightful extent it is in passing through the Customs.

Conclusion.

I lit on the following in the *Home and Colonial Mail* just before going to press, and it is too pertinent to much in preceding pages to omit:—

The China Tea Trade.

The influence of the expansion of the Indian Tea enterprise on the trade in China is being felt. We have more than once adverted to the fact that the growing use of the well-flavoured Teas of India would diminish the consumption of the better grades of China Tea, and that the effect of the competition between the two countries would be first seen in the falling off in the demand for so-called fine China Tea.

The following letter, which appeared in the *Times* Money article lately, confirms this view, and refers to the present unsound condition of the China Tea trade:—

"Sir,—In view of the opening of the Tea season in China, a few remarks upon the present position and future prospects of this important trade may not be inopportune.

"It is no secret that for some years past the losses of merchants have been serious, and that while most of the wealthy firms so long known as connected with China have either entirely ceased to import Tea, or have reduced their operations to a very small compass, the trade has been carried on by new houses possessing but little capital, who are enabled, by the competition of the banks, to do a large business by drawing bills on China, not only for the whole cost of the Teas purchased, but also for their commissions on these purchases— **that is to say, for an unrivalled profit of** 3 **per cent.** The question, Who has so far paid the losses **of** the past two years? is one that greatly exercises the minds of the trade. Many suppose that large balances are being carried over in the books of some of the banks, or by the Chinese, and that it is the hope of recouping a portion of this

CONCLUSION.

loss that induces the banks or the Chinamen to support those who would otherwise be obliged to relinquish the trade. The Chinese have also a further inducement to support such firms, since it is partly through them **that those** high prices are established in China at the **opening of the season which** entail so **much loss** afterwards. As a result of these prices, about 30 per cent. more fine Congou is produced than (on account of the competition of the Indian growth) can be consumed except at the price of medium Tea. How large the excess is may be gathered from the fact that, although 5,000,000 lbs. of this class of Tea was lost last July in the 'Moskwa' and the 'Fleurs Castle,' yet **stocks in** Russia have increased by about 30,000 **half**-chests, and there is still so large a quantity on this market that it **can only be realized at** a loss of from 5d. to 6d. per lb. on the China cost; thus some Teas, said to have cost in Hankow 1s. 8d. to 1s. 9d., have **been** recently sold as low as 1s. 3d., and others costing 1s. 7d. in Foochow, have been sold at 1s. 1d. **per lb.**

"It is evident from the above that merchants **as a rule do not realize** the immense **change that has been brought about in the** conditions of the trade by the enormous increase **in the use of** Indian **Tea,** which **now** forms about one-third of the entire home consumption, **and competes** mostly with the finer qualities of China congou; nor the fact that all engaged in the trade are becoming year by year more averse to holding stock on account of the heavy charges involved, and the risk of deterioration in quality. Yet, **as the whole** twelve months' supply of first crop Tea arrives within three months of the opening of the season, it is plain that some one must hold the balance, which can only be done with safety if the Tea be bought at a very low price.

"**The one remedy for** the present condition of things is that the great bulk of the so-called fine Teas should be bought in China at their present value on this market—viz., at about 5d. to 6d. below the prices given for them **in** recent years. With the large accumulated stocks in **Russia, and** consequently reduced orders from that country, the yearly-**increasing supply of Indian Tea, and** the present prices here, one would think that such a course would at once be adopted. Unfortunately, however, so much of the Tea is bought on commission, and the Russian agents seem **so** reckless as to the prices which they give, that any such prudent action can hardly be hoped for. It would, therefore, be wise for holders of shares in Eastern banks, as well as all who have **been in the habit of intrusting** orders to buying agents in China, to ponder the foregoing facts, which can be easily verified by a reference to any of the trade circulars lest their money should be lost in the crash which must certainly take **place if** the past policy of Tea buyers in China be continued.—I am, &c., "A. B."

Will those warned be **wise in** time, and not swamp the Home Market with China **Teas certain to be** sold at a loss? Who can say? But "A. B." is evidently master of the subject, and if his advice in not taken, the China **Tea** "crash" he predicts will not be a small one.

When China Teas are *not* sent home to realise a certain loss, our Indian Teas will have fairer play.

I cannot conclude without acknowledging the great help **I have derived from** the pages of the *Tea Gazette* in writing these additions to my Fourth Edition.

Since my remarks on Ceylon were printed, I have acquired much further information regarding the Tea industry in that island, and the prospects certainly seem very favourable. Anyhow, there seems to **be** no doubt that Ceylon for Tea offers quite as good a field **as** any part of India, always supposing that good sites are selected and the area to choose from is large.

The future market for Tea is really, as regards Ceylon, the only doubtful point, and consequently (as at page 183) I advise the planters there to act with caution.

Where it is proposed to put coffee lands under Tea, of course one great advantage in economy will be gained, inasmuch as there will be no jungle clearing or previous cultivation. But here again caution is necessary. Make sure the soil is not worn out, for Tea, though it will grow, will not yield largely on such.

June, 1883.

P.S.—The following are the new rules lately issued by the Customs regarding the future treatment of Indian Teas.

The weight of Indian Tea for duty may, if desired by the importers, be ascertained under the following regulations :—

1. The Tea on arrival to be weighed to ascertain the gross weight of each package.
2. With each entry the importer to give an endorsement of the net contents of each package.
3. To test the accuracy of this endorsement, 10 per cent. of each break to be turned out and weighed net.
4. If the difference between the weight given of any package and the weight found exceeds or is less than 3 lbs., the whole parcel should be weighed net.
5. Duty to be charged on the average weight of the packages weighed net, unless the importer elects to weigh the whole parcel in the usual way.
6. When the average of the packages weighed net amounts to so many pounds and a-half, an additional pound will be charged on each of the whole parcel; when the fraction is less than half a pound it is to be rejected.
7. The new system to come into operation on July the 1st next.

ADDENDA

TO THE THIRD EDITION.

THE following from the *Indian Economist*, regarding Indian Teas in general and Neilgherry Teas in particular, is not out of place here. At the same time I do not agree with the writer, for I believe that in the strength and pungency of Indian Teas consists their value :—

INDIAN TEA.

"That the Teas of India have at length come to be fully appreciated in England may be taken, we presume, as an admitted fact ; and it is of importance that planters should direct their attention to modifying their methods of manufacture so as to suit the public taste, and, if possible, turn out an article free from the objections still advanced against the Indian leaf as a daily beverage. There are, we know, those who argue that enough has been done, and that consumers will acquire a taste for the produce of our gardens in time ; but we have daily evidence that in the most trivial matters there is no greater tyrant than the public. It behoves those then who cater for this tyrant to consult its taste and satisfy its demands, however exacting and capricious they may be. The remarks we are about to make are based on experiments and enquiries extending over some years in this country and in England, and we leave those engaged in the enterprise to estimate their value. All Teas grown in the plains of India are known to the trade in London under the general name of Assam, and are chiefly used for mixing, seldom reaching the consumer in a pure state. When they do, the objections raised are that the leaf is too pungent and rough for most palates ; and purchasers are in the habit of mixing it with Chinese to tone down those astringent qualities. In other words, it wants the delicacy of flavour which is the chief characteristic of the Chinese leaf, meaning of course that vended by respectable houses, not the abominable trash that formed part of the cargoes of the *Lalla Rookh* and *Sarpedon*, containing, according to Dr Letheby's Analysis,

'40 to 45 per cent. of iron filings and 19 per cent. of silica.' Nor is this lack of delicacy of flavour to be lightly regarded, for the efforts of our manufacturers have been directed unwittingly and indirectly to foster the peculiarity, as the test of Indian Tea has hitherto been its strength and pungency, to fit it for *salting* weak, thin, inferior sorts of Chinese. This is what the dealers have demanded, and what, consequently, brokers in their turn have insisted on, with the result that the out-turn of our Assam and Cachar plantations is now, if anything, too powerful to suit public taste. Whether means of manipulation may be hit upon by which aroma can be retained without sacrificing strength, we leave those most interested to determine; but it is worthy of note that this objection to strength and roughness is almost confined to women, the sterner sex preferring Assam unmixed, while the working classes of both sexes are unanimous in favour of the unadulterated Indian article. Experiments were further tried by substituting Neilgherry Tea, and after a short interval the verdict of the majority was in its favour. We need now only point out the difference in the manufacture between the two Teas, leaving others to decide questions regarding the bearing of climate or altitude. Up to the time of finishing rolling, the manipulation of the leaf is identical, care being taken to retain the juice; but that made on the hills instead of being almost immediately placed over *choolas* was spread out thinly on tables all night, in a temperature of 54 deg., sustaining consequent loss of strength by evaporation, but developing an aroma that established it at once in favour. So successful has this Neilgherry Tea been at home, that offers are now received by plantation proprietors for their produce at half-a-crown per lb. free on board, in Madras. This would seem to indicate that the aroma is generated by the action of cold upon the damp leaf while in a state of 'suspended fermentation;' for, previous to experimenting with consumers, the samples were submitted to Mincing Lane brokers and pronounced sound, in corroboration of which opinion the bulk from which they were taken sold at auction for 2s. 2½d., so that fermentation (*i.e.* sourness) had been carefully avoided. We know that the climate of Assam and temperature of the Tea-houses render the keeping of rolled leaf even for an hour fatal to soundness; but should the development of this aroma be really due to 'suspension of fermentation' is it not worth while adopting some contrivance for cooling down a chamber set aside for the purpose of spreading out the rolled leaf to the temperature required?

"The question whether delicacy is due to altitude alone and not to manufacture might be ascertained by experiment. Let a quantity of green leaf be **sent** *down* from one of the Neilgherry gardens, **and** worked up in the plains at the foot of the hills, and an equal quantity sent *up* from one of **the** Assam gardens, say to Shillong, and manufactured **on** the Neilgherry principles there, and the result then compared. This experiment would **cost little and determine a not** unimportant question : for all engaged **in Tea are interested in using** their best endeavours to fit it for public **consumption, and to guard it** against Chinese in any shape or **form** whatever."

Note *by the Author.*—That "**delicacy** of flavour," and "want of strength" with **it,** *is* **due to altitude has long** ago been admitted, **and any** experiments **on that head would, I think,** be quite unnecessary. The experiments **as to manufacture on the Neilgherries are** interesting, **and** should be further **looked into.** E. M.

I have **at last completed experiments with a view** to do away with the use of charcoal in Tea manufacture, and **I think** with success.

The "Furnace Teas," for so I purpose naming them, have in most cases been pronounced by the Calcutta brokers to be superior to similar samples **of** the same day's leaf, made in the usual way over charcoal.

Nothing but the heat generated by *any* **fuel placed in furnaces** sunk under ground outside the Tea-house is used. **No motive power** of any kind is employed. **The apparatus is very simple. It is cheap** to erect and very durable in character.

As the apparatus with **which the** Teas up to the present time have been made is a rude and imperfect one, having disadvantages which must tell more or less on the excellence of the Teas so manufactured, and as, even with these disadvantages, the Teas are pronounced by the brokers *at least* equal to charcoal-dried Teas, it is not too much to hope that with a perfect apparatus (one of which will be erected immediately) Teas will be improved in value by this new invention. The following will be shortly the advantages of this new process, even supposing the Teas are no better :—

1. *Economy.*—This will possibly be even greater than what is set out in the extract of the local paper below ; for the fact that the Tea is never placed over charcoal until the whole is ignited, and has become "live charcoal," is not there recognized, much of the caloric thus escapes.

2. Cleanliness and absence of charcoal dust.

3. Absence of the objectionable fumes of charcoal.

4. Immunity from fire in Tea-houses.

5. Greater **speed** in the firing process, and the saving of all the labour employed to make charcoal.

6. **Reduced temperature in Tea-houses.**

If all the advantages are, as I expect they will be, attained, the life of a Tea planter will be more pleasant than hitherto.

The following **is** the opinion of the new process expressed by the *Darjeeling News* of 1st August :—

" It has long been a question, which all planters were desirous to solve, if the fumes of charcoal were necessary to make Tea, that is to say, if any chemical action was produced on the Tea by the said fumes, and if **not, whether it** would **not be** possible to do the firing in some other and far cheaper **way.**

"**The** question **has, we** believe, been solved by Colonel Edward Money, and if so, for the invention is quite a new one, a boon of great magnitude will have been conferred on the Tea interest of India. We congratulate this district **as** being the birthplace of the improvement.

"The apparatus at present **in use at Soom,** and which we have seen working, is a rough and crude one **made on the** spot. This, and the more perfect plans from which larger and better ones are to be **made,** are readily shown by Colonel Money to anyone visiting Soom ; **but until** the invention is patented, it is not well to describe it in print. **Suffice** if we say the invention is a remarkably simple one—cheap to erect—durable in its character, and the working thereof unattended with any expense whatever, beyond the cost of the fuel (which may be of any kind), and which of course will be **many times** less than charcoal.

"If true, as we hear, that it takes 3½ maunds of wood generally to make one maund of charcoal, and if also true, as Colonel Money **suggests, that the caloric in one maund of** wood equals the caloric in two maunds of charcoal, it then follows that each maund of wood, put **into Colonel** Money's furnace, equals seven maunds of wood to make charcoal.

"Of course the above are more or less random figures, but they suffice to show that the **saving of fuel** will be **very great—a** boon of course to planters, but a boon also to the Forest Department and to India.

"We knew of the invention some time back, but we forbore to notice it until the 'brokers' reports on the Tea so made had been received. We have now seen these. Samples of 'charcoal' and 'furnace' Tea were sent down, made from the same leaf, the same day, and manufactured in one up to the "firing" process. Two brokers give the higher value to the furnace Tea, one to the charcoal kind—but the difference is small.

"We believe, as one of our most experienced planters, who has tasted the Teas, been to Soom, and seen the brokers' reports, says, that 'the Tea dried by the furnace apparatus will be *at least* equal to that prepared over charcoal.'

"As Colonel Money is already known as an authority in Tea, and as he has stated to us his belief that 'charcoal days' for Tea are now at an end, we await with confidence the ultimate success of his invention, which even if it makes no better Tea will certainly make it far cheaper, while the dirt from charcoal dust will be done away with, the temperature of the Tea-houses much reduced, and the deleterious fumes of charcoal, so very objectionable from a sanitary point of view in Tea manufacture, will be known no more."

Again, 29th August, a month later, the *Darjeeling News* further remarks :—

"We alluded recently to Colonel Money's very ingenious plan for drying Tea without charcoal. Since then his apparatus has been in full work at Soom, and has been inspected by numbers of the Darjeeling planters, one and all of whom have, we understand, reported most favourably on its working. Samples of Tea manufacture have been from time to time sent to Calcutta brokers for their opinion, and reports have been received from fifteen, of whom seven are in favour of Tea made by the old charcoal process, seven are in favour of the new furnace process, and one reports that the Tea made by each process is exactly the same.

"Colonel Money is now taking steps to erect his improved furnace, which will be in working order by the end of September, and the whole October crop of Soom Tea will be fired by the new furnace.

"Colonel Money has applied for a patent, and as soon as this is granted we hope to give our readers a description of the apparatus.

For obvious reasons it would not be advisable to do so before then. We may mention here that one of the most intelligent and practical planters in this district has ordered one of Colonel Money's flues for his private garden.'

"Of the commercial success of Colonel Money's apparatus we have no doubt whatever, and we trust that Colonel Money will reap a handsome profit from his very ingenious invention, which will be an undoubted boon not only to this district, but to all the Tea-producing districts of India.

"One point which has struck us as good in Colonel Money's apparatus is that the temperature of the Tea-house is considerably lowered during the firing process as compared with the open *chulas*, and that there is no free carbonic acid gas allowed to escape into the Tea-house, so that those very unpleasant symptoms of slow poisoning which often show themselves in planters and Tea-makers will be unknown in future. At our suggestion Colonel Money has decided to keep a register of the maximum temperature of the Tea-house, whilst the open *chulas* continue in use, and to compare it with the temperature when the new apparatus has superseded them, also to test for free carbonic acid gas in the air with each process.

"We are convinced that when the figures are available our readers will be rather astonished at the difference from a sanitary point of view.

"On the whole, we think that Colonel Money's invention is by far the most important application of *common sense* and scientific knowledge to Tea manufacture that we have yet seen, and we are almost certain that his apparatus will before long be adopted throughout the Indian Tea districts." *

* Note to Third Edition.—No. The furnace has been erected but on two or three gardens. Other inventions have since been brought forward, and the whole matter is still in an uncertain state—I mean as to which of the several apparatuses is the best. I believe in mine still, and intend to erect it on the Western Dooar Gardens in which I am interested, but, of course, I am not an impartial judge! One thing, however, I lay claim to, and that is, that I was the first to show by practical results that the fumes of charcoal are in no way necessary to make Tea.

Note to Fourth Edition.—Since the above note was written (now five years ago) many Tea Drying Machines have been invented (see pages 240 to 259), and I most willingly admit they are *all* better than my furnace apparatus. The first inventor rarely attains perfection, and as in my case, he generally labours for the benefit of those who come after!—EDWARD MONEY.

INDEX.

	PAGE
AREA required for a garden	2
— large, a mistake	2
BOXES	147
— cost of	161
CLIMATE	14
— in each district	14 to 25
— wanted	14
— rainfall	14, 28
— rain table	28
— temperature table	26
— elevation table	26
— cold	14
— hot winds	14
— affects flavour of tea	15
— good for tea, bad for man	15, 35
Cultivation	81
— what is it	81
— when a waste of labour	81
— by digging round each plant	82
— weeds not to get ahead	83
— Dutch hoe for	83
— cost each operation per acre	84
— cost of, to 6th year	84
— cost of in full bearing	85
DISTRICTS	13
— which best	30
— rainfall in	28
— cold in	26
— of Assam	15
— of Cachar	16
— of Chittagong	16
— of Terai below Darjeeling	18
— of Dehra Dhoon	18
— of Kangra	19
— of Darjeeling	20
— of Kumaon	22
— of Gurhwal	24

	PAGE
Districts of Hazareebagh	24
— of Neilgherries	24
— of Western Dooars	25
— meteorological table of	26
— comparative advantages of	30
— soil of	13 to 25
— jungle of	13 to 25
— lay of land of	13 to 25
— price waste lands in	4
— elevation of	26
— temperature of	26
Distances for plants	72
— table of	72
— regulated by class	72
— best	72
FLUSHES	97
— number of	97 to 101
— way formed	104
— differ in districts	98
— intervals between	99
HILLS AND PLAINS—	
— comparison of	chap. iii.
— high elevations bad	do.
— table of elevation	26
JUNGLE	34
— what best in Himalayas	34
— not of much consequence in Bengal	34
Jungle, coarse grass	34
— cutting	75
LABOUR	10
— local	10, 11, 12
— imported	10, 11, 12
— government action	10, 11
— cost of imported	10

	PAGE
Labour in tea districts . chap. iii.	
Laying out a garden . . .	42
Lay of land and aspect . .	37
— flat, sloping, steep . 7, 13,	35
— aspect	39
— valleys	40
— narrow valleys . . .	40
Lay of land and selection of steep land 7,	37
— disadvantages of steep land .	37
— lines on steep land . .	46
— plants close on steep land .	45
Leaf-picking	102
— principles of . . .	102
— diagram of shoot . . .	104
— teas made from each leaf .	107
— cannot make separate teas in practice . . .	107
— pruning connected with .	102
— mistakes in	42
— how shoots form . . .	104
— mode of	104
MANUFACTURE	109
— importance of good . .	109
— old and new plan . . .	110
— withering . . 110, 111,	123
— rolling 111,	112
— panning 109,	112
— sunning 112,	128
— tea, how judged . . .	113
— Pekoe tips 105, 106, 114, 115, 116,	122
— strong teas and Pekoe tips incompatible . . .	116
— fermenting or colouring .	127
— firing or dholing . . .	128
— of flowery Pekoe . .	130
Manufacture of green tea . 130,	144
— sifting and sorting 134, 135, 136,	161
— sieves	135
— Chinese sieves best . .	135
— classes of tea . . .	137
— cost of	160
— ignorance of	7

	PAGE
Manufacture, coarse leaf . .	126
— burntness	143
Manure	67
— advantages of . . 17,	67
— how to apply	68
— quantity	69
— cost of	69
— kinds of	67
— results of	69
Management, accounts, forms .	152
— what qualities required for a Manager	152
— forms	153
— accounts	158
Making a garden . . .	73
— general instructions for . .	73
Mechanical contrivances . .	116
— McMeekin's rolling table .	116
— Kinmond's rolling machine .	116
— Nelson's rolling machine .	118
— Jackson's rolling machine .	116
— McMeekin's drawers . .	119
— Money's furnace . . 121,	296
— sifting machines . . .	121
— machine required to separate the leaves	122
— packing machines . .	121
Miscellaneous :—	
Transport . . . chap iii.	
— in each district . . chap. iii.	
Green tea . . 21, 130,	144
Stagnant water . . .	40
Inundation	40
Sections	42
Yield 43,	170
Lines of plants . . 45,	46
Roads	45
Relative price green and black teas	133
Yield first 10 years . .	170
Necessities for tea . . 173,	180
Past, present, and future of Indian tea	174
Strange facts about tea . .	174
Imports	177

INDEX.

	PAGE
Annual consumption	177
Collapse of tea speculation	178
Share list to-day	179
Money matters: **will tea pay?**	1
— **why** has it not **paid** sometimes?	1, 6
— cause of failures	1 to 8
— wilful extensions	6
— price paid for gardens	8
— faulty area sold	8
— **cost** of making **a 300-acre** garden	163
— how **much** profit tea can give	168
— table, result 300 acres for 12 years	172

PACKING	147
— lead case for	147
— larger each **break the better**	151
— cost of	161
Planting at stake	59
— advantages of	57
— disadvantages of	58
— mode of	59
Pruning	86
— time for	86
— instruments for	87
— height to prune	88
— cost of	88

SALE LANDS, WASTE LANDS—	
— sale waste lands	3
— auction system	3
— price waste lands	4
— title	4
Sanitation	35
Seed	54
— transport **of**	55
— **price of**	7
— **shade**, natural	62
— do. artificial	64
— how to sow	57
— when ripe	54
— treatment of	54

	PAGE
Seed as manure	55
— number in 1 maund	56
— proportions that germinate	56
— Government gave seed	51
— indigenous hybrid and China alike	51
— how to **increase**	55
— nurseries or stake planting best	57
Soil	31
— only general rules for	31
— sandy	31
— greasy	32
— poor	32
— Ball on	32
— friable and porous	32
— in Tea districts	13, 25, 31
— clay	33
— decayed vegetation	33
— for seed beds	62

TRANSPLANTING	76
— holes for	59, 76
— mode of	77
— results of bad	77
— when to be finished	78
— best days for	79

VACANCIES	92
— difficult to fill up	92
— why difficult	92
— best plan to fill up	92
— large proportion of	6
Varieties of tea plants	47

WHITE-ANTS, CRICKETS, BLIGHT	89
— harm done by crickets	89
— harm done by white-ants	90
— harm done by blight	91
— remedies for crickets	90
— do. white-ants	91
— do. blight	91
Weeds	82
— ahead of labour	83

INDEX

TO THE ADDITIONS IN FOURTH EDITION.

	PAGE
Agricultural machinery	**223**
America	185, 204, 205, 209
Amsterdam Exhibition	202 to 211
Any fuel *versus* charcoal	239, 258
Australia	201, 202, 204, 205, 207 to 209
Brick tea	212
Calcutta Syndicate	202, 206, **208, 210, 211, 212, 214**
China tea trade	288
China	**194** to 198, **201 to 207, 210 to 212, 288**
Consumption of China and Indian Tea	201
Continent of Europe	202, 211
Damage to tea by procedure in London	272, 273
Darby's digger	225
Date of commencement of tea cultivation in each district	**194**
Deliveries and stocks, 195, **197 to 201**	
Discovery of indigenous tea	194
Dryers, by Robertson, the Typhoon	240, **241**
,, Allen	**242**
,, Davidson, the Sirocco	243, **244**
,, Gibbs and Barry	**244**
,, Shand	244, 245, 246
,, Jackson	246 to 248
,, Kinmond	248 to 257

	PAGE
Fermenting Shelves	239, 258
First tea in India	194
Greatest and least possible loss by Custom House procedure	274, 275
Green tea	203, **204**
Himalayan gardens	212
Hoop iron	**271**
How loss by Custom House procedure could be avoided	275 to 278
Imports into Great Britain 194, 195, 198 to 200, 203	
Increase of Indian Imports into Great Britain	**195**
Indian produce for **1883**	**195**
Indian *versus* China tea	**219**
Jebens' transplanter	**223**
Local market in India	213 to 218
Loss of tea by procedure in London	272, 273
Loss on China teas	288 to 290
Machinery	222 to 271
Making Indian tea known in United Kingdom	218 to **221**
Manufacturing machinery	231 to 271
Markets outside Great Britain	**207** to 217
Money loss to producers and Customs by method of weighing in vogue	278

INDEX.

	PAGE
New mode bulking at warehouse in Crutched Friars	282 to 286
— required further	287, 288
New Zealand	205
Ornamental tin boxes by Harvey Bros. and Tyler	266 to 271
Petition of Indian Tea Districts Association *re* mode of weighing teas	279 to 281
Planting pots	223
Plantations in Northern India	203
Ploughing	223 to 231
Processes of manufacture	231 to 271
Rollers by Jackson	233, 235, 237
,, Kinmond	233, 234, 235, 237
,, Haworth	235, 237
,, Lyle	236
,, Greig	236
,, Thomson	237, 238
Russia	203, 211
Sifters, by Jackson	259
,, Greig	259
,, Pridham	259
,, Ansell	260 to 266

	PAGE
Sorter for green leaf by Greig & Co.	232
Statistics of Indian tea	194 to 206
Tea outside China and India	183 to 192
Ceylon	183
Johore	184
Japan	185 to 188, 205, 210
Java	188
America	188 to 190, 201, 203, 205, 206, 208
Natal	191
Fiji	192
Tea consumption per head	204, 205
Tea Gazette—This is alluded to in most pages (see 290)	
Thibet	212
Weighing and bulking by Customs	272 to 288
Weighing teas by Customs, The new rules	290, 291
Withering machine	232, 253, 257

www.ingramcontent.com/pod-product-compliance
Lightning Source LLC
Chambersburg PA
CBHW022046230426
43672CB00008B/1088